A Modern Book on Economic Geography

A Modern Book on Economic Geography

Debashish Banerjee

RANDOM

RANDOM PUBLICATIONS

NEW DELHI - 110 002 (INDIA)

A Modern Book on Economic Geography

ISBN 978-93-51112-37-2

Published in 2014 in India by

RANDOM PUBLICATIONS

4376-A/4B, Gali Murari Lal, Ansari Road
New Delhi-110 002
Phone: +9111-43580356, 23289044
E-mail: randomexports@gmail.com; sales@randompublications.com; info@randompublications.com

Reprinted 2024

Type Setting by: Friends Media, Delhi-110089
Printed at : Replika Press Pvt. Ltd.

Preface

Economic geography has taken a variety of approaches to many different subject matters, including but not limited to the location of industries, economies of agglomeration, transportation, international trade, economic development, real estate, gentrification, ethnic economies, gendered economies, core-periphery theory, the economics of urban form, the relationship between the environment and the economy, and globalization. The subject matter investigated is strongly influenced by the researcher's methodological approach. Neoclassical location theorists, following in the tradition of Alfred Weber, tend to focus on industrial location and use quantitative methods. Since the 1970s, two broad reactions against neoclassical approaches have significantly changed the discipline: Marxist political economy, growing out of the work of David Harvey; and the new economic geography which takes into account social, cultural, and institutional factors in the spatial economy. Economists such as Paul Krugman and Jeffrey Sachs have also analyzed many traits related to economic geography. Krugman has gone so far as to call his application of spatial thinking to international trade theory the "new economic geography", which directly competes with an approach within the discipline of geography that is also called "new economic geography". The name geographical economics has been suggested as an alternative.

Economic geography is sometimes approached as a branch of anthropogeography that focuses on regional systems of human economic activity. An alternative description of different approaches to the study of human economic activity can be organized around spatiotemporal analysis, analysis of production/consumption of economic items, and analysis of economic flow. Spatiotemporal systems of analysis include economic activities of region, mixed social spaces, and development. Alternatively, analysis may focus on production, exchange, distribution and consumption of items of economic activity. Allowing parameters of space-time and item to vary, a geographer may also examine material flow, commodity flow, population flow and information flow from different parts of the economic activity system. Through analysis of flow and production, industrial areas, rural and urban residential areas, transportation site, commercial service facilities and finance and other economic centres are linked together in an economic activity system. With the rise of the New Economy, economic inequalities are increasing spatially. The New Economy, generally characterized by globalization, increasing use of information and communications technology, growth of knowledge goods, and feminization, has enabled economic geographers to study social and spatial divisions caused by the arising New Economy, including the emerging digital divide. The new economic geographies consist of primarily service-based sectors of the economy that use innovative technology, such as industries where people rely on computers and the internet. Within these is a switch from manufacturing-based economies to the digital economy. In these sectors, competition makes technological changes robust. These high tech sectors rely heavily on interpersonal relationships and trust, as developing things like software is very different from other kinds of industrial manufacturing—it requires intense levels of cooperation between many different people, as well as the use of tacit knowledge. As a result of cooperation becoming a necessity, there is a clustering in the high-tech new economy of many firms.

The primary aim of this book is to present a succinct account of the essential features of this subject. It is being prepared by keeping in view the requirements of the students and academic professionals.

I thank all members of my team who have helped in the preparation of the book. My special thanks go to "Random Publications" who have published the book.

—Debashish Banerjee

Contents

1

Introduction

Economic geography is the study of the economic singularity of countries and regions, of spatial differences in economy on the earth's sphere, that is, differences from place to place, and also of spatial combinations within an economy. If these differences did not exist there would be no economic geography; it could not exist, for there would be no special object for investigation. In order to study these spatial differences, they must first be stated, then described as exactly as possible, and finally, the causes of these differences must be investigated. Ultimately, having investigated all these causes one must develop the mechanisms of these changes in the economy from place to place. In this way one can begin to formulate the problems of economic geography.

It must be emphasized that the differences from place to place in an economy are not due solely to differences in natural conditions. Let us assume that all differences in natural conditions have for some reason or another ended, that all climates have been blended, the seas have been divided evenly with land areas, and the mountains have been erased; even in such a case, contrasts in economy from place to place appear in each given country and at each given moment. These contrasts depend not only on the differences in natural conditions but to a great degree they also depend on the development of productive forces, on the past investment of labour on any part of the earth's surface, and on a number of other socio-historical features.

The Necessity of a Historical Approach

In order to more closely approach and more clearly visualize the problems of economic geography, it is necessary to consider this question historically. Science is not the concern of only one person and a small segment of time; science is a collective experience, the experience of many generations. Only a historical approach to science can show the paths of its development, detect the impasses that must be avoided and, on the other hand, acquaint us with past achievements and thereby prevent the labour of discovering America for the second time. This is way a historical approach to this discipline is needed.

Besides this, we know very well that no discipline develops in a vacuum, that ideas do not fall from the sky, that every system of scientific views and opinions develops in a definite social environment, and that "the demands of life' are the main factors in the development of any science and any ideology.

The stronger the association of a given science with practice, the stronger is the influence of the demands of life. These demands of life in a class society are in the end nothing more than the changing interests of the ruling classes; in this one must see, if not the only, certainly the main stimulus to the development of some sciences. We know that even the emergence itself of the sciences was the result of a social need for them. So geometry appeared, as its name implies, from the word geodesy, measurement of the earth, as the result of a completely practical necessity to divide irregular pieces of land into plots. It is true, geometry has gone far beyond land measurement, but the first social command that gave birth to geometry was geodesy.

Economic geography, as all sciences, was created under the influence of the practical demands of life, and in its development has experienced incessant impulses from social life, definite commands, and has had to react to those practical needs which occurred in a specific historical era. Thus, "a social command" must guide the Marxist in approaching the development of any kinds of sciences and ideas.

With this kind of approach we turn to our subject. What forms did economic-geographic thought take on in the process of its development? What stages did economic geography pass through as a science studying differences from place to place in the economy? First we will give a general outline of the development of economic-geographic learning on the world scale, and then note the special features of the development of this learning in our country.

Financial Statistics

Economic geography attained for the first time a more developed and independent form in the so-called financial statistics that developed in Germany at the beginning of the eighteenth century as the result of special needs of the "police state" that had risen on the ruins of feudalism. Under the feudal system the resources of the country could be made known without a special science, without forming a special branch of learning, and without creating any university courses. In the feudal era the land of the whole country was divided into comparatively small fiefs. Moreover, each feudal lord was not simply a landowner but also the governor of his land; he had the right to collect taxes, to recruit, and to judge those who lived on his territory. All of this belongs, in our opinion, to the area not private rights but of the rights of the state. Yet the lord's sovereign, the feudal king or duke, did not interfere in his internal affairs; the so-called right of immunity existed at that time, which was one of the privileges of the feudal lord.

Immunity as an institution of state law meant the freedom of the feudal lord from interference by the kings it meant also that the king's officials had no right to interfere in the internal affairs of the fiels. Under such a system each feudal lord could obtain directly from his lower lord information concerning how much could be taken from a given land in assessments and recruits and what resources the land had. Thus, the king could find out from each of the feudal lords under his power how much each could give in soldiers, money, and other resources. Hence within a feudalistic "coarse grained" system of government all this information could be obtained informally in a volume sufficient for practical purposes.

With the collapse of the feudal system, the governmental power began to reach the population directly as the government demanded taxes to draft recruits and passed judgment through its officials. As soon as a sizable territory with a large population came within the framework of a single national state so that a government economy could rapidly develop, everything became much more complex. A governmental apparatus had to be created for the administration of this huge state; in order to carry out the functions that had been those of the feudal lords and their administrators, new special cadres of educated officials were needed.

And in Germany a new science was created, *financial statistics.* Achenwall, the father of financial statistics, called this science "a descriptive government science of individual countries." His work, *Abrisse der neuesten Staatwissenschaft,* which initiated financial statistics, appeared in 1739. The aim of financial statistics was to provide the government with information and to train young officials by giving them a university education.

What were the structure and content of financial statistics? Attention was given to the territory of the state, its borders, and its administrative divisons; then came finances, budget, and individual branches of the economy–agriculture, industry, transport, communication, and so forth; then military forces, the fleet, relations with other countries; in one word, the governmental machinery considered as a whole. Thus, the subject of financial statistics was the state, but not so much from the legal viewpoint as from the viewpoint of the resources of the state.

This was a descriptive governmental science. Indeed, in order to understand any state one must know all that has been enumerated, that is, territory, borders, population, form of governmental system, all branches of the economy, military forces, diplomacy; all this is essential. Each educated official must clearly understand what relations his government has with other governments, what financial resources it has, and related information. All of this belongs to the field of education in government.

They were very few geographic elements in financial statistics: mainly directions for the distribution of individual branches of the economy, and sometimes descriptions of separate administrative units were included. Financial statistics created in Germany for the organization and strengthening of the police state, spread from Germany to other countries.

Financial statistics developed its own methodology. These were the times when science was permeated with the scholasticism of the Middle Ages and when methodological rules were brief formulas in Latin. Financial statistics had a formula, "Vires unitae agunt", translated literally: "United forces lead". As a whole this formula seems to recommend: "Describe first the material resources of the country, then describe the governmental organization on this territory, and then show all this in action." Clearly, the methodological formulas were not all useless. In fact, however, it did not go farther than endless lists, and, numerical information.

What was the fate of financial statistics? It had to utilize a large amount of every kind of numerical data. The methods of statistical investigation worked out on this basis were then applied to a number of natural sciences, to the study of genetics by botanists, zoologists, and others. As a result it turned out that financial statistics gave its "soul" so to speak, its method of investigation of mass phenomena, to the discipline we call statistics. And the perishable "body" that was left without a soul, that is, the collection of all kinds of reference information about one country or another, has become an essential element of what is called to sectoral-statistical approach in economic geography, and in this form it drags on its existence to this day.

The Sectoral-Statistical Approach

One must also bear in mind that these various "orders" to financial statistics and commercial geography are not divided by some kind of barrier. They have influenced and penetrated one another and created something with a common nature. It is possible to train simultaneously an official, a merchant, and a military man. Elements of economic geography initiated by various demands have somehow united and become part of general education.

The majority of courses of economic geography that have evolved from financial statistics or commercial geography have retained traces of one approach. In these courses of a so-called traditional or sectoral-statistical approach, prime attention characteristically is given not to separate regions of a country but to individual sectors of the economy. The object of study is not the territory itself but the economy in this territory, not as a whole but by individual sectors.

Economic geography in works of this sectoral-statistical approach is treated as the science of the state of individual sectors of the economy. The economy here is thought of as split into separate sectors, and each chapter is a description of the state of a given sector at a given moment in a given country, but the question of the distribution of this sector and the geography of production is only one of many and diverse interests guiding the author. Technology, history, and economic policy of the government in relation to the economic sector are all treated in the form of endless numerical references and enumeration, and only within all this is there also found some treatment of distribution. However, a minimum of space is given to questions of distribution, and even then the treatment of these questions is for the most part limited to simple references such as where a given industry is located and in what quantity, without explaining the reasons for the distribution.

It is in such consolidated and somewhat modified form–sectoral-statistical economic geography–that these two approaches (financial statistics and commercial geography) exist to this day. Both as financial statistics and as commercial geography, economic geography remained pure description without any inherent regularities, without a real scientific foundation. Economic geography in both these forms is better considered as simply a kind of somewhat dull literature rather than a science. If in these surveys there were some valuable generalizations with respect to science, it was not due to the method but in spite of the method; it was due to the personal talent of the author.

The scientific thought of economic geography did not progress within economic geography itself but in disciplines allied to it, or simply in an amateurish way when scientists of other fields for some reason were temporarily interested in questions of economic geography and contributed some valuable thoughts as was the case with Lomonosov and later Mendeleyev.

Economic-Geographic Descriptions in the Regional Geography [Study of Countries] Literature

Besides financial statistics and commercial geography, general geography, due to its complex content, also had an influence on the development of economic geography. General geography (including general earth science and especially regional geography) had become one of the general-education subjects in public schools during the eighteenth century and even earlier in a number of countries.

With the development of transport, international trade, and general international relations, the need for geographic knowledge began to grow and spread. A certain minimum became necessary not only for persons of narrowly defined professions such as state and trade representatives but for all educated people regardless of profession. This minimum included information on mathematical and physical geography, as well as economic geography. From this complex the school subject evolved under the general name of geography. The main content of this subject consisted of a description of individual countries, including information on the natural environment, population, and economy of each country. Two or three generations later, when geography was firmly established in the curriculum of the secondary school and the number of secondary schools had increased, the time had come to train school teachers of geography, and in the course of the nineteenth century geography penetrated higher education institutions, including the universities.

The immense amount of factual material collected since the beginning of the era of great geographic discoveries about the surface of the earth was so diverse that it demanded generalization and thereafter attracted the interest of brilliant minds who tried to find definite regularities in the distribution of natural phenomena and human society as a whole, and in their combinations within each separate country and in each separate region. With the development of secondary and higher education and with the increased number of educated people, the public demand for geographic literature grew. University courses and compilations on regional geography appeared more and more substantial in volume and content: they no longer had as their aim the training of narrow specialists but rather a general education in geography. The development of such a general, university-level geography could not but exert an influence also on the development of the then incipient forms economic geography.

Instruction in economic geography often had to be turned over not to statisticians, students of commodities, or practitioners (agents or merchants) but to geographers–that is, regional specialists. The same occurred with the composition of textbooks. And if, on the one hand geography in the form of regional specialization influenced financial statistics and commercial geography, then the content of courses in financial statistics and commercial geography conversely penetrated into regional geography. Since no special theoretical knowledge was needed for an economic-geographic description in the sectoral-statistical style, regional geographers could take on this job with little concern. And who was not intelligent enough to find references in statistical collections? For their part, the regional geographers contributed their knowledge of physical geography, knowledge of maps, and sometimes certain skills in general geographic thinking.

Some of the regional specialists who undertook to describe economic activities would adopt, without much concern, the traditions and the structure of the sectoral-statistical school, and thereby ceased for a time to be geographers. Others, on the contrary, tried to describe the economy by taking account of general geographic practice, that is, by locating precisely the objects and phenomena described, by using maps widely, by attempting to tie in the features of the economy with those of natural conditions and finally, by attempting to rearrange this description from a sectoral framework to a regional one. At first such regional geographers who switched to economic geography from physical geography used a network of natural, physical-geographic regionalizations. But after the rapid development of transportation in the era of capitalism and the growth of a geographic division of labour within large national states, there came into being sharply specialized economic regions, and the geographers began a transition from natural regions to economic regions in the economic-geographic section of their descriptions. A new and very positive contribution made by these geographers to economic geography consisted in the strengthening of the geographic components in it.

Many of the major regional geographers who were more interested in the geography of economic activity (or in a wider sense, the geography of man) and better trained in this activity made a sizable contribution to the development of economic geography with their general methodological statements as well as with concerete examples of the economic-geographic characteristics of countries and regions. Or the Russian geographers one can mention K.I. Arsenyev; P.P. Semenov, V.P. Mechnikov and A.I. Voyeykov; of the French, Reclus, Vidal de la Blache and his students Demangeon and Brunhes, as well as Blanchard and Baulig; of the Americans, Smith, Ekblaw, Bowman; of the English, Mackinder, Stamp, Beaver, Herbertson, and others. As examples of great works on regional geography (and the most interesting with respect to economic geography) one can cite *Rossiya* in Russian literature, edited by Semenov-Tyan-Shanskiy, and in French literature, the multivolume *Geographie Universelle.* The French *Geographic Universelle* has many valuable economic-geographic studies of whole countries and individual regions. Of special note is the work of Henri Baulig on North America and of Demangeon on the British Isles.

Standort [Location] Theories

Relatively recently economic geography received one more impetus from the practical demands of life, from capitalist monopolies and trust acting within the framework of an entire country and sometimes extending beyond its borders. Monopolistic groups developed primarily in the United States and Germany in the last decades of the previous century.

The trust, as the higest form of capitalistic union, in contrast to the cartel and the syndicate, assumes a *complete* merger of enterprises. A new stockholding company is created, and each participant sells to it his enterprises for a specific package of stock, and from the moment of founding of the trust the owners of the enterprises that are combined in the trust are no longer owners. A new elective board is created, handling all business, and the former owners become shareholders, with the right to receive dividends and to influence the composition of the board during elections. On this basis, one of the world's largest trusts, the Steel Trust, was created in America in 1901. This was such a powerful organization that at one time its budget exceeded that of France. The main task of a trust is to maximize profits; the means for doing this are to raise prices, lower wages, and decrease production costs. One of the first tasks is the reduction of production to the level of demand and the concentration of production in enterprises with the least production costs.

The experts of such an organization calculate the productive capacity of all plants and come up with, say, 80 million tons. Then they calculate the purchasing power of the market, adjust for growth, and arrive at a total of 40 million tons. Obviously, in the process of capitalistic competition production had been inflated and did not conform to the market. The main problem, as the trust sees it, is overproduction, and the main task is to decrease production, to close superfluous establishments, especially those which are less well equipped and those with higher costs. After these plants have been closed, the productive power is still, let us say, 60 million tons, and the market demands only 40 million tons, which means the productive power must be reduced by another 20 million tons. What other criterion must be taken into account? Another criterion is that of the convenience of location; an enterprise is closed not only if it is more poorly equipped but also if it is inconveniently located. Thus, with the appearance and development of capitalist trusts there arises a very interesting question for the economic geographer: What must be the rational distribution of a given sector in order to maximize proper that is, for a maximum reduction of production costs and transportation expenditures?

If we compare this demand of life with the preceding, we see that there is a great qualitative difference. In the demand for educated officials and agents, the demand was mainly for strictly factual knowledge, purely empirical reference information. However, when we are concerned with the demand for captains of industry, managers of such tremendous unions, we are dealing with a demand not for reference material, but for an entire theory. It concerns the creation of a theory of the most rational distribution of industry under the given capitalist conditions.

The so-called *standort* theories served as an answer to this question posed by monopolistic capitalism. Best known is the theory of Weber in his main work, *Theory of the Location of Industries.* Weber created a whole school in Germany. On the basis of Weber's theory his students compiled a number of monographs on individual branches of German industry. Then there is a theoretical work by Englander, the works of Schroeder, Schilling, and others, and a number of articles in the German journal *Wirtschaft und Statistik.* All these location theories tend to anwer the demands for the most advantageous distribution of industry under capitalist conditions, demands that arose as the result of the creation of industrial trusts. Although they exerted a certain influence by strengthening the theoretical elements in economic geography, they did not create a separate school. The location theories were used in economic-geographic works to explain the existing distribution of industry; examples of such use can be found in *Geographic Universelle.*

Now let us turn to our own country and briefly give the essential characteristics in the development of economic geography before the revolution and then the main directions of development of our economic geography during the Soviet period.

In speaking of characteristic features in the development of economic geography in Tsarist Russia, one must first of all note the role of an exceptional intellectual giant of thought, M.V. Lomonosov. A. scientist-encyclopedist in the full sense of the word, Lomonosov, besides conducting investigations in the fields of nature and technology, also worked in philosophy, history, and philology. He also was very much interested in economic questions and initiated the economic-geographic study of Russia.

Taking account of the needs of economic development in Russia, Lomonosov emphasized the acute necessity of developing industry, especially metallurgy. In a work titled "First Foundations of Metalluargy, or Ore Industries," he wrote: "Warfare, trade, navigation and other necessary government institutions require metals". Lomonosov saw clearly that "the well being, glory and flourishing of the country" depend on the development of trade, "on the mutual exchange of internal surpluses with distant peoples by means of trade." Hence arose the necessity of a complete study of the country. Directing the Geography Department of the Academy of Sciences, Lomonosov considered it necessary to compile an atlas with "a political and economic description of the whole Empire, including Siberia". For this purpose Lomonosov compiled a remarkable questionnaire consisting of thirty questions–a whole programme for the economic-geographic study of Russia. Lomonosov had planned to compile an economic lexicon of Russian products and evidence of their internal and external communications with attached maps. This would have been a detailed trade geography of Russia. In 1764 Lomonosov offered in the Academy of Science an opinion on the utilization of a census for a geography of Russia. Lomonosov was the initiator of expeditions for the geographic study of our country, moreover, he understood this in a comprehensive sense. He gave great attention to the study of the North.

From these brief references, the number of which could be greatly increased, it is clear how broadly Lomonosov understood the tasks of the new science that he had begun to create and for which he used the term *economic geography* for the first time in the 1760s, a term that was based on a correct understanding of problems in the development of Russia. One can not possibly say that Lomonosov coined the expression *economic geography* by chance. This was an exact definition of the new science that was fully developed in his mind and was filled with rich and varied content.

How broadly Lomonosov understood geography as a whole can be seen from his "Word of praise... to Ylizaveta Petrovna" [daughter of Peter the Great] where he wrote: "What is useful to mankind for the mutual sharing of their surpluses, what is more necessary to travelers in foreign lands, than to know the places, the course of rivers, the distances between cities, the size, abundance and proximity of various lands, the customs and habits and governments of various peoples? Geography, which at one glance reveals the vastness of the universe, shows this clearly. This remarkable characterization of geography, "which opens the whole vastness of the universe at a single glance," is also not a random expression by Lomonosov.

In his larger works of great geographic significance, such as *On the Earh's Layers, On Electric Atmospheric Phenomena* and *On Northern Navigation to the East Along the Siberian Ocean,* Lomonosov invariably emphasized the interconnection of phenomena, the necessity to find and explain these relationships, the necessity of a historical approach to phenomena, and the exceptional importance in geography of maps including economic maps. It must be noted, however, that Lomonosov in his view was so far ahead of his time that his brilliant ideas remained without further development for a long time.

Nevertheless, it is to Lomonosov, and no one else in all of world science, that credit belongs both in terms of a broad view of geography, which "reveals the vastness of the universe at a single glance", and in the use of the term economic geography itself, and to the formulation of its main tasks.

The pre-revolutionary history of our economic geography was also characterized by the exclusive attention paid to questions of regionalization of the country, including economic regionalization. Regionalization of the country was of great interest in pre-revolutionary Russia, greater than in almost any country (with the exception perhaps of only the United States). The reason for this one must assume, lay in the vastness of the country itself and the diversity of its parts. Under such conditions it is impossible to know the country without distinguishing the various regions in it; regionalization becomes not only a necessary premise for this knowledge but one of the most important methods. It is not by chance that the greatest number of works on the regionalization of Russia began to appear in the nineteenth century, when, with the development of capitalism, the geographic division of labour rapidly developed, and also the differentiation and specialization of regions. About fifty attempts to regionalize pre-revolutionary Russia can be cited. Some of them, it is true, have a narrowly specialized character and give a regionalization based on only one component of the natural environment (climate or soil), but for the most part these attempts give a regionalization either by totality of all features (nature, population, and economy) or by one pre-dominantly based on the character of the economy.

The best known are the attempts of K.A. Arsen'yev (1818,1848), P.P. Semenov-Tyan-Shanskity (1871-80), D.I. Mendeleyev (1893, and then from census materials in 1897), and A.N. Chelintsev (1910, 1916). Of great methodological interest was the article by N. P. Ogarev on questions of economic regionalization, published in *Moskovskiyae Vedomosti* in 1847. Also of great methodological significance is the classical work by V.I. Lenin, *The Development of Capitalism in Russia,* on questions of economic regionalization. The work showed the possibility and necessity of studying the economy of a capitalist country by regions and at the same time it gave a classical example of Marxist methodology by turning major attention to the singularities of the historical development of the country and its socio-political order.

As a whole, the pre-revolutionary works on regiona-lization made a great contribution to the geographic knowledge of our country and in addition helped to inject the principle of regions into the thinking of our geographers.

Our most outstanding geographers, beginning with V.V.Iockuchayev and ending with L.S. Berg, quite definitely stated that the task of geography is not to study individual components of the geographical environment only in their distribution but to study the inter-connections of these components in definite spatial combinations.

As early as 1912, A.A. Borzov wrote in his article "Geography" (in the *Practical School Encyclopedia).*

Geography is, consequently, a science of the earth's surface and deals not with its individual phenomena but with the totality, taking it as it is found in the various parts of the earth. In other words, geography does not deal separately with ores, plants, animals, or man and does not even study the prevalence of these individual phenomena– all this is the affair of other sciences. Geography examines the forms and landscapes into which all these phenomena are organized in the various places of the earth's surface, how soil, river and water basins as a whole, climate, plants, animals and man are inter-related in each locality, in each landscape and in what forms their influence on each other is expressed; it reveals the influence of an individual landscapes on another and tries to describe the kinds of landscape of which the surface of the earth is composed and to explain the life of each landscape individually as well as the law of their distribution and mutual influence.

During the Soviet period, economic regionalization has received a new meaning and a new significance. Formerly it was the major method of comprehensive geographic perception of territory, but under Soviet conditions, it became the necessary premise of planned development for the whole of Soviet economic planning. In the State Plan for Electrification of Russia (GOELRO), established according to the conception and plan of Lenin, who called it *the second programme of the party,* regionalization of the country was planned in connection with the plan for building electric power stations. Based on the transmission of electric current over a distance of not more then 300 to 400 kilometrs, regions were planned in such a manner that within each region there would be a correspondence between intake of electrical energy (from various sources) and output (for various needs).

This first draft of Soviet economic regionalization quite clearly reflected the characteristic features distinguishing it from the regionalization experiments of per-revolutionary time, namely:

1. a forward-looking nature, a concern with transfor-mation as well as understanding;
2. the conception of a region not as some "statistical homogeneity" but as an economic unit complete in itself (in this case according to the balance of electric energy).

In 1919 the work on economic regionalization was given over for completion to the section of regionalization in the Gosplan (State Planning Committee), which in 1921 drew up a projected economic regionalization scheme in which the USSR was divided into 21 regions. The report of the Sub-commission of the All-Russian Central Executive Committee, under the chair-manship of M.I. Kalinin, which examined this project, stated:

A distinctive and, so far as possible, economically complete territory of the country must be set apart as a region and would represent one of the links in the chain of the national economy because of a combination of natural characteristics cultural traditions, and the specialized training of its populace for productive activity. This principle of economic completeness makes it possible to construct a project of economic development for the region that best utilizes all possibilities with minimum expenditures on the basis of a well-selected complex of local resources, capital values, and the general state plan of the national economy. Other important results are achieved by insuring that regions specialize to a certain degree in those branches that can be most fully developed there and that the exchange between regions is strictly limited to the necessary quantity of expediently directed goods.

Thus, in the Gosplan project of 1921, a region was under- stood to be a productive territorial entity, which was so far as possible complete in itself (but not closed), with productive connections within it developed to a maximum extent, and with a specialization on an All-Union scale.

In contrast to the regions projected in the experiments of pre-revolutionary regionalization schemes, a Gosplan region was thought of not as an area on a map and not as a totality of statistical indices but as an administra-tive-political unit with an organ of local power actively engaged in a struggle for the fulfilment of its share of assignments in the All-Union plan, actively transfor-ming its economy according to the planned specia-lization assigned to it by the center and linking all other branches of its economy with his major specialization. A region in the Gosplan conception must not only be homogeneous, as demanded in pre-revolutionary regionalization systems, but, as a general rule, very heterogeneous; for the most complete industrial combine can be obtained most easily from a combination of heterogeneous parts that complement each other.

A region as an industrial territorial complex with a specialization on an All-Union scale is not only a necessity but also a basic principle of regional development. Each of our regions must develop in such a manner that its economy can become more comprehensive, due to more complete utilization of its resources, and as self-sufficient as possible.

The Gosplan definition of a region contains not only the law of its development but also methodological directions on how this region must be studied and how to draw up and interpret its character. In its time, the 1921 Gosplan project of economic regionalization, which provided a complete and clear methodology linking theory with practice, caused a great deal of methodological and factual literature to be published. The economic-geographic literature connected with GOELRO (State Commission on Electrification of Russia) and the Gosplan project of 1921, together with related works, created a Soviet regional approach that replaced the sectoral-statistical approach. The new approach was accepted by the Party and government in its resolution of 16 May 1934, and in the resolution of the Presidium of the Committee on Courses in Higher Institutions of Learning and Higher Technical Schools of 14 July 1934, "On the Teaching of Geography in Higher Schools of Learning and Higher Technical Schools". In accordance with these resolutions, the entire content of instruction in economic geography in secondary and higher schools of learning was reorganized.

In the process of the work on economic regionalization all knowledge of our territory had to be re-examined when questions were to be solved concerning the network of districts, the borders, and the choice of a center for each district.

Questions on economic regionalization were also posed at the Twelfth party Congress and at the fifteenth through twenty-first congresses; a fact that clearly shows the great significance attached to these questions by the supreme organs of our country. Questions on the rational distribution of industry and agriculture were ranked first in the political report of the Central Committee of the All-Union Communist Party at the Sixteenth Party Congress.

It must be said that the economic geographers, for example N.N. Kolosovskiy, made a great contribution to economic regionalization, rational distribution of the economy, and other practical questions of economic development.

Detailed large-scale investigations of the land, especially of a comprehensive economic-geographic nature, that were conducted as a result of the practical requests emanating from socialist construction of the economy had a great methodolo-gical significance for the development of Soviet economic geography. The economic geographers who formerly used secondary materials in the form of statistical information by large administrative units (by oblast), could now in these expeditionary investigations collect in the field the necessary material with the required detail. Large-scale field work was thereby initiated in economic geography making it possible to discover the regularities not evident in small-scale studies of the literature and statistical tables. Field investigations bring the geographer face to face with nature, with the map, with the appearance of correlations, with conditions at the micro-scale, and thereby help to strengthen the geographic elements of economic geography.

Socialist economies, having separated land from the realm of private property, also create a demand for economic maps, including large-scale maps that under our conditions have the same function as the plan had under capitalistic conditions. Field preparation of large-scale economic maps, which no one had previously even thought about, has received an impetus from the works on the detailed study not only of agriculture but also of drainage and irrigation, and of improvement and development of paved roads. The development of economic cartography, especially on a large scale, connected with the field collection of data contributes even more to strengthening the geographic elements in economic geography and is of great methodological significance. A large-scale economic map plotted in the field fixes the distribution of natural conditions, population, and economy fully, exactly, and to a degree of detail unavailable in textual description. Such an economic map thereby compels the economic geographer to transfer his main emphasis from describing a distribution to explaining it.

Formerly economic geographers could succeed by empirically describing where something could be found, thereby considering their work finished. Now, however, with the appearance of such economic maps it is impossible to limit distribution to a bare description. Stimulating economic geography to explain the distributions on a large-scale economic map by the fullness and detail of portrayal simultaneously helps to point out the pertinent material. In addition, in the process of drawing up economic maps, methodological questions and needs in economic geography arise, and sometimes their solution is hastened. One such problem involves the typology of industrial types of agriculture.

All of the above-mentioned factors economic regionalization under conditions of a planned socialist economy, the rational distribution of industry, the correct regional specialization of agriculture and consolidation of subregions, and the large-scale economic cartography connected with it–greatly stimulates the development of economic geography and raises and expands the demand for economic-geographic knowledge. The principal distinguishing features of Soviet economic geography, with regard to the way it has been shaped by the enumerated factors, can be formulated as follows: First its activity and close connection with the practice of socialist construction of the economy;

the influence of socialist requirements and the dissatisfaction with bare statements of what is where; the desire for an exhaustive explanation on a Marxist-Leninist basis; the establishment of regularities making it possible to establish standards; and the scientific determination of further development plans for each region, large and small. Second, the characteristic feature of Soviet economic geography is its comprehensiveness and, at the same time, its concrete and detailed nature, which is achieved by field investigations and the mapping of the territory. Third, and inseparable from the first two, is the ever-growing technical training of our economic geog-raphers, which is necessary in order to understand more fully the geography of production and to plan the future more correctly.

Under Soviet conditions, both people and occupations grow in conformity with the tasks put upon them by our great era. Therefore, in spite of all kinds of survivals from the past in our discipline, there is no doubt that Soviet economic geography will in coming years be equal to the demands put upon it by our socialist development.

2

Resource

Introduction: Man has to carry on economic activity for the survival of himself, his family and society. For this purpose he has to collect various types of economic products. So the foundation of his economic activity depends on these products, namely, the economic *resource.* The economic activity of man depends very much on the production and utilization of economic resources.

With the development of civilisation the need for various types of resources increases. In earliest times the number of population was small and the demand for resources was also limited. People would meet their demands from local resources. But with the development of civilisation and cultural and technical abilities, man with inherent skill in trying to get and produce various types of resources from local area and from abroad to fulfil his entire satisfaction and needs. Thereby man has developed resource consciousness.

Definition of Resource: According to Zimmermann, a *"resource"* does not refer to a thing or a substance. Rather, it refers to the function which a thing or a substance may perform or to an operation in which it may take part. This function or operation is for attaining a given end, the end is only to satisfy the fundamental needs of a man or a society.

A thing or a substance may be called a *'resource'* when it has some (i) *utility* and (ii) *functionability* to satisfy the needs of man. Coal, a mineral resource, cannot be called a resource unless it is utilized by man for the production of power and its by-products for various economic uses.

The functionability of a substance or a thing may be either actual or potential. For example, India's reserves of workable high grade iron-ore have been estimated at about 1020 crore tonnes. Of these only 3.5 crore tonnes are raised annually. The distribution of the ores in different parts is such that the entire amount can be raised if necessary. Therefore, the potential iron-ore resource of India is 1020 crore tonnes though actual production is about 3.5 crore tonnes.

If due to natural calamities or technical difficulty a particular mine becomes unsuitable for utilization then the mineral of that mine cannot be called a resource. The recent terrible accident in the Chasnala coal mine has made it inoperative. So coal deposits of the mine cannot be considered as resources.

The functionability of a thing or a substance differs from time to time and place to place. The desert area of Rajasthan was unsuitable for human settlement. But thanks to the development of the irrigation system, some of the desert area has been turned into a mighty agricultural region. Thus the resource aspect of the land has been changed. In the continent of Africa there are great possibilities of developing hydro-electricity. But the sources have not yet been used for the generation of power. So these sources cannot be termed as 'resource'.

Classification of Resources

The two major classes of resources, are renewable resources and non-renewable resources.

1. Renewable resources

There are some resources, of which man may use as much as he desires without fear that the supply ever will be exhaused. These may be called the renewable or inexhaustible resources. Water resources, air and solar heat are the example of inexhaustible or renewable resources. These are also known Flow resources. Flow resources are those that are naturally renewed within a sufficient short time span to be of relevance to human beings, they include water, air, animal and plant life, solar radiation, wind power and tidal energy.

Those resources when once they are used, they are gone forever, these are called non-renewable or exhaustible or Fund resources. They are very scarce and their supply may be limited in quantity, not to replenish when they are use. Iron, coal etc. are the example of non-renewable resources. They are known as stock resources.

Classes of Earth Resources

The material phenomena consist of the physical resources such as land resources, soils, water, fuel and mineral resources, and the biotic resources which include natural vegetation or forest resources, native wild life and marine life.

The classification of natural Resources

On the surface of the earth there are generally two major forms of resources, one is Physical resources and second Biotic resources. This classification is very general and is as follows:

Physical Resources

Ginsberg included rocks, surface forms, soil, mineral wealth and water resources in physical resources and showed that these resources are present uniformly everywhere on the earth in the form of natural gifts and they have been used in various forms in the various situations of human civilization. Not only this, ever in the modern scientific age though scientific progress and technological knowledge are most important in determining the utility, shape and change of shape of these resources, their shape has not changed very much. Change of shape in natural resources can be observed where man has established and adjustment with nature. On the contrary, in parts like the Antarctica continent where complete adjustment has not been possible, the shape of physical resources remains the same and their utility is beyond human enjoyment.

Biotic Resources

Ginsberg has included biotic resources in the second class. These are the resources which influence the economic activities of man for a long time and are themselves influenced by human actions. So an inter relation between them continues. These are resources that can increase or decrease according to circumstances and are influenced by human activities, Five destruction of biotic resources, planting trees, hunting animals or breeding their new kinds all these actions are related to human needs and utilization and the determination of their form, amount and consequence depend upon human activities.

Comparison of physical and Biotic Resources

A comparison of physical and Bioric Resources is given below.

Physical Resources

Physical resources are considered immovable resources.

Human actions influence their form. Change in their form is estimated by those actions which are included in the areas of cultural activities rather than physical landscapes. Man alters them by his own will but these changes have very little influence on them. After they have been used, physical resources are finally exhausted, *e.g.*, minerals, when they have been mined, are finished for ever. Such incidents are seen at several places in the mining history of the world. Fertility of soil when finished is exhausted. This is what has caused deserts.

The amount of physical resources is fixed. Man can neither increase them, nor decrease them very much. He can only change their shape. Man can neither increase nor decrease the shape and size of the earth. Man can not product earth. He can only modify natural landscapes by means of cultural landscapes.

Physical resources are spreading in some shape or the other. Resources such as air, water, shape of the earth, soil etc. are present at every place. Biotic resources depend to great extent on the presence of physical resources. Physical resources are called ubiquities.

The amount of physical resources has been large. But it is not equally distributed.

The chief speciality of physical resources is that they are harder than other resources and are longer.

Zoological multiplicity is not found in physical resources. Man can not increase their amount.

Durability is specially found in physical resources and their existence has been coming down from several geological ages. These are several regions which are still untouched by human actions and physical resources aboundend in shape of potential resources.

Use or enjoyment of physical resources or alternation or modification in their shape by human action is effected by long term processes, but the effect of man's action can alter its outer shape but can not destroy it completely.

Physical resources are immovable or they exist at one place in the same shape and there is no change of location in them. Change in their in enter shape has sometimes been observed through biotic resources.

Biotic Resources

Biotic resources are considered as movable resources.

Human actions do influence them but whatever change occurs in their form is again reestablished by nature, *e.g.,* after the destruction of forest, as a result of heat and rain, shrubs and finally forests are again developed in the same part. In the fishing areas, even after fish are caught, there is gradual growth of fish again.

After Biotic resources have been used, some kinds of these are left which, are some time, take up their own shape. In the meadows, as a result of free grazing, grass is finished, but grows again when natural condition are suitable. The same rule applies to forests too.

Man has an important place in the modification or altering the shape of biotic resources. He finished one kind and tries to protect new kinds. On the one hand he destroys forests while on the other he plants trees and protects their new kinds. In the same manner the destruction and protection of animals too are related to human activities.

Biotic resources are not equally distributed in every place and climate and physical resources influence their distribution, Biotic resources are included in the class of rarities. Biotic resources of the kind that are found in the Mediterranean regions are not found in cold regions.

Biotic resources have more variety and more frequency of occurrence than amount.

Less length and less hardness then physical resources has been observed in biotic resources.

Breeding pluralities are found in some shape or the other in biotic resources on the basis of which their generation is continued.

Durability in biotic resources is for a small period of time. It has been observed that durability in biotic resources changes with change in climate or physical resources.

A continuous use of biotic resources reduces their amount and they are finally exhausted. There are some such biotic resources too which are sometimes decorated as pieces of art only in museums. Even today there are several creatures which man has been freely hunting and now they exist only in pictures.

In biotic resources we mainly come across change of location and when physical resources sometimes due to exogenetic or indogenetic forces change their shape, amount, result or traits, biotic resources change their place. This attitude, is specially seen in animals and birds, shows the diversities of climate.

As a result, it is a cluster of several specialization within geography rather than a single clearly defined finely. Its classic divisions are land as a resources, energy or power resources and human resources.

Natural resources comprise the land, menial deposits, climate and all other materials and condition's that are originally furnished by nature. The natural resources may be subdivided almost without limits in terms of use relationship of minerals, power resources or other ubiquarian characteristics. Climate determines the location and distribution of agricultural resources. Cost factors, in turn, are influenced by the relative scareity or abundance of the resource.

Thus western Uttar Pradesh endowed with large amount of fertile soil and relatively little human power and equipment is likely emphasize extensive production of agricultural products; whereas Hooghly region of western Bengal endowed with large aggregates of equipment and skilled labour is likely to emphasize production of more complex manufactured products. The economic utilization of natural resources, of course, is accomplished only by human action. However, only land as resources and the geography of mineral production are highly developed today and their utilization reached at saturation point. Economic geography and geography of agricultural resources are not strictly considered as division with geography of resources, since their fields of interest are so broad as to overlap into many subjects.

Economic Resources—Economic resources, those human and non-human factors which, when used in combination make possible the production of economic goods. Thus economic resources may be classified into two broad groups: labour or human resources and capital equipment ofproduced resources. All production involves labour, nature is likewise always involved as a source of materials. The geographical distribution of economic resources is one of the principal determinants of the character and location of industry, the economic and determinants of the character and location of industry, the economic and political power of nations, and the plane of living of the population.

Labour resources comprise the energy and the skill of all persons engaged in economically productive activity. The potential productivity of the labour resources of a given society is not to be measured alone in terms of the number of people resident in it. The educational level, geographic mobility, versatility and adaptability, ingenuity, ability to use tools and machines, and the educational and legal environments—are all relevant to the character of the labour resource.

Capital consists of all material resources which are suitable for use in productive processes. Capital is usually distinguish in various types according to their functions in the productive organization. Capital equipment resources comprise the tools, machines and building materials that facilitate further production. In a sense, equipment is a secondary rather than a primary resources, since it is the product of the past combination of labour and nature. Some equipment is of a general type and is used by all who are engaged in productive activity, it includes telegraph facilities and similar forms of capital. The importance of capital equipment to the modern economy is so great that is accumulation and maintenance are of national concern is both capitalistic and socialistic communities. Capital is the Resource of all Resources which is the part of that wealth of individuals and of communities, other than land, which is used to assist in the production of future wealth.

Resource Distribution. No doubt, high rates of population growth and low agricultural productivity, together with the lack of resources and technological advancement, have contributed significantly to the perpetuation of poverty in underdeveloped countries. However, no explanation of poverty is more obvious and significant than the existing inequality in the social distribution of productive resources, including both land and capital.

In most underdeveloped countries, land is the basic source of livelihood, income and social status. In spite of the fact that industrial and service activity has expanded in these countries, the agricultural sector (land) remains the most important source of employment and livelihood. Control of land generally means control of capital, other productive resources, and ready access to market distribution networks and outlets.

Given such absolute importance attributed to land in people's lives, the social distribution of land resources becomes a crucial element in the discussion of poverty in undeveloped countries. It has been reported that inequality in resource distribution leads to (I) the exclusion of a large number of people from useful activities, thus making them much less productive than they could be with secure access to resources: (2) the underutilization and low productivity of resources available in a given society; and (3) the lack of incentives among those who possess minimal or no resources of their own and depend on others for their resistance. None of these situations helps to increase productivity and thus reduce poverty.

The unequal distribution of productive resources is analogous to a zero-sum game or gambling situation. Gains to one can be obtained only through losses by others. Whereas those with control over resources enjoy a luxurious life, those who lace resources live in perpetual poverty—at the margin of bare subsistence and starvation.

These income distribution figures clearly show that the lowest 20 percent of the population shares only a tiny fraction of national income. It is as low as 2 percent in the case of Brazil. In no case does it exceed

8.7 percent on the income distribution scale. The highest 20 percent of the population, one the other hand, enjoys the largest portion of national income—from a minimum of 38.8 percent in Great Britain (a highly developed country to a maximum of 66.6 percent for Brazil. As mentioned earlier, the disparity is quite large in the highest-income category between underdeveloped and developed countries.

Global Problem

There is a basic problem. On the hand, it is clear that many resources currently being used are non-renewable, and that the use of some resources destroys others. On the other hand, many elements which are currently considered as resources might be appraised differently in the future as new resources are developed.

As a result, there are many different ways of assessing resource prospects. One extreme is the **Malthusian view** which sees the stock of resources as a finite supply rapidly being depleted by large and increasing demands resulting from uncontrolled population growth and increasing aspirations. The conse-quence of this will be the exhaustion for resources and the impoverishment or even destruction of man. At the other extreme is the **technological view** which concedes that although the stock of resources is ultimately finite, the bounds of possibility within these limits are so extensive that the exhaustion of resources is not a practical problem. Technology may deplete some resources, but it also has a capacity for creating others, and as a result all problems can be solved if technical progress is maintained and economic and social constraints can be overcome.

Between these two extremes, ways have to be found of producing a practical assessment of the earth's supply of resou-rces and of the demand likely to be placed on them so that a coordinated resource policy can be developed to balance them sensibly. Such a policy just also include consideration of the pro-blems of waste and pollution arising from the resource process.

The Supply of Resources

A major task for the planner is to decide which resources are vital and then to discover the size of the available stock. This stock taking has been considerably aided by the development of technique for the **remote sensing of the environment** such as aerial and satellite photography. Resource evaluation from satellites is particularly valuable as infrared photography, radar scanning and other technical developments have supplied new tools to increase our knowledge of the earth and its potentials. The launching of the Earth Resources Technology Satellite ERTS-1 from the USA in 1972 was a major step forward since it was specifically designed to record and transmit resources information back to earth, but there is still a great deal of work to be done before knowledge of the stock of resources is complete. A more difficult task is the assessment of future technological innovations and the forecasting of the economic conditions under which they, and known but currently uneconomic resources, may be profitably used. However, a brief examination of food, mineral and energy supplies will illustrate some resource problems.

At present, enough food is being produced to feed the world population (5,000 millions in 1987), although there are serious problems arising from its maldistribution. It is also possible to increase food supplies as population increase because, of the 25 percent which is potentially pastoral, only about half of each is currently being used. It is also possible to use much of the present agricultural area more intensively. However, this is much more a technical than an economic potential. About one third of the potential arable, of example, lies within the tropics, where leaching and the creation of hard-pan soils will necessitate vast inputs of fertilisers and drainage schemes, thus imposing heavy demands on energy and mineral supplies, in order to produce uncertain returns. Not is the more intensive use of the oceans likely to lead to a vast increase in food supplies. Although fish is a valuable source of protein, it seems unlikely that production will increase to more than 2½ times the present production of 70 million tonnes per annum, and there is already concern about cod stocks around Iceland and herring stocks in the North Sea. Thus, although increases in production are possible, it has been estimated that food supplies are unlikely to increase by more than eightfold under foreseen conditions, and this will put the limit of population growth at about 30,000 millions, with the vast majority at starvation levels. At present rates of increase this figure will be reached in the year 2075.

Mineral ores are localised and exhaustible and are therefore a potential source of friction, but on the whole there are plentiful supplies of minerals. However, the question of whether or not they could become **ores,** capable of being worked at a profit, is dependent on technology and economics, and as a result estimates of reserves are very unreliable. There are already shortages of mercury, tin, tungsten, gold and copper, and alternative sources or substitutes are being sought. The search is very wide ranging but it seems that, as with food supplies, the oceans are unlikely to be a very fruitful source, especially from the rocks beyond the continental shelves, although sediments on the se-bed are potentially valuable. Even in shallower waters, economics and technology place constraints on development and it must be recognised that ore deposits are in finite supply under present economic and technical conditions, and that the exhaustion of some deposits is imminent.

Despite the fact that vast amounts of energy reach the earth every day from the sun, there has been a great deal of concern the possibility that energy supplies may soon be exhausted. It has been estimated that there is only about 50 years' supply of oil and gas, and 200–300 years' supply of coal at present rates of extraction, and some experts believe that these might be better used as raw materials rather than being burned to provide energy. However, the problem is that the vast amount of low-intensity energy coming from the sun is difficult to concentrate, and its conversion into electricity will not be economic until at least the year 2000 in the UK. Similarly, although wind, water and tidal power have long been available to man, their large scale exploitation raises many technical problems, and only hydro-electric power is developed to any great extent. The same is true of attempts to tap geothermal energy. Although geothermal energy is used to produce electricity in volcanic areas, the need to drill to depths of at least, 3,600 m elsewhere raises considerable engineering problems. In fact, current economic and technical conditions make the replacement of fossil fuels as the principal sources of energy very difficult, despite their threatened exhaustion and the pollution problems created by the release of hydrocarbons into the atmosphere as they are burned.

The Demand for Resources

Problems also arise when attempts are made to measure the size and nature of future demand. One thing is certain, the demand for resources will continue to tise, but the two main causes of this rise are difficult to forecast.

The first cause of increased demand is population growth, but how far will, or can, population grow? The problem of forecasting population growth is discussed in Chapter Eight, but many experts agree that only zero growth will provide the long-term solution. One projection suggests that world population must level off below 10,000 millions by the year 2050 to enable reasonable standards to be achieved, but although rates of increase are slackening in some developed countries, there is little sign of an overall abatement of human fertility. As a result, this increase in numbers puts great pressure on resources because more and more people have to be fed, clothed and sheltered, even though this may only be at subsistence levels.

However, when this increase in numbers is combined with rising aspirations and the development of technology capable of sustaining high standards of living, a second cause of increased demand is created. The revolution of rising expectations, especially marked since 1945, has led to the establishment of a consumer society, based on cheap energy, for which demand was increasing at a rate of 12 percent per annum until the oil crisis of 1973. Unfortunately, the consumer society has been base don a robber economy in which large amounts of resources have been used, and the benefits of which have been denied to the vast majority of mankind. In 1975, each person consumed an average energy equivalent to 2,028 kg of coal, but this varied from 221 kg a head in India to 10,999 kg in the USA. The difference between the high consumption/low-population economies with great technical abilities to consume and yet create resources, and the low-consumption/high-population economies with limited technical abilities create great instability and are at potential source of friction. Unfortunately, the greater the level of economic development, the greater the demand for resources, and any attempt to raise living standards in the Third World countries are committed to Western-style development base on urbanisation and industrialization involving high consumption of decreasingly available energy, but even in the West, increasing concern for the 'quality of life' suggests that this may not be the surest path to happiness.

The remarkable developments in science and technology made during the last 200 years have made it possible for many environment to support much greater populations than formerly; however, if population growth and increasing aspirations cause demand for resources to outstrip supply, then overpopulation will be the result.

The Problem of Waste and Pollution

Faced with the danger that demand will outstrip supply, the twin problems of waste and pollution are increasingly important. Unfortunately, the creation of waste and pollution arises during the exploitation, use and dispersal of resources for both economic and technical reasons, and the problems associated with these three stages of the resource process are frequently intensified when accidents occur. Some of these problems are examined in the following sections.

Exploiting Resources

As man's numbers and technology have increased, he has exploited the earth's resources more intensively, but this activity is producing increasing amounts of waste and pollution. The exploitation of minerals has sterilised large areas as pits are dug to remove iron, copper, clay and so on, and as waste from the underground mining of coal or gold is tipped. There were over 100,000 ha of derelict land in Britain in 1967 and despite attempts to reclaim such land, it is increasing at a rate of over 1,400 ha per annum as coal, clay, gravel and sand are worked. On a world scale, much large acreages have been affected by attempts to extend and intensify agriculture, and overcropping and overgrazing have led to the progressive breakdown of soil structure and its erosion by wind and water in many regions. In the USA alone, 5 percent of land suitable for agriculture or forestry has been completely ruined, 15 percent has lost three quarters of its topsoil, and 41 percent is subject to moderate erosion.

Attempt to increase agricultural production have also produced pollution. First, the use of artificial fertilisers is an essential part of high productivity, but as the chemicals are gradually washed from the land by the normal processes of the weather, the resulting concentration of nutrients in rivers and lakes creates problems. This process of nutrient enrichment, especially by nitrogen and phosphorus, is known as **eutrophication,** and its effects on the flora and fauna of lakes such as Lakes Erie and Ontario have been so dramatic that such laws are thought to be in danger of 'dying'. The use of agricultural chemicals has also created a second form of pollution. Herbicides, fugicides and especially insesticides are being used in increasing amounts to maintain and increase production by providing protection against diseases and insect pests. Unfortunately, many insecticides such as DDT or Dieldrin do not break down very quickly and as a result they can build up in animal tissue. This has serious implications fro humans, who are at the top of a food chain, and many Americans are already legally unfit for human consumption because of the high levels of DDT in their bodies. The problem is so serious that countries such as Sweden, Denmark and the USA have banned the use of DDT, but its cheapness and efficacy mean that it is still used in large amounts in many parts of the Third World where priority is necessarily given to increasing food production.

Using Resources

Many resources are used wastefully, especially energy. There are often sound technical reasons for this, for while power stations with

55-60 percent efficiency are planned, the best UK stations are only 36 percent efficient at present. Moreover, some UK power stations are only 20 percent efficient, and as a result, overall UK efficiency was only 29 percent in 1973–4. The magnitude of the problem of resource waste can be illustrated by the fact that if overall efficiency could be increase from 29 to 32 percent, there would be a saving of 10 million tonnes of coal per annum. However, the problem is not only technical but is also associated with Britain's policy of locating larger and larger power stations away from concentrations of population, and a further 10 percent is lost in transmission. In Sweden, thermal power stations are much smaller and are more market-oriented, and this has the added advantage that instead of wasting heat in massive cooling towers, the steam can be used for home heating over distances of up to 25 km.

The use of resources in industry also creates pollution, and this comes about in two ways. First, there is the discharge of pollutant side-effects in manufacture, storage and distribution. Thus, it is estimated that industry in the UK discharges 2 million tonnes of smoke, 1.5 million tonnes of ash and 5 million tonnes of sulphur and gases into the atmosphere every year, adding considerably to the problem of air pollution. This could often be greatly reduced, but the cost would have to be borne by the manufacturer who is thus reluctant to take action, despite the fact that some industrial discharges are highly toxic.

Secondly, the product itself might be a pollutant. The motorcar is an outstanding culprit as it pours out nitrous oxides into the atmosphere, creating petrochemical smog in sunny, motor-dominated areas such as Los Angeles, which in turn does serious damage to people, crops and trees. More recently, there has been concern that the fluorocarbons used as propellant gases in aerosols may be attacking the ozone concentrations in the stratosphere, thus removing the earth's protective barrier against dangerous ultraviolet radiation.

Disposing of Resources

The disposal of resources once they have been used is accompanied by massive waste. This waste is essentially an economic problem because it is usually cheaper, measured simply indirect production costs, for the manufacturer to use new materials than to collect and reuse old ones. However, the economics of the 'throw-away society' are being increasingly questioned because the real costs of dumping are enormous and have to be borne by the community as a whole. It is inevitable that there should be some waste within the resource process, but at present recoverable quantities of limited resources are simply being squandered as 'rubbish' is buried or burned.

Nevertheless, under present economic conditions, large amounts of waste have to be disposed of, and this creates problems which have to be overcome. Social change over the last 40 years has meant that domestic waste percent of the total weight, paper has increased from 15 to 34 percent. As a result, much larger holes have to be found by local authorities in which to bury it, and these are becoming scarce and expensive. Other solid wastes create even more difficult problems, and nuclear wastes, which can remain radioactive for up to 250,000 years, have at present to be stored under very secure conditions to prevent leakage.

On top of the problem of knowing what to do with large amounts of waste material from resource use, there is also the increasing problem of pollution, especially from the liquid wastes of domestic, industrial and agricultural sewage. At present, vast amounts of liquid wastes are simply poured into rivers, lakes and oceans without any form of treatment, with the consequent loss of valuable sources of fertilisers, minerals and so on. Unfortunately this also contaminates water supplies and heightens the risk of diseases such as cholera, dysentery and typhoid. Different sorts of risk arise from industrial pollution, and after the River Cuyohoga had become so heavily polluted with inflammable materials that it ignited and burned down two bridges in Cleveland in 1969, it had to be declared an official fire-risk. More serious, the discharge of mercury waste from a plant near Minamata in Japan led to serious neural damage among many local inhabitants after they had eaten fish and shellfish contaminated with mercury, but despite such warnings the discharge of toxic wastes continues on a world scale, endangering life and polluting other resources.

Accidents

In fact, accidents occur at all three stages of the resource process, and provide spectacular, but usually short-lived, examples of waste and pollution. The most spectacular accidents usually involve oil, due to the fact that of an annual production of over 2,500 million tonnes more than 60 percent is transported by sea in ships of ever-increasing size. Thus, when the *Torrey Canyon* was wrecked in 1967, 120,000 tonnes of oil was lost, and much of it ended up on the holiday beaches of Cornwall and Brittany. Unfortunately, the problem did not end there because 10,000 tonnes of detergent was used to clean up the polluted beaches which were a threat to the tourist industry on which thousands of people depended for there livelihood. The detergents had even greater biological effects than the oil, by killing mollusca such as limpets in vast numbers. Since 25 percent of total oil production passes through the English Channel, and this is the world's busiest shipping lane, the wreck of the *Amoco Cadiz,* spilling 220,000 tonnes of oil onto the Brittany coast in 1978, was not unexpected. Major oil spillages continue, and the tanker *Exxon Valdez* hit a reef in Prince William Sound in 1989. Less oil was spilled, but the introduction of 33,000 tonnes of heavy Alaskan crude into a sensitive environment had a disastrous effect on beaches and wildlife.

Planning Resource Use

In recent years there has been increasing concern that the relationship between man and nature is becoming unbalanced, and that even though man can be considered apart from nature in many ways, he is basically dependent upon it. This recognition of the need for environmental management and planning is not the same as its implementation, but it is an important step in the right direction.

The Need for Planning

Resources planning is necessary fro two main reasons. First, to avoid the possibility of the exhaustion of resources, and second, to avoid disastrous human interference in natural ecosystems.

In view of man's ability to create resources, it seems unlikely that the earth's resources will become exhausted, but on the other hand certain resources are already in short supply, and many others have a very limited availability. There is, therefore, an urgent need for a dynamic equilibrium to be reached in which supply and demand are sensibly balanced. Since demand is very difficult to control, the first priority must be given to increasing supply, and this can be done in a number of ways. First, a full exploration of the earth's supply of resources must be undertaken so that total stocks can be assessed and their useful life calculated. A start has been made with the development of more sophisticated remote sensing techniques, but the stock taking is far from complete. Secondly, once it is known which stocks are seriously depleted, technology must alternative resources before such stocks are totally exhausted. Thirdly, resources must be conserved by the reduction of waste. This will create difficulties because it will require a revolution in attitudes, but if cost-benefit analysis is applied to issues such as the disposal of used resources, it will become clear that much current practice is not only wasteful but is also uneconomic when all costs are accounted. When many resources are in finite supply, **recycling** is essential.

The possibility of an ecocatastrophe in which man's activities create so much pollution that the earth's natural systems begin to disintegrate is the second cause for concern. It is not possible simply to ban pollution because this would mean the end of cars, aircraft, fertilisers, detergents and many other conveniences and aids, but on the other hand it is clear that pollution must be controlled. There is a need to discover which pollutants are harmful and which are simply unpleasant, and then to discover the limits within which man can safely operate and beyond which irreversible damage will take place. There has been some progress, and an international conference in 1972 agreed that there must be a reduction in the dumping of certain wastes into the oceans, but much more international cooperation is necessary. Unfortunately, that is very difficult to achieve, and there are serious obstacles to the planning of resource use on a world scale.

Planning Problems

The obstacles to the effective planning of resources can be examined in two categories. First, there is the problem of controlling demand, and secondly, there is the problem of resource allocation.

The demand for resources is rising because for many groups of people the quality of life is improving, and this must be seen as a positive objective of the whole resource process. Unfortunately, demand is also rising simply to maintain an increase in the quantity of life, but unless this is controlled the resource process will eventually be swamped. Population growth must be controlled, because even at the desperately low rate of resource use achieved by the vast majority of the world's population, its sheer size will lead to the eventual exhaustion of resources without any necessary improvement in living standards. Similarly, although ecosystems have a remarkable ability to absorb high levels of pollution, many are in danger from the enormous population growth brings few benefits and considerable problems, the control of human fertility is beset with social and political constraints. It seems likely that unless rapid world-wide economic growth produces demographic conditions such as those in the developed countries, where voluntary restraint is allowing population to grow slowly, there will almost certainly be involuntary controls on growth such as famine, disease and war.

Because resources are not in unlimited supply and are unevenly distributed, their allocation depends on a number of problematical criteria which are difficult to plan. Even within countries, resource allocation is a difficult problem and conflicts arise over, for example, whether land should be used or farming or housing, or whether forests should be used for timber or amenity. When the question of planning resources on a world scale arises, economic and political divisions raise almost insuperable problems. Until relative scently resources have been plentiful and when shortages occurred they were overcome by territorial or commercial expansion. However, as the supply of resources diminishes and competition for them increases, there is an urgent need for planning and cooperation to avoid conflict, since there is now little room for expansion. It would be Utopian to expect that there could be resource planning on a world scale, but the problems are world-wide nonetheless, and must be confronted.

3

Development of Economic Geography

Economic geography is the study of the economic singularity of countries and regions, of spatial differences in economy on the earth's sphere, that is, differences from place to place, and also of spatial combinations within an economy. If these differences did not exist there would be no economic geography; it could not exist, for there would be no special object for investigation. In order to study these spatial differences, they must first be stated, then described as exactly as possible, and finally, the causes of these differences must be investigated. Ultimately, having investigated all these causes one must develop the mechanisms of these changes in the economy from place to place. In this way one can begin to formulate the problems of economic geography.

It must be emphasized that the differences from place to place in an economy are not due solely to differences in natural conditions. Let us assume that all differences in natural conditions have for some reason or another ended, that all climates have been blended, the seas have been divided evenly with land areas, and the mountains have been erased; even in such a case, contrasts in economy from place to place appear in each given country and at each given moment. These contrasts depend not only on the differences in natural conditions but to a great degree they also depend on the development of productive forces, on the past investment of labour on any part of the earth's surface, and on a number of other socio-historical features.

The Necessity of a Historical Approach

In order to more closely approach and more clearly visualize the problems of economic geography, it is necessary to consider this question historically. Science is not the concern of only one person and a small segment of time; science is a collective experience, the experience of many generations. Only a historical approach to science can show the paths of its development, detect the impasses that must be avoided and, on the other hand, acquaint us with past achievements and thereby prevent the labour of discovering America for the second time. This is way a historical approach to this discipline is needed. Besides this, we know very well that no discipline develops in a vacuum, that ideas do not fall from the sky, that every system of scientific views and opinions develops in a definite social environment, and that "the demands of life' are the main factors in the development of any science and any ideology.

The stronger the association of a given science with practice, the stronger is the influence of the demands of life. These demands of life in a class society are in the end nothing more than the changing interests of the ruling classes; in this one must see, if not the only, certainly the main stimulus to the development of some sciences. We know that even the emergence itself of the sciences was the result of a social need for them. So geometry appeared, as its name implies, from the word geodesy, measurement of the earth, as the result of a completely practical necessity to divide irregular pieces of land into plots. It is true, geometry has gone far beyond land measurement, but the first social command that gave birth to geometry was geodesy.

Economic geography, as all sciences, was created under the influence of the practical demands of life, and in its development has experienced incessant impulses from social life, definite commands, and has had to react to those practical needs which occurred in a specific historical era. Thus, "a social command" must guide the Marxist in approaching the development of any kinds of sciences and ideas. With this kind of approach we turn to our subject. What forms did economic-geographic thought take on in the process of its development? What stages did economic geography pass through as a science studying differences from place to place in the economy? First we will give a general outline of the development of economic-geographic learning on the world scale, and then note the special features of the development of this learning in our country.

Elements of Economic Geography in the Literature of Voyages

First of all we note the embryonic period of the development of economic geography, when as such it did not yet exist independently but only as part of a single complex physical geography and ethnography, in the form of travel journals. Such descriptions of voyages were not only the original written sources of geographic information (in particular, information from the field of economic geography) but also information referring to other disciplines that later evolved and separated from each other, not only the science of geography (including physical, economic, and cultural geography) stems from such sources, but other sciences as well, for example, ethnography.

A description of a voyage is a very complete form of narrative. A person comes to a strange country and everything there is of interest to him. He is surprised and describes everything that he sees; he does not select the facts by categories as do specialists who are interested in only nature (even its individual elements), or only the economy (or only its individual branches) or only the life and customs of the population; the traveler describes absolutely everything that strikes his imagination–mountains, vegetation, climatic phenomena–and if he encounters something surprising in the economy or in the life and customs of the people, he then includes that in his description also. Writing this up along his route he interweaves everything to such an extent that no one can discern where physical geography ends and where economic geography or ethnography begins.

It was quite natural that the descriptive form of voyages was the initial form for geographic and ethnographic sciences. Why? We have already agreed that the essence of geography lies in the study of differences from place to place. But when a person lives in one place he gets accustomed to his surrounding world, to the surrounding nature and forms of economic activity and does not see anything surprising, especially interesting, or worthy of description. But when that person finds himself in other places where there are other natural conditions, other people, and another economy, everything amazes him, and he begins to notice and describe it. Thus, it is natural that literature devoted to voyages became the first form of geography.

This form of literature (descriptions of voyages) is as old as the voyages themselves. Literary monuments of this kind have remained from the ancient Greeks. In the last analysis, the *Odyssey* in nothing but a poetic description of voyages. Descriptions of voyages have remained also from the Egyptians, Carthagenians, and the Arabs. The largest number of voyage reports were made during the era of geographic discoveries, beginning at the end of the fifteenth century with the voyages of Vasco de Gama and Columbus and in the early part of the sixteenth century with the first voyage around the world by Magellan.

Since in the voyage reports the economic-geographic information was not separated specifically but was mixed with other aspects, it is rather difficult to get a full and systematic notion of the economic peculiarity of each country from the description of the traveler who took one route and was not especially concerned with the economy of the country. On the other hand, however, what one has seen with one's own eyes can, of course, be described in a livelier, more buoyant, and more interesting manner, and these voyage descriptions combine economics, nature, and ethnography, all of which make them much more engrossing.

The value of a voyage description depends primarily upon the traveler himself, on this ability to observe, the breadth of his outlook, on the stock of general perceptions that guide him in processing his observations. The very content of the voyage depends on the predominant interests of the traveler. Interest in trade, imperialistic expansion, land acquisition, and so forth had an influence not only on the organization of the voyages and expeditions but also on the direction of the voyages. Many voyages were in essence nothing but a preliminary survery for seizures. The aims of the surveys–military, commercial, and others–were often cloaked under scientific geographic investigations.

Commercial Geography

Another impetus for the development of economic geography was the development of trade relations that followed the era of great discoveries. In the course of the sixteenth, seventeenth and eighteenth centuries there occurred a tremendous expansion of seaways and a corresponding development of transoceanic trade by the leading Western European countries. Earlier the range of European sea trade was limited to the North by the North and Baltic seas, to the South by the Mediterranean Sea. The farthest expeditions within these limits were those between the Mediterranean and North Seas. Beginning with Vasco de Gama and Columbus, little by little, routes were discovered around Africa to India, then from Europe across the Atlantic Ocean to America and, finally, to the islands of the Pacific Ocean. Thus, the range of trade grew greatly, crossed national boundaries and took on an international character. This basic fact could not but affect the demands life placed on economic-geographic knowledge. Actually, in small trade conducted on a local scale there is no need for any special science for the training of agents. Imagine a trade establishment under prerevolutionary conditions in a village that has a trade consisting of two kinds of operations: on the one hand, buying up local agricultural products and on the other hand, selling city goods such as cloth, ready-made clothes, utensils, and agricultural equipment.

What knowledge must a man have who performs trade operations of this type and at this scale? He must know the volume of supply and demand within the limits of his trading sphere, that is, where and when he must buy up the surplus of local agricultural production and the dimension, composition, and season of demand for city goods. His whole scope may be limited to one or two districts. No special science would be needed; since he could get all the necessary information personally. It is quite different when the market widens and even extends beyond national borders. Crossing state borders we find different trade conditions. There are new measures of goods, new monetary systems, special trade rights, new legal procedures, and custom duties. The situation is completely different: quite different natural conditions, other trade customs, approaches, and so forth. To study all the diversity of trade conditions, the whole assortment of goods, and, finally, to study where to buy cheaper and where to sell at a higher price within the framework of the whole world is already a science that demands special studies, a special literature, an special schools.

Just as the interests of the police state gave rise to the demand for educated officials and brought financial statistics to life, so the interest of a trade extending to international dimensions gave rise to the large-scale demand for educated merchants and business agents and resulted in the creation of commercial geography. Here again, there is clearly a transition from quantity to quality. What then must be the scope of geographic knowledge demanded of an educated merchant as distinguished from the scope of knowledge demanded of an educated officials? An educated official could largely limit himself to information with- in the boundaries of his country, but the interests of an important merchant extended over the whole world, and included various countries with completely different natural conditions. Therefore, interest in natural conditions increased. In order to systematize this entire mass of diverse trade knowledge, it is necessary to understand why in one country one can buy such products as sugarcane, coffee, or cocoa, and in another, fur or lumber; it is indeed necessary to have some geographic knowledge. This cannot be done through mechanical cramming of price-lists, reference books, or dictionaries. This knowledge must contain a great deal of geography, including physical geography.

On the other hand, those sections of financial statistics that dealt with governmental organization, finances, army, navy, and diplomatic relations, information that the official needed, where of less interest to the merchant. Thus, the structure of this kind of course changed considerably and was no longer financial statistics but commercial geography; many chapters became superfluous, but the number of countries studies rose, attention to natural conditions, geographic elements, and foreign trade increased. A characteristic feature of textbooks on commercial geography, especially English ones, was the special attention given to a detailed analysis of foreign trade (by countries and commodities). Thus, in addition to financial statistics (and often together with it), commercial geography was created.

This was the time of growing capitalism, when it was still opposed to autocratic monarchical power, when the ideology of the bourgeoisie was in its youth, and its ideologists still believed that the new bourgeois economic order was bringing harmony and universal happiness to mankind. It was assumed therefore that the less there was of official pressure and regulation, the sooner this harmony and general happiness would be established on the earth. This was the time of the dominance of the theories of "laissez faire, laissez passer," a time when one was inclined to look upon the government as a night watchman, and the young bourgeoisie wanted to limit its functions to the preservation of security while preventing its enterference in the economy. Hence one can understand the somewhat disdainful attitude of the leading bourgeoisie and its ideologists toward government and its functions, toward the officials and the knowledge the they needed.

If one says that a merchant is most interested in where to buy cheaply and sell dearly, one is basically correct. This is his main interest and to a considerable degree it predetermines the content of courses in commercial geography. In commercial geography there is surprisingly little or no discussion of the general characteristics of the economy. There are chapters discussing the general character of agriculture and of industry, but the discussion is for the most part limited to strictly tangible branches such as wheat or rye production. Why? It is, quite simply, that agriculture is not traded, but wheat and rye are; and these practical mercantile interests influence to a considerable degree the content of courses in commercial geography. The same preponderance of mercantile interests compelled the inclusion of reference information useful to the merchant, especially that concerning the science of staple commodities, in the courses in commercial geography. Commercial geography in its more practical forms is quite close to a descriptive science of staple commodities in their geographic aspects. And often scientists concerned with staple commodities undertook instruction in commercial geography. In order to conduct trade, one needs more than a mere knowledge of where to buy cheaply and sell dearly; even for commercial capitalism it was of interest to know the conditions of police security in the country where one traded and that is why merchants were interested in law and order in foreign countries.

Another demand on geographic knowledge, in addition to that of an economic geographical order, is the demand for a knowledge of military defense. In this respect the information on the size of the army and military equipment is of prime importance, but this information does not exhaust the question. In order to judge the military strength of a country, it is necessary to know everything that enters into the idea of war potential; and this is a very broad idea, including not only war industries but the whole economy of the country and its concerete spatial manifestation. More than that, it is also important to know national policy, both domestic (including relationship of classes and parties) and foreign (including not only formal declarations but also interests). Thus it is clear how broad and diverse the demands are, from the military-defense point of view, on geographic knowledge, including economic-geographic.

After the period of trade capitalism came that of industrial and financial capitalism when the interest in foreign countries was no longer limited to just trade but included foreign capital investments, which in time acquired greater and greater significance. However, if one is interested in foreign countries not as a merchant but as a representative of financial capital looking for investment possibilities, then his interest in these countries is broader. All the natural resources of a country, of industrial as well as agricultural significance, are of interest: the levels of development of productive fores of the country; the levels of consumption of its population; also its labour skills and much else are of interest, and not only in general and on the average but in its spatial distribution and combination in the various parts of the country. One will also want to know whether a revolution could occur that can cause him to lose everything he has invested. This is an interest of a very general order. It is natural, therefore, that present works of this kind include, together with all kinds of practical information that is frequently quite general detailed and more or less specific descriptions on individual countries. This the interests of a modern merchant or financial man with respect to foreign countries can be rather broad and extend far beyond the framework of a single reference book about where and what to buy more cheaply and where and what to sell more dearly.

Resource

Introduction: Man has to carry on economic activity for the survival of himself, his family and society. For this purpose he has to collect various types of economic products. So the foundation of his economic activity depends on these products, namely, the economic *resource*. The economic activity of man depends very much on the production and utilization of economic resources. With the development of civilisation the need for various types of resources increases. In earliest times the number of population was small and the demand for resources was also limited. People would meet their demands from local resources. But with the development of civilisation and cultural and technical abilities, man with inherent skill in trying to get and produce various types of resources from local area and from abroad to fulfil his entire satisfaction and needs. Thereby man has developed resource consciousness.

Definition of Resource: According to Zimmermann, a *"resource"* does not refer to a thing or a substance. Rather, it refers to the function which a thing or a substance may perform or to an operation in which it may take part. This function or operation is for attaining a given end, the end is only to satisfy the fundamental needs of a man or a society. A thing or a substance may be called a *'resource'* when it has some (i) *utility* and (ii) *functionability* to satisfy the needs of man. Coal, a mineral resource, cannot be called a resource unless it is utilized by man for the production of power and its by-products for various economic uses. The functionability of a substance or a thing may be either actual or potential. For example, India's reserves of workable high grade iron-ore have been estimated at about 1020 crore tonnes. Of these only 3.5 crore tonnes are raised annually. The distribution of the ores in different parts is such that the entire amount can be raised if necessary. Therefore, the potential iron-ore resource of India is 1020 crore tonnes though actual production is about 3.5 crore tonnes. If due to natural calamities or technical difficulty a particular mine becomes unsuitable for utilization then the mineral of that mine cannot be called a resource. The recent terrible accident in the Chasnala coal mine has made it inoperative. So coal deposits of the mine cannot be considered as resources.

The functionability of a thing or a substance differs from time to time and place to place. The desert area of Rajasthan was unsuitable for human settlement. But thanks to the development of the irrigation system, some of the desert area has been turned into a mighty agricultural region.

Thus the resource aspect of the land has been changed. In the continent of Africa there are great possibilities of developing hydro-electricity. But the sources have not yet been used for the generation of power. So these sources cannot be termed as 'resource'.

Physical Resources

Ginsberg included rocks, surface forms, soil, mineral wealth and water resources in physical resources and showed that these resources are present uniformly everywhere on the earth in the form of natural gifts and they have been used in various forms in the various situations of human civilization. Not only this, ever in the modern scientific age though scientific progress and technological knowledge are most important in determining the utility, shape and change of shape of these resources, their shape has not changed very much.

Change of shape in natural resources can be observed where man has established and adjustment with nature. On the contrary, in parts like the Antarctica continent where complete adjustment has not been possible, the shape of physical resources remains the same and their utility is beyond human enjoyment.

Global Problem

There is a basic problem. On the hand, it is clear that many resources currently being used are non-renewable, and that the use of some resources destroys others. On the other hand, many elements which are currently considered as resources might be appraised differently in the future as new resources are developed.

As a result, there are many different ways of assessing resource prospects. One extreme is the Malthusian view which sees the stock of resources as a finite supply rapidly being depleted by large and increasing demands resulting from uncontrolled population growth and increasing aspirations. The conse-quence of this will be the exhaustion for resources and the impoverishment or even destruction of man. At the other extreme is the technological view which concedes that although the stock of resources is ultimately finite, the bounds of possibility within these limits are so extensive that the exhaustion of resources is not a practical problem. Technology may deplete some resources, but it also has a capacity for creating others, and as a result all problems can be solved if technical progress is maintained and economic and social constraints can be overcome. Between these two extremes, ways have to be found of producing a practical assessment of the earth's supply of resou-rces and of the demand likely to be placed on them so that a coordinated resource policy can be developed to balance them sensibly. Such a policy just also include consideration of the pro-blems of waste and pollution arising from the resource process.

The Problem of Supply and Demand

The uneven distribution of the earth's resources and the economic, social and political constraints affecting their exploitation and circulation make any overall assessment of supply and demand very difficult, but the resources problem is a global one which ultimately affects all men.

The Supply of Resources

A major task for the planner is to decide which resources are vital and then to discover the size of the available stock. This stock taking has been considerably aided by the development of technique for the remote sensing of the environment such as aerial and satellite photography. Resource evaluation from satellites is particularly valuable as infrared photography, radar scanning and other technical developments have supplied new tools to increase our knowledge of the earth and its potentials. The launching of the Earth Resources Technology Satellite ERTS-1 from the USA in 1972 was a major step forward since it was specifically designed to record and transmit resources information back to earth, but there is still a great deal of work to be done before knowledge of the stock of resources is complete. A more difficult task is the assessment of future technological innovations and the forecasting of the economic conditions under which they, and known but currently uneconomic resources, may be profitably used. However, a brief examination of food, mineral and energy supplies will illustrate some resource problems.

At present, enough food is being produced to feed the world population (5,000 millions in 1987), although there are serious problems arising from its maldistribution. It is also possible to increase food supplies as population increase because, of the 25 percent which is potentially pastoral, only about half of each is currently being used. It is also possible to use much of the present agricultural area more intensively. However, this is much more a technical than an economic potential. About one third of the potential arable, of example, lies within the tropics, where leaching and the creation of hard-pan soils will necessitate vast inputs of fertilisers and drainage schemes, thus imposing heavy demands on energy and mineral supplies, in order to produce uncertain returns.

Not is the more intensive use of the oceans likely to lead to a vast increase in food supplies. Although fish is a valuable source of protein, it seems unlikely that production will increase to more than 2½ times the present production of 70 million tonnes per annum, and there is already concern about cod stocks around Iceland and herring stocks in the North Sea. Thus, although increases in production are possible, it has been estimated that food supplies are unlikely to increase by more than eightfold under foreseen conditions, and this will put the limit of population growth at about 30,000 millions, with the vast majority at starvation levels. At present rates of increase this figure will be reached in the year 2075.

Mineral ores are localised and exhaustible and are therefore a potential source of friction, but on the whole there are plentiful supplies of minerals. However, the question of whether or not they could become ores, capable of being worked at a profit, is dependent on technology and economics, and as a result estimates of reserves are very unreliable. There are already shortages of mercury, tin, tungsten, gold and copper, and alternative sources or substitutes are being sought. The search is very wide ranging but it seems that, as with food supplies, the oceans are unlikely to be a very fruitful source, especially from the rocks beyond the continental shelves, although sediments on the se-bed are potentially valuable. Even in shallower waters, economics and technology place constraints on development and it must be recognised that ore deposits are in finite supply under present economic and technical conditions, and that the exhaustion of some deposits is imminent.

Despite the fact that vast amounts of energy reach the earth every day from the sun, there has been a great deal of concern the possibility that energy supplies may soon be exhausted. It has been estimated that there is only about 50 years' supply of oil and gas, and 200–300 years' supply of coal at present rates of extraction, and some experts believe that these might be better used as raw materials rather than being burned to provide energy. However, the problem is that the vast amount of low-intensity energy coming from the sun is difficult to concentrate, and its conversion into electricity will not be economic until at least the year 2000 in the UK.

Similarly, although wind, water and tidal power have long been available to man, their large scale exploitation raises many technical problems, and only hydro-electric power is developed to any great extent. The same is true of attempts to tap geothermal energy. Although geothermal energy is used to produce electricity in volcanic areas, the need to drill to depths of at least, 3,600 m elsewhere raises considerable engineering problems. In fact, current economic and technical conditions make the replacement of fossil fuels as the principal sources of energy very difficult, despite their threatened exhaustion and the pollution problems created by the release of hydrocarbons into the atmosphere as they are burned.

4

Poverty and Slums—Impact of Changing Economic Landscape

Western media headlines as usual are as follows – twenty five percent of Indians live on less than a dollar a day and seventy percent live on less than two dollars a day. The forgoing was the headline of May 9, 2005 in a major international newspaper. Others headlines are not any less mischievous. These are all meaningless analysis. It does not reflect that same amount of money has differing values in different places. A more acceptable and bit accurate description of incomes in countries is Purchase Power Parity (PPP), which is, pricing identical products and services as needed by the local population in different countries, thus establishing a new and a more equitable exchange rate. The foregoing is applicable mostly to tradable goods. The PPP will put India's GDP at $3.7 Trillion. This will raise daily monies of twenty five percent of Indians at the lowest rung of the society to seven dollars. The latter is still low but is much higher than the Western media would like to project. The forgoing is not the point; the point is that poverty is a major shame in India's otherwise decent, scientifically advanced, peace loving and at times turbulent image. Poverty creates slums and slums breed hopelessness and crime. Hence it needs to be tackled as an integral part of economic development.

The key question that arises-will the current hype in economical development in India alter the landscape for the very poor? The answer is that, not much will change in next 20 to 25 years. The real impact will be felt later than twenty-five years. That is when 8% growth trajectory will take the PPP daily income of the very poor in India from seven dollars to forty dollars. By then, a $20 Trillion GDP economy

(PPP basis) and $600 billion in exports (year 2001 basis) will add one hundred and fifty million jobs, of which forty to fifty million will go to the very poor segment of the society. This general prosperity will not only put food on the table but will add to better living, better housings etc. In the intervening period of 25 years, rising income levels will definitely add to the exodus from the slums to planned living areas. The forgoing also requires massive governmental effort to house people properly.

Let us examine this issue of poverty and slums in Indian cities and its relationship to the betterment of economic conditions of the masses, a bit further?

What Causes Slums in the Cities in the First Place?

It is vicious cycle of population growth, opportunities in the cities (leading to migration to the cities), poverty with low incomes, tendency to be closer to work hence occupying any land in the vicinity etc. The key reason out of all is the slow economic progress. After independence in 1947, commercial and industrial activity needed cheap labour in the cities. Plentiful was available in the rural area. They were encouraged to come to cities and work. People, who migrated to the cities and found work, brought their cousins and rest of the families to the cities. Unable to find housing and afford it, they decided to build their shelter closer to work. First, one shelter was built, then two and then two thousand and then ten thousand and on and on. Conniving governments provided electricity and drinking water. Politicians looked at the slums as vote bank. They organized these unauthorized dwellers into a political force; hence slums took a bit of a permanent shape. More slums developed as more population moved to the cities. By mid sixties Mumbai, Kolkata, Delhi, and all other large cities were dotted with slums.

Very poor people live in slums. They are not the only one dwelling there. Fairly well to do people also reside there. They are either offspring of the slum dwellers that found education and an occupation. They have prospered but are unable to find affordable housing, hence have continued to stay in the shantytowns. Others are avoiding paying rent and property taxes. The latter is more often the case. It is not unusual that in the dirtiest of slums, where misery prevails that TV sets, refrigerators and radios are also blaring music. This is quite a contrast from the image which one gets in the media or from the opportunist politicians.

India's capital of Delhi has a million and a half out of fourteen million living in slums. Mumbai is worst with greater percentage living in slums. Other big urban centres have done no better. Newly built cities like Chandigarh and surrounding towns where shantytowns could have been avoided altogether have now slums. The forgoing is India's shame despite huge progress.

How will the Growing Economy Impact Poverty and the Slum dwellers?

As stated above, 8% growth rate of Indian economy will push per capita GDP to $2,000 level in about twenty to twenty-five years (PPP per capita GDP will be much higher). The forgoing presupposes that the population does not explode in the near future but continue a healthy 1.5 to 2% growth. That is where the magic equilibrium of prosperity and desire to live a better life begins. These two together could end poverty and slums. With availability of affordable housing and jobs, slum dwelling is the last thought on people's mind.

On the other hand if the above does not happen then slums dwellers will triple in 25 years and so will the poverty. Delhi will have four and a half million-slum dwellers. Kolkata and Mumbai will have even bigger numbers. India's shame will have no end. To avoid that, India's economy has to remain at a high state of growth. Jobs created by the economic growth, hence higher incomes are key criteria for poverty reduction and slum elimination.

The foregoing together with the current urban renewal in progress in the urban areas today will give cities in India a new look. Higher incomes will create a demand for inexpensive housing, which will have to be met with innovative use of land and building techniques. Government provided housing would be a great failure as it has been elsewhere in the world. Instead sufficient cash has to be placed in the people's hands together with inexpensive land that people's housing program become efficient and affordable.

In addition slum living has to be made unattractive with land taxes and denial of social services. Slum colonies, which opt out of current hopelessness, should get a better deal in housing which replaces the slums. This followed with rapidly growing rural economy will kill migration. That will also reduce pressure on housing.

No single policy has ever brought an end to poverty and slums. It is a concerted effort and better policies, which will end it. No country in the world has ever been able to end poverty and slums completely. That includes the richest nation of the world – USA. The point is that if economy progresses and special effort is made to uplift the poor, poverty and slums will be overtaken by better economic conditions of the people.

How did US Tackle its Slums?

US had its share of poverty and slums in around the immigrant dominated cities. New York and Boston had great amount of poverty and slums at the turn of the twentieth century. These slums worsened further with the arrival of newly liberated African-American population from Deep South.

The era pictures give a glimpse of everyday life and it is not pretty. People without jobs and with no prospects crowded cities in the North. A new word, Ghetto was coined, which described these places. Immigrant from different background or race crowded together and gave rise to Ghettos.

At that time US did not have control over its economy and Civil War debt and additional monies borrowed to rehabilitate agriculture and commerce after the Civil War was unpaid. As twentieth century progressed a concerted effort was made to clean up the Ghettos and push people inland with free grant of land and promise of prosperity. Industrial Revolution, which was slow in reaching America from Europe, finally arrived. And it made the difference. It provided the much-needed jobs to the immigrants and coloured. Also, free land in the West gave rise to food self-sufficiency and paying off of all Civil War and post Civil War debts. First World War gave US economy a boost and America joined the select group of countries of Europe in prosperity. Poverty by the end of the Second World War was a thing of the past. In just fifty years, i.e. by 1950, US were nation of 160 million souls, all prosperous and all well employed (forget the habitual lazy). That does not mean that all the Ghettos disappeared. They continued to exist. They exist today, but on a much lower scale. These are not eyesores.

One critical factor which eliminated slums and poverty in US was quadrupling of the US economy from 1900 to 1940. A free wheeling economy created industrial giants and a super rich class. Need for war material during the WWII resulted in creation of huge industrial infrastructure and innovation. Post war reconstruction in Europe added greater impetus to the economy. General well being of the people living in the poorer section of the cities dramatically improved. US raced ahead of Europe and are still ahead, 60 years after the WWII. In most cities, ghettos disappeared or shrunk. Urban renewal and building boom in last sixty years has completely changed the landscape of the country.

There is a parallel here. Poverty and slums in India are at the same level as they were in beginning of the twentieth century in America. Economic growth over fifty years eliminated them. It is possible in India too if the economy sustains the 8% growth trajectory.

Slums and the Great Briton

Great Briton was a great big slum before they became a colonial power in the nineteenth century. For eight hundred years prior, until 1800s, Great Briton was an agrarian society, where the lord lived happily in his Manor and Castles and the masses lived in a great squalor. Slums were everywhere. London had the biggest slums. Colonization brought prosperity and prosperity brought in a huge effort to improve the lot of the people and clean up of the cities.

That is when the unemployed and slum dwellers were pushed to newly developing industrial hubs of Sheffield, Birmingham, Liverpool and Manchester. Compared to that Delhi, Kolkata were heavens. First slums in Kolkata appeared in 1850-70 as a result of systematic destruction of textile industry in Bengal and destruction of trading infrastructure in and around Kolkata. Slums elsewhere followed.

It took all the Victorian age from 1825 to 1900 to vanish poverty and slums in England. Their GDP multiplied 8 times over this period. British factories produced goods and services which were sold at profit in the in the colonies. Work for everybody in England was the cornerstone of building well-serviced cities.

The point is that reduction of poverty and slums follow closely with economic development. Faster the economic development, sooner will the poverty vanish and with it, the slums.

How did China handle its Poverty and Slums?

Chinese had a unique way of making slums disappear from its urban centres. Permit system to live in a city or in a particular neighbourhood was introduced just after the Communist took control in 1949.

That means that a migration of rural population to the urban areas in search of jobs was arrested. In addition the war ravaged eastern provinces where rural population had moved to the cities and into the slums, were emptied out. Nobody questioned Mao Tse Tung's wisdom; hence he had a free hand. People were permitted to return to their homes in the cities only after proof of their residency had been established. Outsiders were sent back to their own homes and land in the rural area. Future residency in the cities was permitted on a permit basis only. Hence the major problem of unplanned urban squatting was prevented. Even today the foregoing policy continues.

The FDI built cities of Guangdong province carry on with the permit system established in 1949. In order to move there, a person has to have a job and place to reside. The latter could be a factory provided bunk bed. This prevents urban squatters. The above is no comparison to how poverty was vanished in UK, US and elsewhere. Major economic progress in last 20 years has re-invigorated the cities with investment and reconstruction. Whether the same is true in the China's rural areas is a debatable issue. China likes to pretend that poverty has been removed. Published reports state otherwise.

Urban Renewal in India

Urban renewal is in progress in India in a big way for the last 50 years. The British starved cities in India of the funds for two hundred years. They only built regal palaces for themselves in Delhi, Shimla and Kolkota. No new funds were made available to the people to renew and rebuild, hence Moghul Delhi presented a decaying and a rundown look, when they finally left India in 1947. The problem got compounded with migration of people from rural areas. Expanding industry and commerce needed them hence migration was encouraged.

Thus urban slums and squatting began in a big way. Today, some estimates place 10 to 15% of Delhi population as slum dwellers. Slums in Kolkata predate Delhi slums. So do the Mumbai slums. They all began the same way – people's livelihood was destroyed or they were invited to work in factories without adequate housing. The problem grew acute with huge population growth after 1950. From 1950 to today, cities lacked funds to renew themselves and help build additional housing. People lacked adequate jobs hence are caught in the poverty cycle.

Only recently a huge building and construction boom has started in all cities in India. Whereas governments are concentrating on building infrastructure and industrial base, private construction is building work places, shopping districts and housing for the middle class. The poor and slum dwellers are not there in any building equation. Cheap housing projects are lowest in the category. Hence slum dwelling has become a way of life.

How Long the Poor have to Wait?

If the experience elsewhere is a guide then poverty, slums and urban squat will be a diminishing phenomenon, if the rapid economic progress keeps its pace. Today we would have smaller of the slums, had economic policies of the present were in place 50 years back. Only now, all signs point to a rapidly rising GDP together with rising per capita GDP. With rise in income level, tendency to head to the slums has lessened. Diehard slum dwellers who wish to pay no taxes and spend nothing on housing will most certainly continue to stay there. Others will prefer to move out.

This is a normal phenomenon. It happened in US and elsewhere. It will happen in India too. An economic equilibrium has not been reached in the society yet, where enough money in people's pocket will persuade them to vacate the slums. This won't we reached for another 20 to 25 years. By about middle of this period with increased availability of housing and higher incomes, the growth in slum dwelling will be arrested. Decline will begin only when much higher incomes are reached, provided India does not make the mistake of regularizing the slums/bustees with land tenure on tenable land and other amenities.

That is a sure fire method to keep the slums going. People will always wait for free grant of land ownership even if these grants never materialize. Even the possibility of this ever happening in a distant future will keep the slum dwellers in the slums.

Slums in India

Baiganwadi

Baiganwadi is a slum located in Govandi (West). This is the laregest slum in Mumbai after Dharavi. Baiganwadi has Mumbai's oldest and largest waste dumping ground. The whole area is divided in Plots and crossing Roads, and gullies.

Geography

Baiganwadi is located between Shivaji Nagar No :1 and Mankhurd. To its North is the mumbais largest waste dumping ground, and to the East lies the Thane Creek.

Populace

Baiganwadi is a very populated place. One can find many people sharing the same room (10 Ft. X 15 Ft.) Most of the population is made up of immigrants from Bihar and Uttar Pradesh. Also one can find many illegal immigirants from Bangladesh.

Economy

As a Slum it don't boast of big companies or a good infrastructure availability like water and Electricity and good roads, Baiganwadi don't have any offices, or other economic activities as rest of the Mumbai. But most of the Residents are of Economically comes under lower middle class, and some comes under BPL.

Water Issue

Baiganwadi is worst hit by water shortage in Mumbai. There is no proper water supply in Area. There are plenty of illegal water connections.

- In the Heart of Bombay: the Dharavi Slum Media.

The Dharavi slum, situated in the heart of Greater Bombay, and the massive redevelopment project that aims to turn it into a swanky neighbourhood for the well-off middle class, is a perfect example of the ultra-liberal leanings of the Indian political class as a whole, which remains persistently deaf and blind to the needs of the poor, who nevertheless represent more than 60% of the population of the Indian megalopolis. A further look:

Dharavi, an Extraordinary Slum

The low-lying slums that stretch out across the land are as much a part of the traditional image of Bombay (renamed Mumbai) as the skyscrapers in India's commercial and financial capital. Seen from above, the intricacy of these two worlds is impressive: the gray blotches formed by the closely packed jumble of corrugated iron roofs contrast with the bright towers and less cluttered areas of the city's residential and business neighborhoods.

Among this multitude of slums, Dharavi is reputed to be one of the biggest in Asia, though it is, above all, one of the oldest. The original inhabitants of Dharavi were the Koli, a community of fishermen whose presence has been visible for centuries in Mahim Creek, located along the Mithi River, which is situated on the northern boundary of Dharavi. In the past, the area over which the slum now spreads out was marshland. It was the migrants, poor and excluded from the wealthier south Bombay neighborhoods, who, decade after decade, precipitated the drying up of the river by filling it with organic waste and other matter, turning it into livable land, on which they could build.

Today, Dharavi occupies a 175-hectare area. The official population is approximately 600,000 people (2001 census) but organizations and researchers working on Dharavi estimate that number to be at least one million individuals, or close to 100,000 families, with an average population density of 350,000 habitants per km2 and one toilet per 1,440 people.

Despite the unifying name "Dharavi," the zone that it designates is a juxtaposition of neighborhoods with their own distinct character that was shaped by the various waves of migrants that came from the four corners of rural India. Apart from the Koli fishermen, who represent only a small percentage of the population, Dharavi is actually the work, in large part, of the men and women who left their villages of origin, most often following natural disasters such as droughts, and came to look for jobs in the attractive megalopolis that is Bombay.

An Area that is Both Residential and Industrial

The first migrants came from Maharashtra (the state of which Bombay is the capital) and Gujarat (the border state north of Bombay). They first settled in the southern neighborhoods of Bombay, but as the city grew, they were pushed farther and farther north to allow the wealthier populations to live in the new residential buildings built on the sites of the former slums. These first migrants settled permanently in Dharavi. Later, such a large wave of migrants came from the Tamil Nadu state (in southern India), particularly from the Tirunelveli district, that today one third of Dharavi's population speaks Tamil. More recently, two very poor and highly populated northern Indian states, Uttar Pradesh and Bihar, were the main sources of new migrants. All these migratory fluxes have contributed to the wide diversity of people and activities in Dharavi: Kumbhar potters from Saurashtra (Gujarat), tanners from Tamil Nadu and Azamgarh (Uttar Pradesh), leather and textile workers from Maharashtra and Bihar, and Valmiki street sweepers from Haryana.

Dharavi also stands out for its bustling informal economic activity in small-scale industry and handicrafts. Unlike Bombay's other slums, where a large majority of inhabitants work outside their place of residence, 80% of Dharavi's residents also work there. In this way, Dharavi is also a full-fledged industrial area, with an estimated 400 million euros in turnover. A study by the SPARC (Society for the Promotion of Area Resource Centres) estimates that Dharavi has 4,902 production facilities, with 1,036 in textiles, 932 in pottery, 567 in the leather, 722 in recycling and scrap metal, 498 in embroidery and 152 in food. Furthermore, there are 111 restaurants and several thousand boutiques in Dharavi.

And yet, this dynamic economic activity should not overshadow the fact that work conditions in this informal sector are very often difficult and precarious. Potters and their families constantly live and work surrounded by heat and toxic smoke emanating from the ovens where they bake their pottery, while leather, textile and food workers spend up to 15 hours a day in dark rooms with no ventilation. Salaries are of course very low and competition between old and new migrants is constantly driving the cost of labour down.

Dharavi, like every other slum, also suffers from a lack of basic infrastructure and sanitation facilities, while access to water and electricity is unpredictable.

But unlike numerous other recent slums, the majority of dwellings in Dharavi are reinforced and built out of cement and bricks (except for the roofs, which are made of simple reused metal sheets or of corrugated iron, or, more rarely, tiles). This points to an older establishment and to progressive improvements to houses, as much as was allowed by financial resources and available space.

How is Urban Poverty Managed?

Journalist and writer Kalpana Sharma warns against a romantic vision of this slum where an economic miracle takes place every day—a triumph of the ingenuity and creativity of the "poor" people living in inhumane conditions. The truth of this image must not eclipse an important point, which is that Dharavi, above all, presents a real problem, one that is still unresolved and largely ignored by the powers that be: the management of urban poverty in an India that is seeing its urban population swell rapidly because of the combined effect of natural population growth and a rural exodus. This phenomenon is most notably due to the absence of any real agricultural policy that would allow rural citizens to make a living from their rural operations, thereby sparing them from the need to pack into the slums. Therefore, Dharavi is also a reminder that such living and working conditions are unacceptable and that it's up to the state and the Indian government to ensure decent living conditions for all their citizens, including, and perhaps especially, the poorest ones, by taking into account their needs in terms of housing and work in the development of their policies.

Until recently, the residents and new arrivals to Dharavi considered it a stable place of settlement. According to Jockin Arputham, founder of the National Slum Dwellers Federation, interviewed on March 31, 2009: "when migrants come to Bombay, they choose Dharavi for two reasons: they are sure that they will find a job there and there is no risk that they will be evicted."

For a long time, the unhealthy conditions in Dharavi actually made it unattractive for real estate investors. Situated on low-lying land, close to the mangrove and the Mithi River, and extremely polluted by the city's waste and sewage, Dharavi is hit each year by monsoon flooding and its associated sanitary risks.

Moreover, since the 1980s, authorities have more or less admitted to the need for improving the situation of the slums without, however, officially acknowledging their existence. Therefore, numerous neighborhoods in Dharavi have been the object of improvement and rehabilitation projects that allowed thousands of residents to be rehoused into apartments buildings, for several major streets to be widened and for the canalization of sewage. Under the leadership of the Slum Rehabilitation Authority (SRA), created in 1995 to promote the implementation of the rehabilitation plans for Greater Bombay's slums, about 70 seven-story buildings have been or are currently being constructed in Dharavi. It is important to remember here that living in a slum does not mean living for free, since residents pay between 500 and 1,000 rupees (or eight to 16 euros) monthly to informal "landlords," a sort of local mafia who, in the absence of the state, dominates the housing market and access to water, electricity, sanitation facilities and arbitrarily imposes its rules on residents.

The results of these projects vary greatly but they have given hope to residents that Dharavi will be officially recognized, which would ensure them ownership or rental security and would allow them to invest more into their housing and business, with the guarantee that the state would provide them with basic public services.

The Dharavi Redevelopment Project (DRP)

But the economic liberalization of the 1990s changed things dramatically. Since 2004, a controversial broad redevelopment plan has been in the works: the Dharavi Redevelopment Project. Dharavi is located in a strategic area, a few steps from the new international financial and business centre, the Bandra Kurla Complex, which is meant to free up the southern area of Bombay. The national stock exchange, the diamond bourse and the headquarters of several important financial institutions and banks are all found here. At a time where space is an increasingly rare commodity in Bombay, the land that Dharavi occupies has therefore, within a few years, become very valuable in a rapidly expanding real estate market and has sparked the interest of Indian and foreign investors. Let's not forget that Dharavi is ideally situated at the crossroads of the two main rail lines serving Bombay.

The Dharavi Redevelopment Project (DRP), which is being constantly modified and delayed and whose cost is continuously increasing (it is estimated to cost 3 billion euros today), is also headed by the Slum Rehabilitation Authority. Generally, the SRA's plans are based on a public-private partnership where private builders or cooperatives build small apartments of approximately 21m2 (225 sq. ft.) and residents who can prove they have lived in the slum before a certain date, are resettled for free, usually on the outskirts of the city. In exchange, property entrepreneurs have the right to build other apartments and commercial sites on this land that has been "freed up" by the slums and sell them at higher market prices, thus allowing them to reap lucrative rewards. The DRP is yet a different project with a wider scope since it aims to rehabilitate the entire slum and to rehouse all of the residents whose names appear on the voters' list prior to 2000, in Dharavi itself. This would mean an official number of 72,000 families.

This project, which is supposed to last seven years, was approved by the government of Maharashtra in 2007, but was developed in 1995 by the architectural firm MM Project Consultants. It is the idea of Mukesh Mehta, a United States-educated Indian architect who has since become a consultant for the Maharashtra government. He defends his so-called "integrated and sustainable" spirit-of-the-times approach, which he has named HIKES for: housing, income, knowledge, environment and socio-cultural development.

He suggests replacing the Dharavi slum with a community of five self-sufficient sectors with residential buildings, shops, industrial centres, schools, hospitals, gardens, golf courses, sports complexes, etc. Unlike in the other SRA projects, the five builders who will be responsible for the redevelopment of these five sectors will also have to ensure the establishment of basic infrastructure: water, electricity, roads, and canalization. This clause ensures that horizontal slums are not turned into vertical slums, as is too often the case. Mr. Mehta's goal is to make the Dharavi Redevelopment Project a redevelopment model that can be internationally reproduced in order to create a slum-free world by 2025.

Problems

On paper, the project may appear attractive, but the reality of it is quite different, and the project has spurred a general outcry from organizations representing the residents of Dharavi, in particular the Dharavi Vikas Samiti collective (the Dharavi development committee), which is made up of the National Slum Dwellers Federation, SPARC and Mahila Milan (a women's association).

The first issue of conflict concerns the number of people who are to benefit from the project. This number appears to have been greatly underestimated, because even by using the year 2000 as a point of reference, the SRA only came to 72,000 families, whereas the NSDF estimates that 100,000 would be a more correct number. This begs the question: where will the non-rehabilitated families go? Will they populate new slums, somewhere farther, with even worse conditions?

The size of the apartments that are to be given for free to Dharavi residents is another problem: 21 m2, is too small an area for families of five to 10 people who often carry out their occupation in the same place as their residence, which they have had to sometimes expand by adding another floor. This would be unthinkable in an apartment building. Through negotiations, the residents' associations succeeded in requiring an area of 28 m2, which seems more acceptable, though some people would prefer 37 m2. This is because numerous business activities require much more space. Owners will either have to buy land at market price—something that few of them can manage—close their business down or move it to another slum.

The fate of pollution-producing informal business activity (soap-making, tanning, pottery) also poses a problem. Does the DRP mean an end to their operations and unemployment for the workers?

There are many questions that have been left unanswered and that indicate the extreme worry of Dharavi residents, small entrepreneurs and artisans who have not received any guarantees about the future of their livelihoods.

Kumbharwada, a Neighbourhood of Potters

The potters of Kumbharwada are another case. This neighbourhood of 2,000 potter families, who came from Gujarat at the start of the 20th century, spreads out over five hectares. For them, space is essential. They estimate that they need at least 92 m2 to store and mould clay, make their pottery and dry it, install ovens where it can be baked, and for some, to have space on the street where they can sell it. The proposed area of 28m2 is very clearly inadequate and their level of poverty makes it impossible for them to buy land. What's more, they absolutely refuse to consider Dharavi as a slum and therefore, want nothing to do with the project. Indeed, they consider themselves as the owners of this land, which was given to them for 99 years at the beginning of the 20th century by British colonists as part of the Vacant Land Tenancy Act. However, Mukesh Mehta believes that this allocation of land became invalid the moment the Maharashtra government adopted the DRP.

Rehabilitation of the Slums or Exclusion of the Poor?

The main criticisms expressed by residents and the associations representing them reflect the absence of any real consultation between the property developers of the Dharavi redevelopment project and the Dharavi residents. Before developing the project, Mukesh Mehta's firm did not carry out any detailed field study to learn about the current situation, the exact number of residents, their economic activity, their needs in terms of housing and industrial, artisanal and commercial space. The DRP is a typical project thought up by a technical expert and imposed "from above" on a population that is clearly for the redevelopment of Dharavi, but certainly not if it clashes with their own interests.

This project is thus, evidence of the unfortunate unwillingness of Indian authorities to create and implement real urban policies that would include low-cost housing for the poor who represent, let's not forget, more than half of India's population. Therefore, this project cannot be considered as an urban development plan because in the end, far from taking into account the current living and work conditions of the residents, it only envisions the financial gain to be had not only by the property developers and builders, but also by the state, which expects to gain a profit of 20 million rupees thanks to the interest that will be paid to it by its private "partners."

Eventually, if the project as it stands now is carried out, there is a fear that, just like in many other cases, the resettled residents will leave Dharavi, either by will or by force. Either they will no longer have enough space to carry out their business activity, or maintenance costs will be so high (more than 1,500 rupees per month, not including municipal taxes and electricity and water fees) that residents will have no other choice but to rent out or sell their apartments and move to another slum, despite being forbidden from moving for 10 years (as experience would have it). Dharavi will then become what Mukesh Mehta and the government of Maharashtra likely want: a neighbourhood for the middle class who will benefit from all of the basic and luxury services close to home.

An Uncertain Future

Right now, it is hard to predict the evolution of this project, which, despite being constantly pushed back for 12 years, is still progressing in stages. A request for proposals was launched in June 2007 and interested property developers, both Indian and foreign, started submitting the non-financial technical aspects of their projects in February 2009. Some are already predicting the replacement of Dharavi as a working-class neighbourhood with a residential and commercial middle-class area. Others affirm that the residents will oppose any plan that would force them to leave. They were the ones who, through their hard labour, turned the Dharavi marshland into livable land. For example, they threaten to block railway traffic, which would effectively paralyse all of Bombay's economic activity.

Political parties are no strangers either to the difficulties encountered in the implementation of the DRP. Today, the coalition led by the Congress party, which governs Maharashtra (the state where Bombay is located) defends the Dharavi Redevelopment Project. The opposition parties, BJP and Shiv Sena, firmly rooted in Dharavi, completely reject the project, even though they approved it when they were in power in 2004.

We must now wait for the results of the April-May 2009 national election. Another important economic issue is the global economic crisis, which puts this massive project into question. But this is also a unique opportunity for the residents' associations to suggest alternatives that may have a greater chance of being taken seriously by the authorities. It's what Jockin Arputham hopes for anyway. Recently appointed to a government advisory committee, he believes that he "can convince builders to meet certain needs of the residents." But which ones? He has not said.

Kathputhli Slum

The Kathputhli Slum Area is an urban slum in Jaipur, India, with a population of approximately 10,000 people.

Population

The population of the slum in Kathputhli is mainly inhabited by the low-caste sweepers, rag-pickers, artisans and general labourers, who have migrated from rural areas to a more urban setting. The main draw for these people to urban areas is the hope of better jobs, higher pay, modern housing and an upgrading of their lifestyle from rural workers to middle-class landowners, enjoying the benefits of life in a globalised world.

Kathputhli dwellers are normally migrants from Rajasthan rural areas and there is a strong cottage industry within the slums of puppet making. Local artisans, some of them itinerant puppet performers, have settled in the area to continue making puppets, performing shows and selling their handiwork to tourists and the large number of wealthy people who site see around Jaipur.

Government

The Kathputhli housing structures there are mainly semipermanent. And it is now legally considered to be a colony, rather than a "slum" which generally denotes illegal squatters. Constructed of claybrick, cow dung and concrete. A few of the informal canteens and tea stalls have access to mains power and water. The development level of the slum matches the early stages of the residential areas of Maharashtra's Ichalkaranji, which started off as a more informal squatter community before the graduation to land rights, water, electricity and permanent housing took place.

Development

There is only one development agency working in Kathputhli, which is the Helping Hand Society Jaipur, providing vocational training and education to the unskilled of the population in sewing and tailoring, shoemaking, computer literacy, English language, general deportment and gradual exposure to amenities associated with modern urban living.

Pavement Dwellers

Pavement dwellers refers to Mumbai dwellings built on the footpaths/pavements of city streets, which use the walls or fences which separate building compounds from the pavement and street outside. Materials include cloth, corrugated iron, cardboard, wood, plastic, and sometimes also bricks or cement. According to Sheela Patel of SPARC, pavement dwellers are primarily first generation migrants who moved to Mumbai sometimes 30 to 50 years ago, and who have lived on the pavement of public roadways ever since. They are completely invisible as far as local, state, and national policies are concerned.

SPARC conducted a study in 1985 about the pavement dwellers called "*We the Invisible*" based on a census of about 6,000 households. It showed approximately half of the pavement dwellers to be from the poorest districts in the state of Maharashtra, with the other half came from the poorest parts of wider India. Many came as victims of drought, famine, earthquakes or religious persecution or riots. Others came as a result of a complete breakdown in their livelihoods where they had been living. Pavement dwellers migrate to Mumbai hoping to capitalize on the wealth and job opportunities that the city offers. They are typically forward-thinking, seeking to build lives in the city that give the next generation better opportunities than would have been possible in the village.

1985 Eviction Crisis

In 1985 the Supreme Court of India granted the Municipal Corporation of Greater Mumbai authority to demolish household structures on the sidewalks of Mumbai. With the aid of SPARC, the rights of Mumbai's pavement dwellers were recognised able coexistence was successfully negotiated.

Yamuna Pushta

Yamuna Pushta is the *Pushta* (embankment) on both sides of the Yamuna River in Delhi, starting from the ITO bridge and up to the Salimgarh Fort. It has also been home to riverbed cultivators, and over 100,000 residents a string of slum colonies (shantytown) for some 40 years, mostly on the western banks, like those near the Nigambodh Ghat (cremation ghats) near Old Delhi and a few on the eastern banks like those near Sakarpur in East Delhi. Many of these slums were being demolished in 2004, after court orders which were part of the beautification drive of the Government ahead of the 2010 Commonwealth Games and for creating a "green belt".

Yamuna Pushta Slums

Yamuna Pushta slums were developed by the migrant populations who could not afford land in the city, encroached upon the riverbed. The Master Plan of the city described the area as "floodable" hence permanent structures were never built by the government. Early settlers bought land from local farmers, some reclaimed land which others encroached. Thus grew several *jhuggi* clusters on both side of the Yamuna river. With the Yamuna flooding each monsoon, the resident of many of lower lying slums were uprooted, took refuge within the city. Yet year after year, these slums grew despite remaining outside the purview of urban development within city, and basic facilities remain minimal, and many stayed on because they developed into valuable vote banks. Another important reason for their development right up to the Nizamuddin bridge in recent years was the availability of work opportunities in the vicinity.

First resettlement drive in Yamuna Pushta took place in 1967, and the resident of the slum near Jamuna Bazar near Nigambodh Ghat were settled in Welcome Colony in East Delhi, however with more migrants regularly pouring in this these slums kept on refilling. Then,

1982 Asian Games saw nearly a million migrants labourer coming in to construct games related infrastructure.

Then in early 2000s, government activated its plans for the 118-acre Games Village to house the 8,500 athletes and other sports persons visiting Delhi during the 2010 Commonwealth Games, and also started an ambitious project of restoring and beautifying the 22 km-long stretch of Yamuna floodplain. The Delhi High Court gave orders for demotion of the slums at Yamuna Pushta in May 2002, and in MCD had issued an eviction notice to the *jhuggi* (makeshift huts) dwellers on January 12 2004 and at least 5,000 school-going children were to be affected by the drive. Slumdwellers have been asked to pay up Rs 7,000 per house as the residents offered to shift to resettlement colonies at like Holambi Kalan, Bawana, Narela and Madanpur Khadar, by the Slum and Jhuggi Jhonpari Department of the Municipal Corporation of Delhi (MCD), though most of them became homeless since they could not even afford these costs, and further city has virtually no low-income housing that is affordable and legal. The slums were eventually demolished in a drive that started March 2004, after the Election Commission gave its permission ahead of the Lok Sabha elections, and registration forms were issued to the residents.. In this drive 1,000 slum clusters from Gautampurui-I and Koyla Basti of Yamuna Pushta were demolished, in all more than 18,000 slum clusters from both sides of the Yamuna river. As later studied revealed, the income of most of resettled residents decreased by 50 percent.

Subsequently, a eight-lane express highway has been opened there in 2007, paving way for construction of the 2010 Commonwealth Games Village and beautification drive of the Yamuna banks prior to it. By October 2009, nearly 400,000 people from three large slum clusters, of Yamuna Pushta, Nanglamachi and Bhatti mines has been relocated

Aftermath

In 2006, a book *Yamuna Gently Weeps: A Journey into the Yamuna Pushta Slum Demolitions* was been published about the demolition of Yamuna Pushta., and a documentary film by the same name made by Ruzbeh N Bharucha was also released.

As of 2010, the area continues to be a home for numerous homeless people, out of the 1,00,000 homeless living on the streets of Delhi, where after cold deaths here, the revenue department put up tents in January 2010

5

Rural Economy

The success story of Indian economy is spreading its wings towards India's districts and rural areas which accounts for over 65% of the nation's total populace. Currently, the rural sector of India is not only observing a massive increase in its per capita income but also in its expenditure and production. To enhance the rural economy of India, the Indian government has increased the monetary incentives allotted for the National Rural Employment Guarantee Act (NREGA) to USD 8.04 bn in its 2009 Union Budget. Moreover, the government has also allotted USD 34.74 bn in its Bharat Nirman Programme for enhancing rural road and rail network.

Surprisingly, the rural economy was unaffected by the recent global financial meltdown as per the research conducted by Rural Marketing Association of India (RMAI). The research also revealed that the rural economy in India is soon to witness an increase in its earnings which will be largely triggered by the incessant expansion in agriculture for the last four successive years.

Rural Consumer Market of India

The rural consumer market of India is expected to attain its target of USD 425 bn by 2010-2011, which can be translated as double of 2004-05 economy size, as per the report by CII-Technopark.

Indian Rural Retail Industry

As per the report by Associated Chambers of Commerce and Industry of India (ASSOCHAM), the Indian rural retail economy is worth USD 113 bn which can be translated as 40% of the total Indian retail market worth USD 280 bn. Some of the firms which have already established their base in rural areas are Reliance, AV Birla and Godrej, while firms like DCM, Pantaloon-Godrej JV, Tata, Hindustan Unilever, etc. are all set to expand their retail business in rural market.

Demand for FMCG in Indian Rural Areas

During the fourth quarter of the FY 2009, the demand for fast moving consumer goods (FMCG) increased steadily as compared to its urban counterparts, as per the research conducted by AC Nielsen.

Companies like Dabur, HUL, Godrej, etc have started recruiting more and more deserving candidates from rural districts in an attempt to elevate their network and market. Firms like Nestle and GlaxoSmithkline Consumer Healthcare (GSK) are all set to introduce new products for the rural areas in order to promote their brand. This indicates that the FMCG firms no longer treat rural markets as an appendage to their metropolitan strongholds and are targeting the market for positioning their brands and for industrial set-ups.

Indian rural Healthcare Industry

The Indian rural Healthcare market is expected to expand at a pace of 44% by 2015, totaling its worth to USD 8.8 bn, according to a survey carried out by McKinsey. Conglomerates like Sanofi-Aventis, has currently introduced a promotional activity to advertise generics in rural provinces called 'Prayas'. This initiative is considered as an attempt to share medicinal information with practicing medicos in rural districts through seminars.

Indian Rural Automobiles Industry

The recent development that the Indian rural Automobiles Industry saw was the declaration of the establishment of new sales and service channels in rural India by the President of Mahindra and Mahindra Group (M&M) Rajeev Dubey. These service outlets have a premeditated target of manufacturing 1,00,000 automobiles by FY 2015.

Indian Rural Services Industry

Surprisingly, more than 60% of the services industry of the nation is based in the rural areas, as per the research conducted by National Sample Survey Organisation (NSSO). In the fiscal year 2007, there were around 85% of the own account enterprises (OAEs) in India which deployed 76% of the manpower in rural districts of India.

Indian Rural Telecommunication Industry

According to the research carried out by Confederation of Indian Industries (CII), the Indian rural Telecommunication Industry is expected to account for more than 65% of the entire telecom subscribers in India.

In an attempt to envelop rural subscribers, many telecom giants in India have willingly invested in rural telecom industry to benefit from its massive potential. Mobile equipments manufacturing firms like Intex Technologies, Karbonn, etc have allocated USD 21.03 mn for its promotional activities for 2010.

Indian Rural Agricultural System

Although agriculture contributes only 21% of India's GDP, its importance in the country's economic, social, and political fabric goes well beyond this indicator. The rural areas are still home to some 72 percent of the India's 1.1 billion people, a large number of whom are poor.

Most of the rural poor depend on rain-fed agriculture and fragile forests for their livelihoods. The sharp rise in foodgrain production during India's Green Revolution of the 1970s enabled the country to achieve self-sufficiency in foodgrains and stave off the threat of famine. Agricultural intensification in the 1970s to 1980s saw an increased demand for rural labor that raised rural wages and, together with declining food prices, reduced rural poverty.

Sustained, although much slower, agricultural growth in the 1990s reduced rural poverty to 26.3 percent by 1999/00. Since then, however, the slowdown in agricultural growth has become a major cause for concern. India's rice yields are one-third of China's and about half of those in Vietnam and Indonesia. With the exception of sugarcane, potato and tea, the same is true for most other agricultural commodities.

The Government of India places high priority on reducing poverty by raising agricultural productivity.

However, bold action from policymakers will be required to shift away from the existing subsidy-based regime that is no longer sustainable, to build a solid foundation for a highly productive, internationally competitive, and diversified agricultural sector.

Issues and Challenges

Slow Down in Agricultural and Rural Non-Farm Growth: Both the poorest as well as the more prosperous 'Green Revolution' states of Punjab, Haryana and Uttar Pradesh have recently witnessed a slow-down in agricultural growth. Some of the factors hampering the revival of growth are:

- Poor composition of public expenditures: Public spending on agricultural subsidies is crowding out productivity-enhancing investments such as agricultural research and extension, as well as investments in rural infrastructure, and the health and education of the rural people. In 1999/2000, agricultural subsidies amounted to 3 percent of GDP and were over 7 times the public investments in the sector.
- Over-regulation of domestic agricultural trade: While economic and trade reforms in the 1990s helped to improve the incentive framework, over-regulation of domestic trade has increased costs, price risks and uncertainty, undermining the sector's competitiveness.
- Government interventions in labor, land, and credit markets: More rapid growth of the rural non-farm sector is constrained by government interventions in factor markets — labor, land, and credit — and in output markets, such as the small-scale reservation of enterprises.
- Inadequate infrastructure and services in rural areas.

Weak Framework for Sustainable Water Management and Irrigation:

- Inequitable allocation of water: Many states lack the incentives, policy, regulatory, and institutional framework for the efficient, sustainable, and equitable allocation of water.
- Deteriorating irrigation infrastructure: Public spending in irrigation is spread over many uncompleted projects. In addition, existing infrastructure has rapidly deteriorated as operations and maintenance is given lower priority.

Inadequate Access to Land and Finance:

- Stringent land regulations discourage rural investments: While land distribution has become less skewed, land policy and regulations to increase security of tenure (including restrictions or bans on renting land or converting it to other uses) have had the unintended effect of reducing access by the landless and discouraging rural investments.
- Computerization of land records has brought to light institutional weaknesses: State government initiatives to computerize land records have reduced transaction costs and increased transparency, but also brought to light institutional weaknesses.

- Rural poor have little access to credit: While India has a wide network of rural finance institutions, many of the rural poor remain excluded, due to inefficiencies in the formal finance institutions, the weak regulatory framework, high transaction costs, and risks associated with lending to agriculture.

Weak Natural Resources Management: One quarter of India's population depends on forests for at least part of their livelihoods.

- A purely conservation approach to forests is ineffective: Experience in India shows that a purely conservation approach to natural resources management does not work effectively and does little to reduce poverty.
- Weak resource rights for forest communities: The forest sector is also faced with weak resource rights and economic incentives for communities, an inefficient legal framework and participatory management, and poor access to markets.

Weak delivery of basic services in rural areas:

- Low bureaucratic accountability and inefficient use of public funds: Despite large expenditures in rural development, a highly centralized bureaucracy with low accountability and inefficient use of public funds limit their impact on poverty. In 1992, India amended its Constitution to create three tiers of democratically elected rural local governments bringing governance down to the villages. However, the transfer of authority, funds, and functionaries to these local bodies is progressing slowly, in part due to political vested interests. The poor are not empowered to contribute to shaping public programs or to hold local governments accountable.

Priority Areas for the World Bank Support

Enhancing Agricultural Productivity, Competitiveness, and Rural Growth

Enhancing productivity: Creating a more productive, internationally competitive and diversified agricultural sector would require a shift in public expenditures away from subsidies towards productivity enhancing investments.

Second it will require removing the restrictions on domestic private trade to improve the investment climate and meet expanding market opportunities. Third, the agricultural research and extension systems need to be strengthened to improve access to productivity enhancing technologies. The diverse conditions across India suggests the importance of regionally differentiated strategies, with a strong focus on the lagging states.

Improving Water Resource and Irrigation/Drainage Management: Increase in multi-sectoral competition for water highlights the need to formulate water policies and unbundle water resources management from irrigation service delivery. Other key priorities include: (i) modernizing Irrigation and Drainage Departments to integrate the participation of farmers and other agencies in irrigation management; (ii) improving cost recovery; (iii) rationalizing public expenditures, with priority to completing schemes with the highest returns; and (iv) allocating sufficient resources for operations and maintenance for the sustainability of investments.

Strengthening rural non-farm sector growth: Rising incomes are fueling demand for higher-value fresh and processed agricultural products in domestic markets and globally, which open new opportunities for agricultural diversification to higher value products (e.g. horticulture, livestock), agro-processing and related services.

The government needs to shift its role from direct intervention and overregulation to creating the enabling environment for private sector participation and competition for agribusiness and more broadly, the rural non-farm sector growth. Improving the rural investment climate includes removing trade controls, rationalizing labor regulations and the tax regime (i.e. adoption of the value added tax system), and improving access to credit and key infrastructure (e.g. roads, electricity, ports, markets).

Improving Access to Assets and Sustainable Natural Resource Use

Balancing poverty reduction and conservation priorities: Finding win-win combinations for conservation and poverty reduction will be critical to sustainable natural resource management. This will involve addressing legal, policy and institutional constraints to devolving resource rights, and transferring responsibilities to local communities.

Improving access to land: States can build on the growing consensus to reform land policy, particularly land tenancy policy and land administration system. States that do not have tenancy restrictions can provide useful lessons in this regard. Over the longer term, a more holistic approach to land administration policies, regulations and institutions is necessary to ensure tenure security, reduce costs, and ensure fairness and sustainability of the system.

Improving access to rural finance: It would require improving the performance of regional rural banks and rural credit cooperatives by enhancing regulatory oversight, removing government control and ownership, and strengthening the legal framework for loan recovery and the use of land as collateral. It would also involve creating an enabling environment for the development of micro-finance institutions in rural areas.

Strengthening Institutions for the Poor and Promoting Rural Livelihood

Promoting Community-Based Rural Development: State Government efforts in scaling up livelihood and community-driven development approaches will be critical to build social capital in the poorest areas as well as to expand savings mobilization, promote productive investments, income generating opportunities and sustainable natural resource management. Direct support to self-help groups, village committees, user's associations, savings and loans groups and others can provide the initial 'push' to move organizations to higher level and access to new economic opportunities. Moreover, social mobilization and particularly the empowerment of women's groups, through increased capacity for collective action will provide communities with greater "voice" and bargaining power in dealing with the private sector, markets and financial services.

Strengthening Accountability for Service Delivery: As decentralization efforts are pursued and local governments are given more prominence in the basic service delivery, the establishment of accountability mechanisms becomes critical. Local governments' capacity to identify local priorities through participatory budgeting and planning needs to be strengthened. This, in turn, would improve the rural investment climate, facilitating the involvement of the private sector, creating employment opportunities and linkages between farm and non-farm sectors.

Agriculture Sector

Agriculture in India has a long history dating back to ten thousand years.

Today, India ranks second worldwide in farm output. Agriculture and allied sectors like forestry and logging accounted for 16.6% of the GDP in 2007, employed 52% of the total workforce and despite a steady decline of its share in the GDP, is still the largest economic sector and plays a significant role in the overall socio-economic development of

India. India is the largest producer in the world of milk, cashew nuts, coconuts, tea, ginger, turmeric and black pepper.

It also has the world's largest cattle population (281 million). It is the second largest producer of wheat, rice, sugar, groundnut and inland fish. It is the third largest producer of tobacco. India accounts for 10% of the world fruit production with first rank in the production of banana and sapota.

India's population is growing faster than its ability to produce rice and wheat.

Initiatives

The required level of investment for the development of marketing, storage and cold storage infrastructure is estimated to be huge. The government has not been able to implement various schemes to raise investment in marketing infrastructure. Among these schemes are *Construction of Rural Go downs, Market Research and Information Network*, and *Development/Strengthening of Agricultural Marketing Infrastructure, Grading and Standardization.*

The Indian Agricultural Research Institute (IARI), established in 1905, was responsible for the research leading to the "Indian Green Revolution" of the 1970s. The Indian Council of Agricultural Research (ICAR) is the apex body in agriculture and related allied fields, including research and education. The Union Minister of Agriculture is the President of the ICAR.

The Indian Agricultural Statistics Research Institute develops new techniques for the design of agricultural experiments, analyses data in agriculture, and specializes in statistical techniques for animal and plant breeding. Recently Government of India has set up Farmers Commission to completely evaluate the agriculture program.. However the recommendations have had a mixed reception.

Mixed Farming

In August 2001 India's Parliament passed the Plant Variety Protection and Farmers' Rights Act, a sui generis legislation. Being a WTO member, India had to comply with TRIPS and include PVP. However, farmers' rights are of particular importance in India and thus the Act also allows for farmers to save, sow and sell seeds as they always have, even if it is of a protected variety.

This not only saves the livelihoods of many farmers, it also provides an environment for the continuing development and use of landraces, says Suman Sahai. The way it always was

Problems

Slow agricultural growth is a concern for policymakers as some two-thirds of India's people depend on rural employment for a living. Current agricultural practices are neither economically nor environmentally sustainable and India's yields for many agricultural commodities are low. Poorly maintained irrigation systems and almost universal lack of good extension services are among the factors responsible. Farmers' access to markets is hampered by poor roads, rudimentary market infrastructure, and excessive regulation. —World Bank: "India Country Overview 2008".

The low productivity in India is a result of the following factors:

- According to World Bank, Indian Branch: Priorities for Agriculture and Rural Development", India's large agricultural subsidies are hampering productivity-enhancing investment. Overregulation of agriculture has increased costs, price risks and uncertainty. Government intervenes in labour, land, and credit markets. India has inadequate infrastructure and services. World Bank also says that the allocation of water is inefficient, unsustainable and inequitable. The irrigation infrastructure is deteriorating. The overuse of water is currently being covered by over pumping aquifers, but as these are falling by foot of groundwater each year, this is a limited resource.
- Illiteracy, general socio-economic backwardness, slow progress in implementing land reforms and inadequate or inefficient finance and marketing services for farm produce.
- Inconsistent government policy. Agricultural subsidies and taxes often changed without notice for short term political ends.
- The average size of land holdings is very small (less than 20,000 m^2) and is subject to fragmentation, due to land ceiling acts and in some cases, family disputes. Such small holdings are often over-manned, resulting in disguised unemployment and low productivity of labour.
- Adoption of modern agricultural practices and use of technology is inadequate, hampered by ignorance of such practices, high costs and impracticality in the case of small land holdings.
- Irrigation facilities are inadequate, as revealed by the fact that only 52.6% of the land was irrigated in 2003–04, which result in farmers still being dependent on rainfall, specifically the Monsoon season. A good monsoon results in a robust growth for the economy as a whole, while a poor monsoon leads to a

sluggish growth. Farm credit is regulated by NABARD, which is the statutory apex agent for rural development in the subcontinent. At the same time overpumping made possible by subsidized electric power is leading to an alarming drop in aquifer levels.

History

Indian agriculture began by 9000 BC as a result of early cultivation of plants, and domestication of crops and animals. Settled life soon followed with implements and techniques being developed for agriculture. Double monsoons led to two harvests being reaped in one year. Indian products soon reached the world via existing trading networks and foreign crops were introduced to India. Plants and animals—considered essential to their survival by the Indians—came to be worshiped and venerated.

The middle ages saw irrigation channels reach a new level of sophistication in India and Indian crops affecting the economies of other regions of the world under Islamic patronage. Land and water management systems were developed with an aim of providing uniform growth. Despite some stagnation during the later modern era the independent Republic of India was able to develop a comprehensive agricultural program.

Agricultural Produces

Agriculture is the production, processing, marketing, and use of foods, fibers and byproducts from plant crops and animals. Agriculture was the key development that led to the rise of human civilization, with the husbandry of domesticated animals and plants (i.e. crops) creating food surpluses that enabled the development of more densely populated and stratified societies. The study of agriculture is known as agricultural science. Agriculture is also observed in certain species of ant and termite.

Agriculture encompasses a wide variety of specialties and techniques, including ways to expand the lands suitable for plant raising, by digging water-channels and other forms of irrigation. Cultivation of crops on arable land and the pastoral herding of livestock on rangeland remain at the foundation of agriculture. In the past century there has been increasing concern to identify and quantify various forms of agriculture. In the developed world the range usually extends between sustainable agriculture (e.g. permaculture or organic agriculture) and intensive farming (e.g. industrial agriculture).

Modern agronomy, plant breeding, pesticides and fertilizers, and technological improvements have sharply increased yields from cultivation, but at the same time have caused widespread ecological damage and negative human health effects. Selective breeding and modern practices in animal husbandry such as intensive pig farming (and similar practices applied to the chicken) have similarly increased the output of meat, but have raised concerns about animal cruelty and the health effects of the antibiotics, growth hormones, and other chemicals commonly used in industrial meat production.

The major agricultural products can be broadly grouped into foods, fibers, fuels, and raw materials. In the 21st century, plants have been used to grow biofuels, biopharmaceuticals, bioplastics, and pharmaceuticals. Specific foods include cereals, vegetables, fruits, and meat. Fibers include cotton, wool, hemp, silk and flax. Raw materials include lumber and bamboo. Other useful materials are produced by plants, such as resins. Biofuels include methane from biomass, ethanol, and biodiesel. Cut flowers, nursery plants, tropical fish and birds for the pet trade are some of the ornamental products.

In 2007, one third of the world's workers were employed in agriculture. The services sector has overtaken agriculture as the economic sector employing the most people worldwide. Despite the size of its workforce, agricultural production accounts for less than five percent of the gross world product (an aggregate of all gross domestic products).

Overview

Agriculture has played a key role in the development of human civilization. Until the Industrial Revolution, the vast majority of the human population labored in agriculture. Development of agricultural techniques has steadily increased agricultural productivity, and the widespread diffusion of these techniques during a time period is often called an agricultural revolution. A remarkable shift in agricultural practices has occurred over the past century in response to new technologies. In particular, the Haber-Bosch method for synthesizing ammonium nitrate made the traditional practice of recycling nutrients with crop rotation and animal manure less necessary.

Synthetic nitrogen, along with mined rock phosphate, pesticides and mechanization, have greatly increased crop yields in the early 20th century. Increased supply of grains has led to cheaper livestock as well. Further, global yield increases were experienced later in the 20th century when high-yield varieties of common staple grains such as rice, wheat, and corn (maize) were introduced as a part of the Green Revolution. The Green Revolution exported the technologies (including pesticides and synthetic nitrogen) of the developed world to the developing world. Thomas Malthus famously predicted that the Earth would not be able to support its growing population, but technologies such as the Green Revolution have allowed the world to produce a surplus of food.

Many governments have subsidized agriculture to ensure an adequate food supply. These agricultural subsidies are often linked to the production of certain commodities such as wheat, corn (maize), rice, soybeans, and milk. These subsidies, especially when instituted by developed countries have been noted as protectionist, inefficient, and environmentally damaging.

In the past century agriculture has been characterized by enhanced productivity, the use of synthetic fertilizers and pesticides, selective breeding, mechanization, water contamination, and farm subsidies. Proponents of organic farming such as Sir Albert Howard argued in the early 20th century that the overuse of pesticides and synthetic fertilizers damages the long-term fertility of the soil. While this feeling lay dormant for decades, as environmental awareness has increased in the 21st century there has been a movement towards sustainable agriculture by some farmers, consumers, and policymakers.

In recent years there has been a backlash against perceived external environmental effects of mainstream agriculture, particularly regarding water pollution, resulting in the organic movement. One of the major forces behind this movement has been the European Union, which first certified organic food in 1991 and began reform of its Common Agricultural Policy (CAP) in 2005 to phase out commodity-linked farm subsidies, also known as decoupling. The growth of organic farming has renewed research in alternative technologies such as integrated pest management and selective breeding. Recent mainstream technological developments include genetically modified food.

In late 2007, several factors pushed up the price of grains consumed by humans as well as used to feed poultry and dairy cows and other cattle, causing higher prices of wheat (up 58%), soybean (up 32%), and maize (up 11%) over the year. Food riots took place in several countries across the world. Contributing factors included drought in Australia and elsewhere, increasing demand for grain-fed animal products from the growing middle classes of countries such as China and India, diversion of foodgrain to biofuel production and trade restrictions imposed by several countries.

An epidemic of stem rust on wheat caused by race Ug99 is currently spreading across Africa and into Asia and is causing major concern. Approximately 40% of the world's agricultural land is seriously degraded. In Africa, if current trends of soil degradation continue, the continent might be able to feed just 25% of its population by 2025, according to UNU's Ghana-based Institute for Natural Resources in Africa.

History

Agricultural practices such as irrigation, crop rotation, fertilizers, and pesticides were developed long ago, but have made great strides in the past century. The history of agriculture has played a major role in human history, as agricultural progress has been a crucial factor in worldwide socio-economic change. Division of labor in agricultural societies made commonplace specializations rarely seen in hunter-gatherer cultures. So, too, are arts such as epic literature and monumental architecture, as well as codified legal systems. When farmers became capable of producing food beyond the needs of their own families, others in their society were freed to devote themselves to projects other than food acquisition. Historians and anthropologists have long argued that the development of agriculture made civilization possible.

Ancient Origins

The Fertile Crescent of Western Asia, Egypt, and India were sites of the earliest planned sowing and harvesting of plants that had previously been gathered in the wild. Independent development of agriculture occurred in northern and southern China, Africa's Sahel, New Guinea and several regions of the Americas. The eight so-called Neolithic founder crops of agriculture appear: first emmer wheat and einkorn wheat, then hulled barley, peas, lentils, bitter vetch, chick peas and flax.

By 7000 BC, small-scale agriculture reached Egypt. From at least 7000 BC the Indian subcontinent saw farming of wheat and barley, as attested by archaeological excavation at Mehrgarh in Balochistan. By 6000 BC, mid-scale farming was entrenched on the banks of the Nile. About this time, agriculture was developed independently in the Far East, with rice, rather than wheat, as the primary crop. Chinese and Indonesian farmers went on to domesticate taro and beans including mung, soy and azuki. To complement these new sources of carbohydrates, highly organized net fishing of rivers, lakes and ocean shores in these areas brought in great volumes of essential protein. Collectively, these new methods of farming and fishing inaugurated a human population boom that dwarfed all previous expansions and continues today.

By 5000 BC, the Sumerians had developed core agricultural techniques including large-scale intensive cultivation of land, monocropping, organized irrigation, and the use of a specialized labor force, particularly along the waterway now known as the Shatt al-Arab, from its Persian Gulf delta to the confluence of the Tigris and Euphrates. Domestication of wild aurochs and mouflon into cattle and sheep, respectively, ushered in the large-scale use of animals for food/fiber and as beasts of burden. The shepherd joined the farmer as an essential provider for sedentary and seminomadic societies. Maize, manioc, and arrowroot were first domesticated in the Americas as far back as 5200 BC.

The potato, tomato, pepper, squash, several varieties of bean, tobacco, and several other plants were also developed in the New World, as was extensive terracing of steep hillsides in much of Andean South America. The Greeks and Romans built on techniques pioneered by the Sumerians but made few fundamentally new advances. Southern Greeks struggled with very poor soils, yet managed to become a dominant society for years. The Romans were noted for an emphasis on the cultivation of crops for trade.

In the Americas, a parallel agricultural revolution occurred, resulting in some of the most important crops grown today. In Mesoamerica wild teosinte was transformed through human selection into the ancestor of modern maize, more than 6000 years ago. It gradually spread across North America and was the major crop of Native Americans at the time of European exploration. Other Mesoamerican crops include hundreds of varieties of squash and beans. Cocoa was also a major crop in domesticated Mexico and Central America. The turkey, one of the most important meat birds, was probably domesticated in Mexico or the U.S. Southwest. In the Andes region of South America the major domesticated crop was potatoes, domesticated perhaps 5000 years ago. Large varieties of beans were domesticated, in South America, as well as animals, including llamas, alpacas, and guinea pigs. Coca, still a major crop, was also domesticated in the Andes.

A minor center of domestication, the indigenous people of the Eastern U.S. appear to have domesticated numerous crops. Sunflowers, tobacco, varieties of squash and Chenopodium, as well as crops no longer grown, including marshelder and little barley were domesticated. Other wild foods may have undergone some selective cultivation, including wild rice and maple sugar. The most common varieties of strawberry were domesticated from Eastern North America.

Middle Ages

During the Middle Ages, farmers in North Africa, the Near East, and Europe began making use of agricultural technologies including irrigation systems based on hydraulic and hydrostatic principles, machines such as norias, water-raising machines, dams, and reservoirs. This combined with the invention of a three-field system of crop rotation and the moldboard plow greatly improved agricultural efficiency.

In the European medieval period, agriculture was considered part of the set of *seven mechanical arts*.

Modern Era

After 1492, a global exchange of previously local crops and livestock breeds occurred. Key crops involved in this exchange included the tomato, maize, potato, manioc, cocoa bean and tobacco going from the New World to the Old, and several varieties of wheat, spices, coffee, and sugar cane going from the Old World to the New. The most important animal exportation from the Old World to the New were those of the horse and dog (dogs were already present in the pre-Columbian Americas but not in the numbers and breeds suited to farm work). Although not usually food animals, the horse (including donkeys and ponies) and dog quickly filled essential production roles on western-hemisphere farms.

The potato became an important staple crop in northern Europe. Since being introduced by Portuguese in the 16th century, maize and manioc have replaced traditional African crops as the continent's most important staple food crops.

By the early 19th century, agricultural techniques, implements, seed stocks and cultivated plants selected and given a unique name because of its decorative or useful characteristics had so improved that yield per land unit was many times that seen in the Middle Ages. Although there is a vast and interesting history of crop cultivation before the dawn of the 20th century, there is little question that the work of Charles Darwin and Gregor Mendel created the scientific foundation for plant breeding that led to its explosive impact over the past 150 years.

With the rapid rise of mechanization in the late 19th century and the 20th century, particularly in the form of the tractor, farming tasks could be done with a speed and on a scale previously impossible. These advances have led to efficiencies enabling certain modern farms in the United States, Argentina, Israel, Germany, and a few other nations to output volumes of high-quality produce per land unit at what may be the practical limit.

The Haber-Bosch method for synthesizing ammonium nitrate represented a major breakthrough and allowed crop yields to overcome previous constraints. In the past century agriculture has been characterized by enhanced productivity, the substitution of labor for synthetic fertilizers and pesticides, water pollution, and farm subsidies. In recent years there has been a backlash against the external environmental effects of conventional agriculture, resulting in the organic movement.

The cereals rice, corn, and wheat provide 60% of human food supply. Between 1700 and 1980, "the total area of cultivated land worldwide increased 466%" and yields increased dramatically, particularly because of selectively bred high-yielding varieties, fertilizers, pesticides, irrigation, and machinery. For example, irrigation increased corn yields in eastern Colorado by 400 to 500% from 1940 to 1997.

However, concerns have been raised over the sustainability of intensive agriculture. Intensive agriculture has become associated with decreased soil quality in India and Asia, and there has been increased concern over the effects of fertilizers and pesticides on the environment, particularly as population increases and food demand expands. The monocultures typically used in intensive agriculture increase the number of pests, which are controlled through pesticides. Integrated pest management (IPM), which "has been promoted for decades and has had some notable successes" has not significantly affected the use of pesticides because policies encourage the use of pesticides and IPM is knowledge-intensive.

Although the "Green Revolution" significantly increased rice yields in Asia, yield increases have not occurred in the past 15–20 years. The genetic "yield potential" has increased for wheat, but the yield potential for rice has not increased since 1966, and the yield potential for maize has "barely increased in 35 years". It takes a decade or two for herbicide-resistant weeds to emerge, and insects become resistant to insecticides within about a decade. Crop rotation helps to prevent resistances.

Agricultural exploration expeditions, since the late 19th century, have been mounted to find new species and new agricultural practices in different areas of the world. Two early examples of expeditions include Frank N. Meyer's fruit-and nut-collecting trip to China and Japan from 1916-1918 and the Dorsett-Morse Oriental Agricultural Exploration Expedition to China, Japan, and Korea from 1929-1931 to collect soybean germplasm to support the rise in soybean agriculture in the United States.

In 2009, the agricultural output of China was the largest in the world, followed by the European Union, India and the United States, according to the International Monetary Fund. Economists measure the total factor productivity of agriculture and by this measure agriculture in the United States is roughly 2.6 times more productive than it was in 1948.

Six countries-the US, Canada, France, Australia, Argentina and Thailand-supply 90% of grain exports. The United States controls almost half of world grain exports. Water deficits, which are already spurring heavy grain imports in numerous middle-sized countries, including Algeria, Iran, Egypt, and Mexico, may soon do the same in larger countries, such as China or India.

Crop Production Systems

Cropping systems vary among farms depending on the available resources and constraints; geography and climate of the farm; government policy; economic, social and political pressures; and the philosophy and culture of the farmer.

Shifting cultivation (or slash and burn) is a system in which forests are burnt, releasing nutrients to support cultivation of annual and then perennial crops for a period of several years. Then the plot is left fallow to regrow forest, and the farmer moves to a new plot, returning after many more years (10-20).

This fallow period is shortened if population density grows, requiring the input of nutrients (fertilizer or manure) and some manual pest control. Annual cultivation is the next phase of intensity in which there is no fallow period.

This requires even greater nutrient and pest control inputs. Further industrialization lead to the use of monocultures, when one cultivar is planted on a large acreage. Because of the low biodiversity, nutrient use is uniform and pests tend to build up, necessitating the greater use of pesticides and fertilizers.

Multiple cropping, in which several crops are grown sequentially in one year, and intercropping, when several crops are grown at the same time are other kinds of annual cropping systems known as polycultures.

In tropical environments, all of these cropping systems are practiced. In subtropical and arid environments, the timing and extent of agriculture may be limited by rainfall, either not allowing multiple annual crops in a year, or requiring irrigation. In all of these environments perennial crops are grown (coffee, chocolate) and systems are practiced such as agroforestry. In temperate environments, where ecosystems were predominantly grassland or prairie, highly productive annual cropping is the dominant farming system.

The last century has seen the intensification, concentration and specialization of agriculture, relying upon new technologies of agricultural chemicals (fertilizers and pesticides), mechanization, and plant breeding (hybrids and GMO's). In the past few decades, a move towards sustainability in agriculture has also developed, integrating ideas of socio-economic justice and conservation of resources and the environment within a farming system.

This has led to the development of many responses to the conventional agriculture approach, including organic agriculture, urban agriculture, community supported agriculture, ecological or biological agriculture, integrated farming and holistic management, as well as an increased trend towards agricultural diversification.

Crop Statistics

Important categories of crops include grains and pseudograins, pulses (legumes), forage, and fruits and vegetables. Specific crops are cultivated in distinct growing regions throughout the world. In millions of metric tons, based on FAO estimate.

***Table:** Top Agricultural Products, by crop types (million tonnes) 2004 data*

Cereals	2,263
Vegetables and melons	866
Roots and Tubers	715
Milk	619
Fruit	503

Meat	259
Oilcrops	133
Fish (2001 estimate)	130
Eggs	63
Pulses	60
Vegetable Fiber	30

Source: *Food and Agriculture Organization (FAO)*

Table: *Top agricultural products, by individual crops (million tonnes) 2004 data*

Sugar Cane	1,324
Maize	721
Wheat	627
Rice	605
Potatoes	328
Sugar Beet	249
Soybean	204
Oil Palm Fruit	162
Barley	154
Tomato	120

Source: *Food and Agriculture Organization (FAO)*

Livestock Production Systems

Animals, including horses, mules, oxen, camels, llamas, alpacas, and dogs, are often used to help cultivate fields, harvest crops, wrangle other animals, and transport farm products to buyers. Animal husbandry not only refers to the breeding and raising of animals for meat or to harvest animal products (like milk, eggs, or wool) on a continual basis, but also to the breeding and care of species for work and companionship. Livestock production systems can be defined based on feed source, as grassland-based, mixed, and landless.

Grassland based livestock production relies upon plant material such as shrubland, rangeland, and pastures for feeding ruminant animals. Outside nutrient inputs may be used, however manure is returned directly to the grassland as a major nutrient source.

This system is particularly important in areas where crop production is not feasible because of climate or soil, representing 30-40 million pastoralists. Mixed production systems use grassland, fodder crops and grain feed crops as feed for ruminant and monogastic (one stomach; mainly chickens and pigs) livestock. Manure is typically recycled in mixed systems as a fertilizer for crops. Approximately 68% of all agricultural land is permanent pastures used in the production of livestock.

Landless systems rely upon feed from outside the farm, representing the de-linking of crop and livestock production found more prevalently in OECD member countries. In the U.S., 70% of the grain grown is fed to animals on feedlots. Synthetic fertilizers are more heavily relied upon for crop production and manure utilization becomes a challenge as well as a source for pollution.

Production Practices

Tillage is the practice of plowing soil to prepare for planting or for nutrient incorporation or for pest control. Tillage varies in intensity from conventional to no-till. It may improve productivity by warming the soil, incorporating fertilizer and controlling weeds, but also renders soil more prone to erosion, triggers the decomposition of organic matter releasing CO_2, and reduces the abundance and diversity of soil organisms.

Pest control includes the management of weeds, insects/mites, and diseases. Chemical (pesticides), biological (biocontrol), mechanical (tillage), and cultural practices are used. Cultural practices include crop rotation, culling, cover crops, intercropping, composting, avoidance, and resistance. Integrated pest management attempts to use all of these methods to keep pest populations below the number which would cause economic loss, and recommends pesticides as a last resort.

Nutrient management includes both the source of nutrient inputs for crop and livestock production, and the method of utilization of manure produced by livestock. Nutrient inputs can be chemical inorganic fertilizers, manure, green manure, compost and mined minerals. Crop nutrient use may also be managed using cultural techniques such as crop rotation or a fallow period. Manure is used either by holding livestock where the feed crop is growing, such as in managed intensive rotational grazing, or by spreading either dry or liquid formulations of manure on cropland or pastures.

Water management is where rainfall is insufficient or variable, which occurs to some degree in most regions of the world. Some farmers use irrigation to supplement rainfall. In other areas such as the Great Plains in the U.S. and Canada, farmers use a fallow year to conserve soil moisture to use for growing a crop in the following year. Agriculture represents 70% of freshwater use worldwide.

Processing, Distribution, and Marketing

In the United States, food costs attributed to processing, distribution, and marketing have risen while the costs attributed to farming have declined. This is related to the greater efficiency of farming, combined with the increased level of value addition (e.g. more highly processed products) provided by the supply chain. From 1960 to 1980 the farm share was around 40%, but by 1990 it had declined to 30% and by 1998, 22.2%. Market concentration has increased in the sector as well, with the top 20 food manufacturers accounting for half the food-processing value in 1995, over double that produced in 1954. As of 2000 the top six US supermarket groups had 50% of sales compared to 32% in 1992. Although the total effect of the increased market concentration is likely increased efficiency, the changes redistribute economic surplus from producers (farmers) and consumers, and may have negative implications for rural communities.

Crop Alteration and Biotechnology

Crop alteration has been practiced by humankind for thousands of years, since the beginning of civilization. Altering crops through breeding practices changes the genetic make-up of a plant to develop crops with more beneficial characteristics for humans, for example, larger fruits or seeds, drought-tolerance, or resistance to pests. Significant advances in plant breeding ensued after the work of geneticist Gregor Mendel. His work on dominant and recessive alleles gave plant breeders a better understanding of genetics and brought great insights to the techniques utilized by plant breeders. Crop breeding includes techniques such as plant selection with desirable traits, self-pollination and cross-pollination, and molecular techniques that genetically modify the organism. Domestication of plants has, over the centuries increased yield, improved disease resistance and drought tolerance, eased harvest and improved the taste and nutritional value of crop plants. Careful selection and breeding have had enormous effects on the characteristics of crop plants. Plant selection and breeding in the 1920s and 1930s improved pasture (grasses and clover) in New Zealand. Extensive X-ray an ultraviolet induced mutagenesis efforts (i.e. primitive genetic engineering) during the 1950s produced the modern commercial varieties of grains such as wheat, corn (maize) and barley.

The green revolution popularized the use of conventional hybridization to increase yield many folds by creating “high-yielding varieties”. For example, average yields of corn (maize) in the USA have increased from around 2.5 tons per hectare (t/ha) (40 bushels per acre) in 1900 to about 9.4 t/ha (150 bushels per acre) in 2001. Similarly, worldwide average wheat yields have increased from less than 1 t/ha in 1900 to more than 2.5 t/ha in 1990. South American average wheat yields are around 2 t/ha, African under 1 t/ha, Egypt and Arabia up to 3.5 to 4 t/ha with irrigation. In contrast, the average wheat yield in countries such as France is over 8 t/ha. Variations in yields are due mainly to variation in climate, genetics, and the level of intensive farming techniques (use of fertilizers, chemical pest control, growth control to avoid lodging).

Genetic Engineering

Genetically Modified Organisms (GMO) are organisms whose genetic material has been altered by genetic engineering techniques generally known as recombinant DNA technology. Genetic engineering has expanded the genes available to breeders to utilize in creating desired germlines for new crops. After mechanical tomato-harvesters were developed in the early 1960s, agricultural scientists genetically modified tomatoes to be more resistant to mechanical handling. More recently, genetic engineering is being employed in various parts of the world, to create crops with other beneficial traits.

Herbicide-tolerant GMO Crops

Roundup Ready seed has a herbicide resistant gene implanted into its genome that allows the plants to tolerate exposure to glyphosate. *Roundup* is a trade name for a glyphosate-based product, which is a systemic, nonselective herbicide used to kill weeds. *Roundup Ready* seeds allow the farmer to grow a crop that can be sprayed with glyphosate to control weeds without harming the resistant crop. Herbicide-tolerant crops are used by farmers worldwide. Today, 92% of soybean acreage in the US is planted with genetically modified herbicide-tolerant plants.

With the increasing use of herbicide-tolerant crops, comes an increase in the use of glyphosate-based herbicide sprays. In some areas glyphosate resistant weeds have developed, causing farmers to switch to other herbicides. Some studies also link widespread glyphosate usage to iron deficiencies in some crops, which is both a crop production and a nutritional quality concern, with potential economic and health implications.

Insect-resistant GMO Crops

Other GMO crops used by growers include insect-resistant crops, which have a gene from the soil bacterium *Bacillus thuringiensis* (Bt), which produces a toxin specific to insects. These crops protect plants from damage by insects; one such crop is Starlink. Another is cotton, which accounts for 63% of US cotton acreage.

Some believe that similar or better pest-resistance traits can be acquired through traditional breeding practices, and resistance to various pests can be gained through hybridization or cross-pollination with wild species. In some cases, wild species are the primary source of resistance traits; some tomato cultivars that have gained resistance to at least nineteen diseases did so through crossing with wild populations of tomatoes.

Costs and benefits of GMOs

Genetic engineers may someday develop transgenic plants which would allow for irrigation, drainage, conservation, sanitary engineering, and maintaining or increasing yields while requiring fewer fossil fuel derived inputs than conventional crops. Such developments would be particularly important in areas which are normally arid and rely upon constant irrigation, and on large scale farms. However, genetic engineering of plants has proven to be controversial. Many issues surrounding food security and environmental impacts have risen regarding GMO practices. For example, GMOs are questioned by some ecologists and economists concerned with GMO practices such as terminator seeds, which is a genetic modification that creates sterile seeds. Terminator seeds are currently under strong international opposition and face continual efforts of global bans. Another controversial issue is the patent protection given to companies that develop new types of seed using genetic engineering. Since companies have intellectual ownership of their seeds, they have the power to dictate terms and conditions of their patented product. Currently, ten seed companies control over two-thirds of the global seed sales. Vandana Shiva argues that these companies are guilty of biopiracy by patenting life and exploiting organisms for profit Farmers using patented seed are restricted from saving seed for subsequent plantings, which forces farmers to buy new seed every year.

Since seed saving is a traditional practice for many farmers in both developing and developed countries, GMO seeds legally bind farmers to change their seed saving practices to buying new seed every year.

Locally adapted seeds are an essential hertitage that has the potential to be lost with current hybridized crops and GMOs. Locally adapted seeds, also called land races or crop eco-types, are important because they have adapted over time to the specific microclimates, soils, other environmental conditions, field designs, and ethnic preference indigenous to the exact area of cultivation. Introducing GMOs and hybridized commercial seed to an area brings the risk of cross-pollination with local land races Therefore, GMOs pose a threat to the sustainability of land races and the ethnic heritage of cultures. Once seed contains transgenic material, it becomes subject to the conditions of the seed company that owns the patent of the transgenic material. There is also concern that GMOs will cross-pollinate with wild species and permanently alter native populations' genetic integrity; there are already identified populations of wild plants with transgenic genes. GMO gene flow to related weed species is a concern, as well as cross-pollination with non-transgenic crops. Since many GMO crops are harvested for their seed, such as rapeseed, seed spillage in is problematic for volunteer plants in rotated fields, as well as seed-spillage during transportation.

Modern Agriculture

Modern agriculture is a term used to describe the wide majority of production practices employed by America's farmers. The term depicts the push for innovation, stewardship and advancements continually made by growers to sustainably produce higher-quality products with a reduced environmental impact. Intensive scientific research and robust investment in modern agriculture during the past 50 years has helped farmers double food production while essentially freezing the footprint of total cultivated farmland.

Safety

The agriculture industry works with government agencies and other organizations to ensure that farmers have access to the technologies required to support modern agriculture practices. Farmers are supported by education and certification programs that ensure they apply agricultural with care and only when required.

Sustainability

Technological advancements help provide farmers with tools and resources to help reduce their environmental footprint and to make farming more sustainable. New technologies have given rise to innovations like conservation tillage, a farming process which helps prevent land loss to erosion, water pollution and enhances carbon sequestration. The World Bank, the Bill & Melinda Gates Foundation and others have noted that integrated crop management is based on agro-ecological principles and can increase yields while reducing environmental damage.

Affordability

Modern agriculture practices help farmers to provide an affordable supply of nutritious food to meet the demands of a growing population. With modern agriculture, more crops can be grown on less land allowing farmers to provide an increased supply of food at an affordable price.

Food Safety, Labeling and Regulation

Food security issues also coincide with food safety and food labeling concerns. Currently a global treaty, the BioSafety Protocol, regulates the trade of GMOs. The EU currently requires all GMO foods to be labeled, whereas the US does not require transparent labeling of GMO foods. Since there are still questions regarding the safety and risks associated with GMO foods, some believe the public should have the freedom to choose and know what they are eating and require all GMO products to be labeled.

The Food and Agriculture Organization of the United Nations (FAO) leads international efforts to defeat hunger and provides a neutral forum where nations meet as equals to negotiate agreements and debate food policy and the regulation of agriculture. According to Dr. Samuel Jutzi, director of FAO's animal production and health division, lobbying by "powerful" big food corporations has stopped reforms that would improve human health and the environment. The "real, true issues are not being addressed by the political process because of the influence of lobbyists, of the true powerful entities," he said, speaking at the Compassion in World Farming annual forum. For example, recent proposals for a voluntary code of conduct for the livestock industry that would have provided incentives for improving standards for health, and environmental regulations, such as the number of animals an area of land can support without long-term damage, were successfully defeated due to large food company pressure.

Environmental Impact

Agriculture imposes external costs upon society through pesticides, nutrient runoff, excessive water usage, and assorted other problems. A 2000 assessment of agriculture in the UK determined total external costs for 1996 of £2,343 million, or £208 per hectare. A 2005 analysis of these costs in the USA concluded that cropland imposes approximately $5 to 16 billion ($30 to $96 per hectare), while livestock production imposes $714 million. Both studies concluded that more should be done to internalize external costs, and neither included subsidies in their analysis, but noted that subsidies also influence the cost of agriculture to society. Both focused on purely fiscal impacts. The 2000 review included reported pesticide poisonings but did not include speculative chronic effects of pesticides, and the 2004 review relied on a 1992 estimate of the total impact of pesticides.

A key player who is credited to saving billions of lives because of his revolutionary work in developing new agricultural techniques is Norman Borlaug. His transformative work brought high-yield crop varieties to developing countries and earned him an unofficial title as the father of the Green Revolution.

Livestock Issues

A senior UN official and co-author of a UN report detailing this problem, Henning Steinfeld, said "Livestock are one of the most significant contributors to today's most serious environmental problems". Livestock production occupies 70% of all land used for agriculture, or 30% of the land surface of the planet. It is one of the largest sources of greenhouse gases, responsible for 18% of the world's greenhouse gas emissions as measured in CO_2 equivalents. By comparison, all transportation emits 13.5% of the CO_2. It produces 65% of human-related nitrous oxide (which has 296 times the global warming potential of CO_2) and 37% of all human-induced methane (which is 23 times as warming as CO_2. It also generates 64% of the ammonia, which contributes to acid rain and acidification of ecosystems. Livestock expansion is cited as a key factor driving deforestation, in the Amazon basin 70% of previously forested area is now occupied by pastures and the remainder used for feedcrops. Through deforestation and land degradation, livestock is also driving reductions in biodiversity.

Land Transformation and Degradation

Land transformation, the use of land to yield goods and services, is the most substantial way humans alter the Earth's ecosystems, and is considered the driving force in the loss of biodiversity. Estimates of the amount of land transformed by humans vary from 39–50%. Land degradation, the long-term decline in ecosystem function and productivity, is estimated to be occurring on 24% of land worldwide, with cropland overrepresented. The UN-FAO report cites land management as the driving factor behind degradation and reports that 1.5 billion people rely upon the degrading land. Degradation can be deforestation, desertification, soil erosion, mineral depletion, or chemical degradation (acidification and salinization).

Eutrophication

Eutrophication, excessive nutrients in aquatic ecosystems resulting in algal blooms and anoxia, leads to fish kills, loss of biodiversity, and renders water unfit for drinking and other industrial uses. Excessive fertilization and manure application to cropland, as well as high livestock stocking densities cause nutrient (mainly nitrogen and phosphorus) runoff and leaching from agricultural land. These nutrients are major nonpoint pollutants contributing to eutrophication of aquatic ecosystems.

Pesticides

Pesticide use has increased since 1950 to 2.5 million tons annually worldwide, yet crop loss from pests has remained relatively constant.

The World Health Organization estimated in 1992 that 3 million pesticide poisonings occur annually, causing 220,000 deaths. Pesticides select for pesticide resistance in the pest population, leading to a condition termed the 'pesticide treadmill' in which pest resistance warrants the development of a new pesticide.

An alternative argument is that the way to 'save the environment' and prevent famine is by using pesticides and intensive high yield farming, a view exemplified by a quote heading the Center for Global Food Issues website: 'Growing more per acre leaves more land for nature'.

However, critics argue that a trade-off between the environment and a need for food is not inevitable, and that pesticides simply replace good agronomic practices such as crop rotation.

Climate Change

Climate change has the potential to affect agriculture through changes in temperature, rainfall (timing and quantity), CO_2, solar radiation and the interaction of these elements. Agriculture can both mitigate or worsen global warming.

Some of the increase in CO_2 in the atmosphere comes from the decomposition of organic matter in the soil, and much of the methane emitted into the atmosphere is caused by the decomposition of organic matter in wet soils such as rice paddies.

Further, wet or anaerobic soils also lose nitrogen through denitrification, releasing the greenhouse gas nitric oxide. Changes in management can reduce the release of these greenhouse gases, and soil can further be used to sequester some of the CO_2 in the atmosphere.

International Economics and Agriculture

Differences in economic development, population density and culture mean that the farmers of the world operate under very different conditions.

A US cotton farmer may receive US$230 in government subsidies per acre planted (in 2003), while farmers in Mali and other third-world countries do without. When prices decline, the heavily subsidized US farmer is not forced to reduce his output, making it difficult for cotton prices to rebound, but his Mali counterpart may go broke in the meantime.

A livestock farmer in South Korea can calculate with a (highly subsidized) sales price of US$1300 for a calf produced. A South American Mercosur country rancher calculates with a calf's sales price of US$120–200 (both 2008 figures). With the former, scarcity and high cost of land is compensated with public subsidies, the latter compensates absence of subsidies with economics of scale and low cost of land.

In the Peoples Republic of China, a rural household's productive asset may be one hectare of farmland. In Brazil, Paraguay and other countries where local legislature allows such purchases, international investors buy thousands of hectares of farmland or raw land at prices of a few hundred US$ per hectare.

Energy and Agriculture

Since the 1940s, agricultural productivity has increased dramatically, due largely to the increased use of energy-intensive mechanization, fertilizers and pesticides. The vast majority of this energy input comes from fossil fuel sources. Between 1950 and 1984, the Green Revolution transformed agriculture around the globe, with world grain production increasing by 250% as world population doubled. Modern agriculture's heavy reliance on petrochemicals and mechanization has raised concerns that oil shortages could increase costs and reduce agricultural output, causing food shortages.

Modern or industrialized agriculture is dependent on fossil fuels in two fundamental ways: 1) direct consumption on the farm and 2) indirect consumption to manufacture inputs used on the farm. Direct consumption includes the use of lubricants and fuels to operate farm vehicles and machinery; and use of gas, liquid propane, and electricity to power dryers, pumps, lights, heaters, and coolers. American farms directly consumed about 1.2 exajoules (1.1 quadrillion BTU) in 2002, or just over 1 percent of the nation's total energy.

Indirect consumption is mainly oil and natural gas used to manufacture fertilizers and pesticides, which accounted for 0.6 exajoules (0.6 quadrillion BTU) in 2002. The energy used to manufacture farm machinery is also a form of indirect agricultural energy consumption, but it is not included in USDA estimates of U.S. agricultural energy use. Together, direct and indirect consumption by U.S. farms accounts for about 2 percent of the nation's energy use. Direct and indirect energy consumption by U.S. farms peaked in 1979, and has gradually declined over the past 30 years.

Food systems encompass not just agricultural production, but also off-farm processing, packaging, transporting, marketing, consumption, and disposal of food and food-related items. Agriculture accounts for less than one-fifth of food system energy use in the United States.

Oil shortages could impact this food supply. Some farmers using modern organic-farming methods have reported yields as high as those available from conventional farming without the use of synthetic fertilizers and pesticides. However, the reconditioning of soil to restore nutrients lost during the use of monoculture agriculture techniques made possible by petroleum-based technology takes time.

In 2007, higher incentives for farmers to grow non-food biofuel crops combined with other factors (such as over-development of former farm lands, rising transportation costs, climate change, growing consumer demand in China and India, and population growth) to cause food shortages in Asia, the Middle East, Africa, and Mexico, as well as rising food prices around the globe. As of December 2007, 37 countries faced food crises, and 20 had imposed some sort of food-price controls. Some of these shortages resulted in food riots and even deadly stampedes.

The biggest fossil fuel input to agriculture is the use of natural gas as a hydrogen source for the Haber-Bosch fertilizer-creation process. Natural gas is used because it is the cheapest currently available source of hydrogen. When oil production becomes so scarce that natural gas is used as a partial stopgap replacement, and hydrogen use in transportation increases, natural gas will become much more expensive. If the Haber Process is unable to be commercialized using renewable energy (such as by electrolysis) or if other sources of hydrogen are not available to replace the Haber Process, in amounts sufficient to supply transportation and agricultural needs, this major source of fertilizer would either become extremely expensive or unavailable. This would either cause food shortages or dramatic rises in food prices.

Mitigation of Effects of Petroleum Shortages

One effect oil shortages could have on agriculture is a full return to organic agriculture. In light of peak-oil concerns, organic methods are more sustainable than contemporary practices because they use no petroleum-based pesticides, herbicides, or fertilizers. Some farmers using modern organic-farming methods have reported yields as high as those available from conventional farming. Organic farming may however be more labor-intensive and would require a shift of the workforce from urban to rural areas. It has been suggested that rural communities might obtain fuel from the biochar and synfuel process, which uses agricultural *waste* to provide charcoal fertilizer, some fuel *and* food, instead of the normal food vs fuel debate. As the synfuel would be used on-site, the process would be more efficient and might just provide enough fuel for a new organic-agriculture fusion.

It has been suggested that some transgenic plants may some day be developed which would allow for maintaining or increasing yields while requiring fewer fossil-fuel-derived inputs than conventional crops. The possibility of success of these programs is questioned by ecologists and economists concerned with unsustainable GMO practices such as terminator seeds, and a January 2008 report shows that GMO practices "fail to deliver environmental, social and economic benefits." While there has been some research on sustainability using GMO crops, at least one hyped and prominent multi-year attempt by Monsanto Company has been unsuccessful, though during the same period traditional breeding techniques yielded a more sustainable variety of the same crop. Additionally, a survey by the bio-tech industry of subsistence farmers in Africa to discover what GMO research would most benefit sustainable agriculture only identified non-transgenic issues as areas needing to be addressed. Nevertheless, some governments in Africa continue to view investments in new transgenic technologies as an essential component of efforts to improve sustainability.

Position of Farmers

A farmer is a person, engaged in agriculture, who raises living organisms for food or raw materials, generally including livestock husbandry and growing crops such as produce and grain. A farmer might own the farmed land or might work as a labourer on land owned by others; but in advanced economies, a farmer is usually a farm owner, while employees of the farm are farm workers, farmhands, etc.

India is an agricultural country. India lives in villages. The villagers depend on agriculture. They are either farmers or workers on the agricultural fields. Ours industries and urban business also depend on agriculture. Thus, an Indian farmer truly represents India. He can be called the son of the soil. It is on his sweet and labour that our progress and prosperity depend.

It is he who feeds and clothes the people. An Indian farmer is very hard working. He is very busy throughout the year. For him there is no rest. He is engaged in tilling the soil, sowing the seeds, watering the fields, reaping and harvesting the crop and then taking it to the market to sell it. And yet he is very poor. He is being exploited by the money-lenders, the middlemen and the government servants.

His needs are few and simple and yet they are not met. Most of the Indian farmers or tenants. Their exploitation should be stopped. They should be distributed agricultural land. They should be given cheap loans and other facilities. They should be given better seeds, fertilizers and return for their produce. The irrigation facilities should be improved.

India cannot prosper until Indian farmer is poor and miserable. He is the very soul of the country. He is as important as a soldier, a doctor or an engineer. That is why the then Prime Minister Lal Bahadur Shastri gave us the slogan: "Jai Jawan, Jai Kisan." But it should not remain only a slogan. The Indian farmer should be given his due regard and status. Every effort should be made to make him happy, rich and comfortable. His labours and sweat should not go unrewarded.

He should be taught how to read and write. Education should be taken to his door-steps so that his children do not remain illiterate. He should be provided with better medical and health facilities. He is the bread-earner of the country and should be treated accordingly. If he himself remains hungry, illcad or ignorant how India can make progress? Some schemes have been started to improve his economic and social condition. But many more such schemes need to be started.

Indian Farmers Position on WTO

The farmers of India are very much concerned with the recent developments in the WTO negotiations on agriculture. In the current negotiations to conclude the modalities on agriculture before the General Council in end July, it is becoming clearer that once again the interest of India and other developing countries and their farmers are in danger. And we fear that the Indian government, driven by its offensive interest in services, would try to push through a deal for conclusion of the Doha round even at the cost of its million of farmers and industry workers. We had witnessed this in Hong Kong where India betrayed other developing countries in joining hands with US and EU to protect services text in exchange of minor gains in agriculture.

Today it is clear that the Indian position in WTO is driven by its offensive interest in services negotiations. India has no stake in agricultural negotiations and we are quite apprehensive that any tradeoff in services negotiations can change Indian position in agriculture.

When UPA government came in power largely with the support of farmers and rural India, Indian farmers were quite hopeful that their interest would be paramount in its agenda. But last two years of UPA rule has brought misery and destitution for the rural community and never before there were such severe agrarian crisis as it is today. Every day dozens of farmers are committing suicide yet Mr. Sharad Pawar, Union Minister for Agriculture, in a live television interview (CNN-IBN-June 4) said that "100,000 farmers suicide per year is a normal thing that we have been seeing for a number of years". This is the height of government's apathy towards farmers. And ironically even the relief packages announced by this government to deal with agrarian crisis are corporate driven and only promote the interest of the US biotech industries like Monsanto and their agribusiness like Cargill and ADM. And quite obviously three giant US corporations (Monsanto, Wal-Mart and Archer Daniels Midland) along with an Indian agribusiness ITC have got formal entry in the Indian government system as board members of the "Indo-US Knowledge Initiative on Agricultural Research and Education", launched during the US President's recent visit to India.

In last two years the UPA government has done a lot to protect interest of the corporate India at the cost of the poor and marginal class. Most of the agricultural related policy introduced by the UPA government has been to further the agenda of corporate globalization. The introduction of seed bills 2004; changes in the agriculture produce marketing act (APMC Act); the food safety and standards bill; withdrawal of food subsides for the poor under BPL programme; the contract farming; liberalization of imports for seeds and planting material; increased commercialization of GM cotton and field trials for GM food crops; providing data exclusivity to MNCs in agro-chemicals; and completely liberalizing imports of food grains are some of those decisions which favours only the corporations. Recently we witnessed a classic example of anti farmer and pro corporate policy of the UPA government when it signed a deal with AWB Ltd of Australia for import of 5 lakh tonne of wheat, at the time of harvest in India and at a price much above the MSP price for procurement of wheat from farmers. Though the government refused to pay an MSP of above Rs. 7000/-per tonne to Indian farmers but it is paying Rs. 10500 per tonne to AWB, which is procuring wheat from Indian mandies at a little extra price than the MSP and supplying the same Indian wheat to the government.

In view of the above, we fear that in the ongoing negotiations on agriculture as well, the UPA government will jeopardize the interest of Indian farmers by accepting whatever scrap being offered by US and EU. And this will be done on the name of protecting the export interest of an small section of big "farmers" and corporations like ITC.

In the current negotiations on agriculture, the main issue is about deciding the formulae for tariff cuts and subsidy cuts. In view of the impact of removal of quantitative restrictions, Indian farmer stand to lose from the proposed large tariff cuts under negotiations. Any further lowing of tariff on agricultural goods would be disastrous for small and marginal farmers of the country and would lead to an epidemic of farmers' suicide. It would jeopardize our self-sufficiency in food, increase our dependency on agricultural imports and reduce the margin between applied and bound rates, thereby restricting future governments from freely changing tariffs.

In return for the increased market access, the US and EU are offering artificial reduction in their domestic support and the proposed cut will not make any change in their applied level of support. Instead it allows them to raise their overall subsidies level.

This was made clear in the recent Domestic Support Simulations conducted by Canada which proved that neither the U.S. nor the E.C. will have to make reductions in their domestic support payments (as per their current proposals) and the U.S. in particular, will be able to increase overall spending in the amber and blue boxes and the de minimis. It found that under the U.S. proposal, U.S. agriculture spending could legally increase to $22.5 billion a year, from last year's estimated $19.6 billion, simply by re-categorizing existing payments.

The US trade official also claim that they are under extreme pressure from number of leading U.S. agriculture organizations who demand lowering of U.S. ambitions on domestic support. That means there can't be any further increase in the current US offer for reduction in domestic support.

Moreover, the US is not ready to concede an effective protection for the developing countries through SPs and allows only five tariff lines (against a demand of 20% by the G20) to be self designated as SPs (US framework paper on SP of 6th April 2006) which is less than 1% of India's total tariff line (680) in agriculture. Even on Special Safeguard Mechanism (SSM), US intentions are not very clear and it is trying to limit the scope of this safeguard to an extent that recourse to such mechanism becomes useless (US proposal of 24th April 2006).

In fact all the so-called gains from the Hong Kong Declaration are proving to be illusionary. Even though SP and SSM are not effective safeguard mechanisms to deal with cheap subsidized imports, but these are the only safeguard available to the developing nations given the proposed deepest cut in import tariff. But US and EU does not want to offer even these minimal safeguard to the developing countries to protect their farmers from cheap subsidized imports. Therefore there going to be a complete disaster for the farmers and agriculture of the developing countries if this present offers on the table goes through.

It is now clear how tough it is to get so little from the developed countries on any issues which is of the interest of the developing countries and LDCs in the agricultural negotiations. We therefore reassert our demand that agriculture must be kept out of the perview of the WTO.

Several recent studies have also indicated the same and predicted loses for developing countries including India from the Doha Development Round, in the agriculture as well as industrial sectors. Contrary to commonly held view, research from the World Bank, the Carnegie Endowment and the European Commission reveal that the majority in Asia and Africa will be faced with losses in both agriculture and industrial goods liberalisation. Even EU's own impact assessment of the Doha Round foresee that many of the world's developing economies will lose out from the Round, including parts of South Asia and much of Sub-Saharan Africa.

Rural Recreation

Recreation is any activity performed during one's leisure or free time. Recreational activities are often done for amusement, enjoyment or pleasure and are considered to be 'fun'. Almost any activity can be considered recreational when engaged in during one's free time.

Rural tourism focuses on participating in a rural lifestyle. It can be a variant of ecotourism. Any village can be a tourist attraction, and many villagers are very hospitable. Agriculture is becoming highly mechanized and therefore requires less manual labor. This is causing economic pressure on some villages, leading to an exodus of young people to urban areas.

Benefits

Rural tourism allows the creation of an alternative source of income in the non-agricultural sector for rural dwellers. The added income from rural tourism can contribute to the revival of lost folk art and handicrafts. It is an ideal and natural method of rural and urban economic exchange.

Relevance in Developing Nations

Rural tourism is particularly relevant in developing nations wherein farmland has become fragmented due to population growth.

Relevance in Developed Nations

Rural tourism exists in developed nations in the form of providing accommodation in a scenic location ideal for rest and relaxation.

United States: Niche Tourism in Rural Areas

Many niche tourism programs are located in rural areas. From wine tours and eco-tourism, to agritourism and seasonal events, tourism can be a viable economic component in rural community development. According the USDA, Cooperative State, Education and Extension Service, "Tourism is becoming increasingly important to the U.S. economy. A conservative estimate from the Federal Reserve Board in Kansas, based on 2000 data, shows that basic travel and tourism industries accounted for 3.6 percent of all U.S. employment. Even more telling, data from the Travel Industry Association of America indicate that 1 out of every 18 people in the U.S. has a job directly resulting from travel expenditures."

The publication *Promoting Tourism in Rural America* explains the need for planning and marketing rural community and to weigh the pros and cons of the impacts of tourism. Local citizen participation is helpful and should be included in starting any kind of a tourism program. Being prepared by planning tourism can assist in a successful program that enhances the community.

6

Economics and Population

Until now most economic study has been preoccupied with the reasons one country's economy is healthier than another's. The comparisons help us discover the best practices. Over the years, we've improved economies by learning from each other and adopting the models that are most successful. On the whole, the evidence has demonstrated that nations with market-directed economies are more successful than those with centrally planned economies. The big centrally planned economies of China and the former Soviet Republics have, over the last few decades, converted to more market-driven systems. And they have found new prosperity.

Economists have paid a lot more attention to the relative success or failure of national economies than to the larger dynamics of the world's economy. Students of economics understand the reasons why one nation outperforms another better than they understand the fundamental forces that direct the human economy as a single entity or the symbiotic relationships that support groups of national economies. Likewise we find it hard to track economics across long periods of time.

What events occurred in the 19th century that made some nations prosperous in the 20th century? Are events occurring today that might undermine our economic health 30 years from now? We're pretty comfortable looking at one national economy and its condition today. When we aggregate more than one national economy and then try to track economic trends over time, the equation's complexity increases by orders of magnitude. It's difficult for the economist to get his or her arms around the global economy as it evolves across the decades.

Economists are aware of this gap in understanding. They recognize the complexity of their subject matter. They make allowances for what they call "externality." In economics, "externality" refers to the effects of an economic event on parties not directly involved – people in faraway places, in the past or in the future. The most vivid illustrations of externality, these days, come from the environmental realm.

The carbon we've added to the atmosphere by burning fossil fuels has had relatively little effect on the people who pumped the oil, sold the oil or burned the oil. Most economic studies quantify our reliance on fossil fuels as a logical reliance on a relatively abundant natural resource. Viewed in this way, fossil fuels have been a precious resource fueling prosperity and innovation for more than 100 years with almost no bad effects.

If negative environmental consequences are not felt within the economy where the petroleum is produced or where it is burned, then those consequences are "externalities." It is increasingly evident, however, that burning fossil fuels has a generalized effect on the health of the planet overall and that it will have an effect on the health and welfare of future generations.

Those Effects are External to Most Economic Models, and it's Hard to Quantify Them.

Economists are attempting to measure the effects of externalities like long-term environmental consequences. Economies that accurately evaluate the costs of their products are more efficient. If oil were taxed to pay reparations for the long-term environmental consequences of its extraction and consumption, then governments could use the additional revenues to mitigate the damage. Consumers might use less oil because it would be more expensive. Either way, the "externality" of environmental damage would be a measured factor in the economic equation. We would at least be aware of the true economic effects of our behaviour.

Nigeria's birthrate would be external to most equations measuring economic growth in the United States even though Nigerian labour provides a lot of affordable oil to Western industrialized nations, and lots of Nigerians emigrate to wealthy countries where they provide high-quality, low-cost labour. Africa's population increase is not routinely measured as a factor in the economics of England, France or the United States. But effects are felt nonetheless in both negative and positive ways. Some economists conclude that stable populations are good for national economies because the most prosperous nations record the lowest birth rates – the demographic-economic paradox again. Though we can speculate on the effects of stable population on economies, the fact is we don't have any real-world knowledge to draw on. A few nations have stabilized their populations, but they depend on population growth in other parts of the world to supply cheap labour and new consumers.

Every nation in Western Europe is supplementing its population with immigrants. In 2005, the most recent year for which I could find a firm number, 1.8 million new people moved to Europe from elsewhere. Somewhere between 45 million and 60 million people living in the United States today are in first-generation immigrant households. About 17 percent of people living in the United States are immigrants.

Bluntly, we have no examples of economic growth occurring in the absence of human population growth. The expansion of our species has always supported the expansion of our economies for as long as we've been keeping track, yet wealthy nations generally ignore the growth in foreign populations when they measure their own prosperity.

It appears that the United States is an economic success story standing on its own two feet, but to what extent does our prosperity depend on a steady stream of ambitious immigrants? On the other hand, how prosperous will we be when North America's population reaches a billion people? Population growth is a Ponzi scheme and we're setting up future generations as its victims. We are paying into the base of the pyramid with our natural resources.

Overcoming the Problems of Population Growth

Implementing any human development programme has become a daunting challenge due mainly to the increasing population. Demographic transition over time paints an alarming picture of the state of population. The country's population growth has been showing an alarming trend over a couple of decades and has now reached the height of overpopulation with 14.45 people. If there is no attempt to arrest the growth of population the total population will double. With this growth of population it has become difficult to meet the nutritional demands of the citizens. With the growing number of poor, it has become even more difficult to get them within the reach of development programmes. The reproductive health sector is also deficient.

The dire consequences of rapid population growth is the depletion of natural resources. We now see devastation of resources caused by non-ecological human behaviour. Demographic imbalance, unplanned settlements and economic growth tend to harm the natural order of things dismantling ecological settings.

Public policy through resource mobilisation and allocation cannot do much in determining which way things should move unless the government plans to combat overpopulation. Only observing population day on 11th July is not enough. Of course this day is a reminder to all the citizens thinking rationally at the level of awareness with the global policy community reaffirming its commitment to sustainable level of population growth. There can hardly be any argument with the fact that a swelling population threatens to put at risk all implementation strategies of development in the substantive areas of public policy. Even a high budgetary allocation against any policy moves for a change can hardly be implemented in a country with a rising population.

The policymakers may look at demographic transition over time — bulge and decline of population on a comparative scale in all groups respective of age, sex, class, religion and sect or location. Time series data is available to surmise population growth at various levels. Nevertheless it is more important to probe the fact that we are lagging behind the western countries as far as population control measures are concerned.

With advances in science and technology come new challenges. In fact tangible progress of the nation requires institutional capacity to combat them. It has been increasingly important for the state to comply with fiscal demands of the increasing number of young people and their share in economic participation. The energetic youth can be used to deal with birth control measures if it can be put into a productive force.

The current development intervention does not incorporate any concern about maintaining demographic balance through a streamlined population policy and conserving environmental resources. When the population base is extremely high it harms 'per capita well being' and per capita consumption. The fundamental condition for resilient economic growth is population growth at the desired level. It cannot be done only by allocation on reproductive health.

The government has a plan to formulate a 'pragmatic population policy' realising the weaknesses in the family planning intervention. Its new policy move is to increase the contraceptives prevalence rate upto 80 per cent by 2021. The government has earmarked Tk.498 crore, development and non-development combined, for the procurement of birth control related materials and equipment.

The theme of Population Day this year (2009) is 'Responding to the Economic Crisis: Investing in women is a Smart Choice.' The comment of the UNFPA representative, Bangladesh, deserves mention: "In time of economic hardship women in developing countries are likely to be disproportionately affected which in turn inversely impacts their children and communities That's why it is so important that people's basic needs, including for reproductive health and family planning are being addressed even more urgently..." The situation of women nowadays presents the world with an opportunity to generate income and reduce poverty.

Because of human development achievements of the past decades many young daughters are going to schools and combating childhood diseases. But to succeed in competitive global economy they should be equipped with better skills. Despite rising awareness about gender equality and birth control resulting in lower fertility rates in many developing countries the family planning movement has yet to attain any remarkable success. It still remains to be seen how population control measures are being managed in patriarchal societies. There is a need to test the level of acceptability of birth control methods considering the variables of sex, class and outlook.

Family planning in Bangladesh needs to be strengthened as a movement involving a large number of rural and urban women as activists. Fiscal demands for reproductive health for mother and child, education for the vulnerable and employment should be redeemed all within a broad brush of social security net. What is urgently needed is persuasion through motivation. It's high time to enhance social security of the disadvantaged group.

The state should compensate those women who cannot have children. The state should also provide all logistics and support including allowances and social insurance for health, education and old age to the parents blessed with only one baby. Confidence building measures to be institutionally dealt with of course has a positive impact on the married couples willing to take contraceptives. The new health policy may incorporate a special section on family planning with indices like reproductive and protective health services including safe birth, safe abortions and prenatal and antenatal services in clinics and proper nursing of the newborn baby. There should have been a provision for the prevention of early marriage and premature pregnancy. I think with well thought measures of birth control in the proposed health policy voluntary family planning movement will be reinforced.

Ending Population Growth: Why Family Planning is Key to a Sustainable Future

The widespread assumption that world population, now at 6.9 billion, will inevitably grow to 9 billion by midcentury is wrong. The equally widespread belief that an earlier, lower population peak would require coercive "population control" is also incorrect. Population growth rates and average family size worldwide have fallen by roughly half over the past four decades, as modern contraception has become more accessible and popular.

Population could peak before then and at a lower level, ameliorating environmental risks associated with climate change, water scarcity, biodiversity loss, and food and energy insecurity. Don't Take Demographic Projects At Face Value. Those who ponder humanity's future in the twenty-first century generally take at face value demographic projections suggesting that the world population will reach something like 9 billion around 2050 and will then stabilize at about that level. The widespread belief that this 30 percent increase from today's 6.9 billion people is inevitable undermines consideration of the role of population size in climate change, water scarcity, biodiversity loss, rising energy prices, and food security.

Contributing to this is the related view that efforts to prevent population growth would require coercive government policies that constrain couples from having the children and the family sizes they want. While some analysts are confident that the world can feed, house, and otherwise support 9 billion or more people, others are less certain, and voices of caution about population growth are heard more often than in the past. A logical application of the precautionary principle in the face of current environmental problems would suggest that humanity could more easily accomplish these feats in an environmentally sustainable manner with a smaller population.

In a joint statement in 1993, representatives of 58 national scientific academies stressed the complexities of the population-environment relationship but nonetheless concluded, "As human numbers increase, the potential for irreversible changes of far-reaching magnitude also increases. ... In our judgment, humanity's ability to deal successfully with its social, economic, and environmental problems will require the achievement of zero population growth within the lifetime of our children." In 2005, the United Nations' Millennium Ecosystem Assessment identified population growth as a principal indirect driver of environmental change, along with economic growth and technological evolution.

In October 2010, a group of US and European climate and demographic researchers published findings from an integrated assessment model calculating the impact of various population scenarios on fossil-fuel carbon dioxide emissions over the coming century. If world population peaked at close to 8 billion rather than 9 billion, along the lines described in a low-fertility demographic projection published by the UN Population Division, the model predicted there would be a significant emissions savings: about 5.1 billion tons of carbon dioxide by 2050 and 18.7 billion tons by century's end.

What if we could prove wrong the popular conviction that a future with 9 billion people and a growing population is inevitable? Suppose we could demonstrate that world population size might peak earlier and at a lower level if government policies aimed not at reproductive coercion but at individual reproductive freedom? Suppose such policies aimed to help all women and girls prevent unwanted pregnancies and conceive only when they want to bear a child? This article presents new data on births resulting from women's active intentions to become pregnant. The hypothesis it probes may appear counterintuitive: if, starting at any moment, all pregnancies in the world resulted from each woman's intent to give birth, human population would immediately shift course away from growth towards decline within a few decades.

Key Concepts

- Even though most women of reproductive age now use contraception, we are far from a world in which all births result from intended pregnancies. Based on survey data, approximately 40 percent of pregnancies are unintended in developing countries, and 47 percent in developed ones.
- More than one in five births worldwide result from pregnancies women did not wish to occur.
- An estimated 215 million women in developing countries have an unmet need for family planning: they are sexually active, don't want to become pregnant, and yet for various reasons—including lack of access—are not using contraception.
- If all births resulted from women actively intending to conceive, fertility would immediately fall slightly below the replacement level; world population would peak within a few decades and subsequently decline.
- Assuring that all women are fully in control of the timing and frequency of childbearing is not expensive. Religious, cultural,

and political opposition to contraception or the possibility of population decline is the key obstacle to such assurance. More research and a public better educated about sexuality and reproduction could engender a global social movement that would make possible a world of intended pregnancies and births.

- *Total Fertility Rate*: Refers to the average number of children a woman would bear over her lifetime if at each point in her reproductive age she had the number of live births typical of women at that age. Note that the total fertility rate differs from the population growth rate, which is the percentage by which a population grows each year, and from the birthrate, which is the number of live births each year per thousand people in the population. The global total fertility rate currently stands at 2.53 children per woman.
- *Replacement Fertility Rate*: Refers to the total fertility rate in a population that, if held steady over time and absent net migration, would result in a nonchanging population. This rate is often mischaracterized as uniformly and precisely 2.1 children per woman, but not all children survive to reproductive age, and the proportion of those who do not varies over time and by population. For the world as a whole, with many low-income regions still experiencing high death rates among young people, the replacement fertility rate currently stands at 2.35 children per woman. Surprisingly, the gap between global total fertility and replacement fertility is now less than one-fifth of one birth.

Even achievement of global replacement fertility would not stop population growth for several decades, due to population momentum. This is the tendency of a population, influenced by its age structure, to continue its current growth dynamic even as fertility changes. Because there are so many young people of reproductive age in any population that has had above-replacement fertility for some time, for example, even low fertility can produce an overall number of births that statistically overwhelms deaths among the smaller cohorts of older individuals. It can take decades before subreplacement fertility actually halts growth. If total fertility falls well below replacement however, this momentum is weakened and a peak in population will come sooner, followed by a decline. These demographic phenomena are evident in Japan, with a total fertility rate of 1.3 children per woman and a population that has already peaked and is now slowly shrinking.

An Ethical Basis for Action to Slow Population Growth

What can societies that value democracy, self-determination, human rights, personal autonomy, and privacy do to include demographic change among strategies for environmental sustainability? An important answer may lie in a relatively untested set of principles adopted by almost all the world's nations at a 1994 UN conference held in Cairo. The third of three once-a-decade governmental conferences on population and development, it produced a programmer of action that abandoned the strategy of "population control" by governments in favour of a focus on the health, rights, and well-being of women.6 An operating assumption of this programmer is that when women have access to the information and means that allow them to choose the timing of pregnancy, the intervals between births lengthen, average family size shrinks, and teen births become less frequent. All of these improve maternal and child survival and slow population growth.

Experts disagree on how reproductive autonomy compares with other strategies in slowing that growth. Some assume economic growth is the most effective means, although birthrates rose along with prosperity in many countries after World War II and remain relatively high in several wealthy oil-exporting nations in which women have fewer rights and lower status than men. Moreover, some analysts argue that the arrow of causation operates more in the other direction, with low fertility stoking economic growth.

There is a more robust and demonstrable correlation between female educational attainment and fertility. Worldwide, women with no schooling have an average of 4.5 children, while those who have spent at least a year or more in primary school have just three. Women who complete at least a year or two of secondary school have 1.9 children—well below replacement fertility rates. With one or two years of advanced education for women, average childbearing rates fall even further, to 1.7. On this basis alone, those interested in depressing population growth rates might want to focus on improving women's educational attainment. Questions remain about whether education alone can bring about declines in fertility without other supporting conditions, especially easy, affordable access to a range of contraceptive options. Similar uncertainties cloud understanding of exactly how improved child survival and the empowerment of women affect fertility. Improving both factors certainly contributes to later births and smaller families and is valuable regardless of its demographic impacts. But without clear data on the magnitude of these influences, interventions related to schooling, child survival, and women's empowerment are rarely seen as core aspects of governmental population policy.

This brings us to family planning. Access to safe and reliable contraception has exploded since the mid-twentieth century. An estimated 55 percent of all heterosexually active women worldwide now use modern contraceptive methods, while an additional seven percent use less reliable traditional methods. As the use of birth control has spread, fertility has plummeted from a global average of five children per woman in 1950 to barely more than 2.5 today.

While not necessarily sufficient to depress fertility on a population-wide basis, family planning is essential to the phenomenon. Women may begin sexual activity later in life and may resort to abortion to terminate unwanted pregnancies. But humanity's average family size could not have plummeted simply because women had diplomas, contractual rights, or confidence that their children would survive. To have small families, heterosexually active women and their partners need safe and effective contraception—modern birth control.

Lessons from history suggest that women have sought and employed contraceptives since ancient times to avoid unwanted pregnancy when circumstances were inauspicious for the 15 to 18 years of parental commitment a new birth entails. Egyptian papyri that date back 4,000 years describe pessaries, ancient precursors to the diaphragm, made of acacia oil and crocodile dung. Literature from Asia to North America documents herbs used for centuries as emmenagogues, substances that induce immediate menstruation and hence expel recently fertilized eggs. In the Mediterranean, in the ages of ancient Greece and Rome, a booming trade in the contraceptive, or possibly abortifacient, silphium helped drive its source, a wild giant fennel, into extinction. And an ecclesiastical court record from 1319 preserves the personal account of a young widow in southwestern France who provided details of her use of an herbal contraception during an extended affair with a priest. We know, too, that women and their partners historically have moderated their reproduction in response to their external environments, natural and economic. (Until modern times, these were generally the same thing.) In eighteenth- and nineteenth-century Sweden, for example, birthrates neatly tracked the price of grain crops with a roughly nine-month delay. The Japanese population during the eighteenth-century Tokugawa shogunate declined during several decades of food scarcity—until a government propaganda campaign against infanticide (the dominant method of family-size control at the time) pushed fertility well above replacement levels in the nineteenth century, restoring demographic growth.

Similar responses of fertility to external circumstances are evident today. The high cost of housing in Japan is prominent among the reasons offered by young people for delaying marriage and childbearing. In the United States, a two percent decline in the country's birthrate in 2008 was attributed largely to the deterioration of the economy.

Implications of Personal Fertility-Management Aspirations

History and recent fertility phenomena thus suggest the likelihood that the interest in safely and effectively managing the timing of pregnancy and childbirth may be nearly universal among women. Lack of education, affluence, and equality may simply be barriers—along with others related to patriarchal, pronatalist, and even medical cultural norms—to existing aspirations to avoid unwanted pregnancies.

Data exist for the likely demographic impact of establishing conditions worldwide that would facilitate women's choices about the timing of pregnancy. According to the Guttmacher Institute, a US reproductive health-care research organization, an estimated 215 million women in developing countries have an "unmet need for family planning." This applies to women who are sexually active and express the desire to avoid pregnancy yet are not using contraception.

Estimates of their number derive from demographic and health surveys conducted in certain developing countries every few years. Many women in developed countries may be in the same circumstances, but data are insufficient in most cases to suggest their numbers. In early 2010, researchers with the Futures Group in Washington, DC, estimated the demographic impact of meeting unmet family-planning demand in 99 developing countries and one developed one. The researchers excluded China, on the assumption that government population policies aimed at limiting most families to a single child rule out births from unintended pregnancies. And they supplemented their country list with the United States, the world's most populous developed county and one for which there is some data suggesting the magnitude of unmet need.

Using accepted models for the impact of rising contraceptive prevalence on birthrates, the researchers concluded that satisfying unmet need for contraception in these 100 countries—with a cumulative 2005 population of 4.3 billion—would produce a population of 6.3 billion in 2050. Under the United Nations' medium projection, the countries' population would be 400 million higher, at 6.7 billion. Average global fertility at midcentury would be 1.65 children per woman, well below the population replacement fertility level—and would continue to fall.

This conclusion, if backed up by further research, is momentous. By implication, simply providing safe and effective contraceptive options to all sexually active women who do not want to become pregnant would end and then reverse world population growth. The effect is independent of any further fertility reductions that might occur as a result of greater educational attainment for women, improved child survival, women's empowerment, and general economic advancement.

To some experts the idea that simply facilitating women's childbearing intentions would end population growth, without significant demand creation for family planning through cultural shifts and other means, goes against survey findings from many African and some Asian countries.

These findings suggest that in parts of these continents women's average desired family size is as high as six or seven children. Wouldn't facilitating these women's childbearing intentions undermine any hope of ending world population growth? Not necessarily. For one thing, women expressing such high desired family sizes are at most a relatively small proportion of the world's population (albeit significant in Africa's). But the more important point is that a high desired family size can easily coexist with high levels of unintended pregnancy that, if prevented, would result in significantly lower birthrates than if not prevented.

The reason for this is not hard to understand: women's individual reproductive decisions arrive at their desired family size, if at all, only cumulatively. Decisions about the desirability of pregnancy are made singly, in individual acts of sexual intercourse in which conception is possible. Whatever one's hopes for an eventual number of children, pregnancy decisions occur in the context of current personal, economic, and social circumstances. Desired family size can be compared to house size and the number of cars owned. We may wish to have a large house and many cars, but our circumstances may not allow for us to have either without endangering our finances and well-being. We decide moment by moment whether working towards that goal makes sense for us. So it is with reproductive intentions; every step of a woman and her partner's reproductive lives is governed by their immediate circumstances.

It seems likely that even in countries where women respond in health surveys that they desire six or seven children, they would end up with fewer, possibly many fewer, if at each step of their reproductive lives they were able to choose precisely when to become pregnant. In some developed countries with low fertility, women express a desire to have two children yet have closer to one on average. With the right partner, the right job, the right apartment, and the right economic and social-support systems, a woman in Japan, for example, might have the two children she desires. But with options to prevent or terminate pregnancies, many Japanese women have one child or none; the national average is 1.3. All of this suggests the value of developing and testing the hypothesis that meeting the needs of women and their partners for personal control of pregnancy could lead to the end of population growth. Physician and reproductive specialist Malcolm Potts has found that in all countries where women can choose from a range of contraceptive options, backed by access to safe and legal abortion services, total fertility rates are at or below replacement fertility levels.

If these findings can be borne out consistently by additional research, those who worry about the impact of global population growth on environmental and social sustainability might usefully advocate for worldwide universal access to family-planning services. The need for such access is enshrined in the second target of the fifth UN Millennium Development Goal, which calls for developing countries to "achieve, by 2015, universal access to reproductive health." This concept embraces more than family planning, including a holistic state of sexual and reproductive well-being that encompasses maternal and child health, prevention of AIDS and other sexually transmitted infections, access to safe abortion services (where these are legal), and post-abortion care.

A Thought Experiment With Data

The Futures Group study has not yet gained the widespread attention its findings merit. Among the reasons for this may be that the concept of "unmet need" for contraception is not widely understood among the public, news media, and policymakers. Moreover, because of lack of data the study excluded not only China, with a fifth of the world's population, but dozens of other developing countries—and all the world's industrialized countries other than the United States.

Newly available data on unintended pregnancy in many countries, assembled by the Guttmacher Institute, support an alternative research approach to the question of the demographic impacts of births that result from pregnancies women never sought or wanted to have. These data, based on a range of surveys worldwide, provide the basis for beginning to answer an intriguing and valuable question: What would happen to world population growth if every pregnancy worldwide, starting tomorrow, were the outcome of a woman's active intention to become pregnant and bear and help raise a child? If no pregnancies were unintended, in other words, how many births would there be compared to current births, and how would this new birthrate affect the future of human population?

Averaged over the 73 countries for which data exist, and comprising 83 percent of the world's births, just under ten percent of births result from pregnancies occurring among women who never wanted to have another child. Even under the most conservative scenario—extrapolated globally, with all births from pregnancies that are merely mistimed considered equivalent to births from intended pregnancies—a hypothetical world population in which women only become pregnant when they want to would reduce today's global total fertility rate to 2.29 births per woman.

That figure is slightly below today's global replacement fertility rate—placing world population on a direct path towards future decline, albeit at a very slow pace given population momentum (and assuming neither future fertility decline nor improvement in mortality among young people). Under the less conservative assumption that one-quarter of births from mistimed pregnancies are equivalent to unwanted pregnancies, the total fertility rate sinks lower, to 2.22 births per woman—resulting in a somewhat faster track towards a human population peak, even with no future fertility decline. These calculations are, at best, first-order analyses of the impact on world population growth of an idealized scenario in which all births are the outcomes from intended pregnancies. As noted, they do not take into account the possibility that global fertility would continue its decline once all births resulted from intended pregnancies.

More survey research and data on pregnancy intention among individual women in all countries would be needed to make a more robust determination of demographic impacts. But the essence of research on this question remains hopeful—and little known: a successful global effort that assured all women the capacity to decide for themselves whether and when to become pregnant would also place world population on a path towards a reasonably imminent peak followed by slow demographic decrease. Additional efforts to see that women have the educational, economic, legal, and political opportunities they deserve would accelerate this transition.

Toward a World of Intended Pregnancies and Wanted Children

Given the feasibility of such a transition, why isn't it happening today? Why aren't higher proportions of births the result of intended pregnancies? And what might we do to overcome the obstacles and actually bring that world about?

Popular as it is with women and couples, contraception remains a deeply sensitive issue for much of the public. Vehemently opposed by the Catholic Church and regarded with suspicion by many other Christian, Islamic, and even some Jewish religious leaders, open advocacy for contraceptive availability and use inevitably risks stoking religious opposition. Influence of the Catholic Church hierarchy has blocked efforts in the Philippines, for example, to include access to modern contraception in the country's government health system. Opposition from the Holy See, which has permanent observer status within the UN system, led to silence on reproductive health in the UN Millennium Development Goals when they were forged in 2000—even though representatives of the world's governments had pledged to achieve universal access to reproductive health by 2015 at the UN conference in Cairo in 1994. Only in 2007 was language aiming at that reproductive health access target added to Millennium Development Goal number five. Seven years of opportunities to achieve the target had been squandered.

Perhaps more destructive than religious opposition is a relative denigration in most cultures of concerns that lie principally in the sphere of women. Access to contraception is clearly one such concern, since women bear the babies and undergo most of the risks to life and health associated with reproduction. At least since the rise of agricultural, urban, and hierarchical societies, male interests in reproduction have differed markedly from those of women. Men are often anxious to produce a multitude of future heirs, soldiers, labourers, farmers, and followers. Women tend to be strategically concerned with the survival and well-being of each of their children. These gender differences are anything but ironclad, and in many cultures the gender gap in attitudes has narrowed in recent decades, especially as women's status has risen relative to men's. In other cultures, however, the gap not only remains wide, it demands the subjugation of women, sex, and reproduction to male needs.

Beyond male reproductive dominance lies the conviction among neoclassical economists that endless economic growth is possible and that it requires endless population growth. Politicians often measure their self-worth based on the size of their electorates. They happily side with economists on the idea that endless economic and demographic growth is both possible and desirable. With all these factors in play, it is not surprising that the world's governments are nowhere close to allocating the resources the Cairo conference had estimated would be needed for all women in developing countries to have reasonable access to decent family-planning services. This was roughly $18 billion for the year 2010, a third of which was to be contributed by industrialized-country governments (the 1993 dollars in the UN document are here converted to current dollars). Despite that commitment—and an increase in the population of reproductive-age people in developing countries, from 2.3 to 2.9 billion—actual expenditures from these governments on international family-planning assistance fell from $723 million in 1995 to $338 million in 2007. Assistance has changed little since the latter year.

A global social movement is needed to pressure policymakers and influential cultural and thought leaders to reverse this dismal trend. Raising $9 billion a year from wealthy governments that currently spend just a few hundred million on international family-planning assistance shouldn't be as difficult as it is. As much money is allocated for a few days worth of military activities worldwide. A comparable or greater amount probably would be needed to assure that the vast majority of pregnancies in wealthy countries are intentional, but this sum has never been estimated. Significant investments in all countries in education on sexuality and reproduction are also needed, but what these should be is unknown as well. Still, the point undoubtedly still holds: a world in which almost all births result from intended conceptions would not be prohibitively expensive or difficult, aside from cultural barriers, to bring about.

Yet due to contraception's sensitivity—complicated by a history pockmarked with episodes of contraceptive coercion in China, India, Peru, and a few other countries—environmentalists and advocates for women's rights and health have never succeeded in forging an activist alliance capable of raising the modest sums needed for all to have access to family planning. Several elements are needed if a global social movement to promote family planning and intentional pregnancy is ever to have its own birth.

One is more research about the likely population and environmental outcomes of a world of fully intended pregnancies—and the policies, programmes, and costs that could lead to such a world. Another is agreement that any such policies and programmes must be based on reproductive rights rather than on coercion, and therefore on the intentions of women and their partners rather than on those of anyone else. And a third is the creativity to shape—or the courage to stand up to—the religious, economic, and other cultural forces that promote population growth and oppose the gender and reproductive health conditions that undermine it.

There is nothing fated about a world of 9 billion people—in 2050, or ever. While true control of population is beyond our aspirations and capacities, policy choices are available that will nudge our numbers closer to environmentally and socially sustainable levels. The choices are rooted in human development and human rights, specifically the right of all, and most directly of women, to decide for themselves when it is the right time to bring a new child into the world.

Population Growth and Food Security in the Horn of Africa

The current food crisis in the Horn of Africa has fast become a humanitarian disaster. According to World Vision UK, the crisis has affected in excess of 6 million people in Ethiopia, 2 million in Uganda, 3 million in Somalia and 10 million in Kenya. The ongoing effects of the food crisis are devastating. In northern Kenya, the impact of the drought and rising food costs has been largely felt amongst the pastoralist community, where in excess of 70% of people's livelihoods have been affected. In Turkana, for example, one in four children suffer from acute malnutrition. Across Ethiopia, the cost of food has increased by more than 50% and in the Karamoja region of Uganda, 70% of residents are receiving food aid following insufficient rains over three consecutive years. In Somalia, a country that has existed without a formal government for the past 18 years, increased fighting and instability has resulted in a steep increase in the price of food and water, a problem compounded by the inability of aid agencies to deliver vital supplies. In some regions water costs have increased by 1,000% in recent months. With widespread malnutrition across the country, it is currently estimated that one in six Somali children are acutely malnourished.

Multiple Factors

There is not one single catalyst for the current food crisis. A myriad of factors including drought, poverty, rising food prices, unemployment, landlessness, lack of drinking water and civil conflict are all commonly cited as contributing factors. The impact of population growth on food crises, however, is commonly overlooked.

The countries currently affected by the food crisis in the Horn of Africa have all witnessed a decrease in fertility rates over recent decades. In spite of this decrease, population momentum, where high fertility in the previous generation has resulted in a large portion of the population being of childbearing age, means that the populations of these countries continue to grow rapidly. In Kenya, for example, where according to the US Census Bureau fertility has decreased from 7.6 in 1980 to its current rate of 4.2, the country's population continues to increase at a rate of 2.6% per year. The sustained and rapid population growth occurring in the Horn of Africa raises serious concerns over food supply. According to the Principal Policy Analyst at the Kenya Institute for Public Policy Research and Analysis, John Omiti, "population growth is higher than our ability to produce food. We need to address the demographic challenge to balance supply and demand."

A Malthusian Trap?

Although food production was largely able to cater for the exponential growth in world population that occurred during the 20th century, population growth within Africa is beginning to outpace food supply. Between 2007 and 2025, food production in Africa must increase from its current production level of 2.2 billion tonnes to 3 billion tonnes to keep up with population growth. In light of this and the recent food crisis, the question arises: are we heading towards the Malthusian trap, whereby population growth will outstrip food supply? Due to trade, aid and increased technological innovation as a result of the Industrial Revolution, it is unlikely that Malthus' visions will be felt on a large scale. It is plausible, however, to suggest a strong correlation between high fertility and food insecurity. Continuously high rates of fertility amongst subsistence farmers and the associated increase in population density result in the further sub-division of family plots, thereby placing increased pressure on the success of crops. When food shortages do occur, moreover, it is the poor who are most affected. With decreases in food supply, those already forced to live on the smallest of rations are confronted with a simultaneous increase in the price of food. Food affordability therefore becomes a major concern, as the poorest members of society already spend 50-70% of their incomes on food.

High fertility as a barrier to development

With poverty inextricably linked to hunger, high fertility rates in the countries of the Horn of Africa have proven a major hurdle to economic prosperity and therefore food security. The persistence of high fertility in the Horn of Africa has precluded the countries in the region from capitalising on what is commonly referred to as the "demographic dividend". This occurs in countries in transition from high to low fertility, where there is a window of opportunity to achieve economic growth via an increased ratio of workers to non-workers. When coupled with government initiatives and increased foreign investment, a demographic dividend can induce economic growth and increase government revenue via the collection of income tax. A decrease in the number of dependents not only minimises the impact of sub-dividing land within families, it also reduces constraints to family savings that can in turn provide families with a valuable safety net. Although Malthus's grand claim that unchecked population growth will inevitably result in widespread food shortages remains unproven, high fertility rates do provide a significant obstacle to food security. A decrease in fertility would therefore go some way to minimising the risk of future food crises.

Population and the Environment

Stress on the environment and the depletion of natural resources both reinforce and are exacerbated by gender inequality, poor health and poverty, the Cairo conference emphasized. Environmental stress is increasing, due to both "unsustainable consumption and production patterns" (including high resource consumption in wealthy countries and among better-off groups in all countries) and demographic factors such as rapid population growth, population distribution and migration.

Affirming that "meeting the basic human needs of growing populations is dependent on a healthy environment", ICPD Programme of Action(1) addressed the interrelationships among population, economic growth and protection of the environment, reiterating principles of Agenda 21, adopted by the United Nations Conference on the Environment and Development in Rio in 1992.

A Virtuous Circle

Efforts to slow down population growth, to reduce poverty, to achieve economic progress, to improve environmental protection, and to reduce unsustainable consumption and production patterns are mutually reinforcing. Slower population growth has in many countries increased those countries' ability to attack poverty, protect and repair the environment, and build the base for future sustainable development.

At both the Cairo conference and its five-year review, the global community affirmed that greater equality between men and women is an essential component of sustainable development, including environmental protection. Boosting the status of women is now accepted as a prerequisite for lowering fertility and ensuring sound management of natural resources. And awareness is increasing of the need to address environmental crises, demographic realities, gender inequity and rising consumption amid persistent poverty in a holistic manner.

At both the Cairo conference and its five-year review, the global community affirmed that greater equality between men and women is an essential component of sustainable development, including environmental protection. Boosting the status of women is now accepted as a prerequisite for lowering fertility and ensuring sound management of natural resources. And awareness is increasing of the need to address environmental crises, demographic realities, gender inequity and rising consumption amid persistent poverty in a holistic manner. The 2003 UNFPA global survey found that countries have made progress in addressing population issues within the context of poverty, environment, and decentralized planning processes. One hundred and twenty-two countries reported developing plans or strategies on population-environment linkages. Forty countries have developed specific policies, and 22 have put in place laws or legislation on population dynamics and the environment.

Still, the stakes are high, as human activity continues to alter the planet on an unprecedented scale. More people are using more resources with more intensity and leaving a bigger "footprint" on the earth than ever before.

Signs of Ecological Change

Over the past century and especially over the past 40 years, people have effected vast changes in the global environment. Those most directly affected by environmental challenges, from water pollution to climate change, are also the poorest—and least able to change livelihoods or lifestyles to cope with, or combat, ecological decline. Some snapshots:

- Farmers, ranchers, loggers, and developers have cleared about half the world's original forest cover, and another 30 per cent is degraded or fragmented.
- Over the last half century, land degradation has reduced cropland by an estimated 13 per cent and pasture by 4 per cent. In many countries, population growth has raced ahead of food production in recent years. Some 800 million people are chronically malnourished and 2 billion lack food security.

- Three quarters of the world's fish stocks are now fished at or beyond sustainable limits. Industrial fleets have fished out at least 90 per cent of large ocean predators —including tuna, marlin and swordfish—in the last 50 years.
- Since the 1950s, global demand for water has tripled. Groundwater quantity and quality are declining due to over-pumping, runoff from fertilizers and pesticides, and leaking of industrial waste. Half a billion people live in countries defined as water stressed or water-scarce; by 2025, that figure is expected to surge to between 2.4 billion and 3.4 billion.
- Climate change. As a result of fossil fuel consumption, carbon dioxide levels today are 18 per cent higher than in 1960 and an estimated 31 per cent higher than at the onset of the Industrial Revolution in 1750. Accumulation of greenhouse gases in the atmosphere, including carbon dioxide, is tied to rising and extreme change in temperatures, and more severe storms.
- Sea level has risen an estimated 10-20 centimetres, largely as a result of melting ice masses and the expansion of oceans linked to regional and global warming. Small island nations and low-lying cities and farming areas face severe flooding or inundation.

Population's Impact on Resource Use

Numbers alone do not capture the impact of the interactions between human populations and the environment. The size and weight of the environmental footprint each person plants on Earth is determined by the ways people use resources, which affects the quantities they consume. For instance, a vegetarian who primarily uses a bicycle has a much smaller impact than someone who eats meat and drives a sport utility vehicle.

The ecological footprint of an average person in a high-income country is about six times bigger than that of someone in a low-income country, and many more times bigger than in the least-developed countries. The combined footprints of people in a region determine the prospects for saving or permanently losing the biological diversity found there. Many economists and environmentalists use an equation that ties together population, consumption and technology to describe their relative impacts (I=PAT: Impact=Population x Affluence x Technology).

As birth rates fall, consumption levels and patterns (affluence), coupled with technology, will take on new importance in determining the state of the global environment. But population will remain the critical factor where lack of access to reproductive health services and family planning, shortfalls in education for girls and women, poverty and women's limited power relative to men continue to fuel high fertility. Global Consumers And Persistent Poverty. A rapidly growing global consumer class, now around 1.7 billion people, accounts for the vast majority of meat eating, paper use, car driving, and energy use on the planet, as well as the resulting impact of these activities on its natural resources.

This class is not limited to industrialized countries; as populations surge in developing countries and as the world economy becomes increasingly globalized, more and more people have the means to acquire a greater diversity of products and services than ever before. Meanwhile, 2.8 billion people—two in five—still struggle to survive on less than $2 a day. In 2000, 1.1 billion people did not have reasonable access to safe drinking water, and 2.4 billion people worldwide lived without basic sanitation.

Lack of access to clean water and sanitation in the developing world led to 1.7 million deaths in 2000.(3). Differential Impacts. Where population growth and high levels of consumption coincide, as they do in some industrial nations, the impact of growth is significant. For instance, even though the United States' population is only a fourth as large as India's, its environmental footprint is over three times bigger—it releases 15.7 million tons of carbon into the atmosphere each year compared with India's 4.9 million tons. Hence the impact of the current 3 million annual population increase in the United States is greater than that of India's 16 million increase.

Environmental impact can continue to grow even as population growth levels off. In China, population growth has slowed dramatically, but consumption of oil and coal and the resulting pollution continues to rise. While the Chinese Government is promoting greater fuel efficiency for cars, it is not promoting increased use of public transportation, biking and walking, or efficient urban planning so people would not have to drive.

Besides reducing overall resource use, governments can reduce the environmental impacts of increased consumption by promoting appropriate technology that uses resources more efficiently. Industrial countries can help the developing world by assisting with the dissemination and adoption of cleaner technologies. Other demographic trends intersect with consumption in surprising ways. As a result of rising incomes, urbanization, and smaller families, the average number of people living under one roof declined between 1970 and 2000—from 5.1 to 4.4 in developing countries and from 3.2 to 2.5 in industrial countries—while the total number of households increased. Each new house requires land and materials. And with fewer people in each household, savings from shared use of energy and appliances are lost. A one-person household in the United States, for example, uses 17 per cent more energy per capita than a two-person household. Even in some European nations and in Japan, where population growth has stopped, changing household dynamics are important drivers of increased consumption.

Promoting More Efficient Use of Energy

A number of initiatives suggest countries are taking seriously the challenge of reducing harmful production and consumption patterns. For example, China last year began to regulate its rapidly growing auto industry, requiring new family vehicles sold in major cities to meet air pollution standards as strict as those in the United States and Western Europe. Starting this year, new fuel economy standards for cars will be significantly more stringent than those in the United States. The transfer of energy-efficient technology is also growing. China has become the world's largest manufacturer of efficient compact fluorescent light bulbs, in part through joint ventures with lighting firms in Japan, the Netherlands and elsewhere. India has become a major manufacturer of advance wind turbines using technology obtained through joint ventures and licensing agreements with Danish, Dutch, and German firms.

Economic Impact of Population Dynamics

There is clear evidence that enabling people to have fewer children, if they want to, helps to stimulate development and reduce poverty, both in individual households and at the macro-economic level. Family Size And Well-being. Recent research supports the premise that having many (and unplanned for) children imposes a heavy burden on the poor, while smaller families have higher upward economic mobility.

Fertility impacts on a family's poverty in several ways:

- Smaller families share income among fewer people, and average income per capita increases. A family of a certain size may be below the poverty line, but with one less member may rise above the poverty threshold.
- Fewer pregnancies lead to lower maternal mortality and morbidity, and often to more education and economic

opportunities for women. A mother's death or disability can drive a family into poverty. Her ability to earn income can lead the family out of poverty.

- High fertility undermines the education of children, especially girls. Larger families have less to invest in the education of each child. In addition, early pregnancy interrupts young women's schooling, and in large families mothers often remove daughters from school to help care for siblings. Less education typically implies increased poverty for the family as well as the inter-generational transmission of poverty.
- Families with lower fertility are better able to invest in the health of each child, and to give their children proper nourishment. Malnourishment leads to stunted growth, cerebral underdevelopment and subsequent inability to achieve high levels of productivity in the labour force.

MACRO-ECONOMIC IMPACT. High fertility impedes development in a variety of ways. The World Health Organization (WHO) Commission on Macroeconomics and Health noted in 2001, "At the societal level, rapid rural population growth in particular puts enormous stress on the physical environment and on food productivity as land-labour ratios in agriculture decline. Desperately poor peasants are then likely to crowd cities, leading to very high rates of urbanization, with additional adverse consequence in congestion and in declining urban capital per person." Lower fertility, on the other hand, is linked to economic gains. A 2001 study of 45 countries found that if these countries had reduced fertility by 5 births per 1,000 people in the 1980s, the average national incidence of poverty of 18.9 per cent in the mid-1980s would have been reduced to 12.6 per cent between 1990 and 1995.(3)

At the time of Cairo, econometric proof of this "population effect" on economic growth was difficult to obtain, and mainstream economists tended to dismiss it or play down its importance. A 1986 study by the National Research Council in the United States. concluded that population growth had little or no effect on overall economic growth, despite its important effects at the household level; but it relied on data from the 1960s and 1970s, when many developing countries were early in their demographic transition. The Demographic Window. A new round of research in the mid-1990s, (5) using data from longer periods, showed clearly that falling fertility opens a "demographic window" of economic opportunity. With fewer dependent children relative to the working age population, countries can make additional investments which can spur economic growth and help reduce poverty. This window opens only once and closes as populations age and the ratio of dependants (children and the elderly) eventually starts to rise again.

Several countries in East Asia—the so-called Asian Tigers—and a few others have taken advantage of this economic bonus. China has seen a dramatic drop in the incidence of poverty. One study estimated that declining fertility in Brazil has raised the annual growth of GDP per capita by 0.7 percentage points. Mexico and other Latin American countries have registered similar effects. On the other hand, some countries have largely squandered the opportunity for a one-time "windfall" because of a lack of good governance or policies that have led to unproductive investments. In the poorest countries where fertility remains high, the demographic window will not open for some time, but investments now—particularly in improving reproductive health service delivery—could hasten its arrival and ensure future dividends. The world's regions are at different stages of the demographic transition. South Asia will reach its peak ratio of working-age to dependent-ages between 2015 and 2025. In Latin America and the Caribbean, the proportion in working ages started to increase earlier than in East Asia and will peak during 2020-2030, but the proportional change has been less marked, and the economic bonus will be correspondingly less sudden and less intense. Some Arab and Central Asian countries will approach their demographic opportunity within two decades, while others are farther away.

In much of sub-Saharan Africa the demographic bonus is still a long way off. The population is still very young and the proportion in working ages relatively low. Many countries are just beginning the demographic transition, and others have not even started. Only 11 countries are projected to reach their maximum working-age proportion before 2050. Unmet need for contraception in the region is high, however, suggesting the expansion of quality programmes could hasten the arrival of the bonus.

Global Resources and Population

In his famous text *An Essay on the Principle of Population* (1798), English clergyman Thomas Malthus argued that the human population tends to increase more rapidly than food supplies and that population growth would ultimately lead to disease, starvation, and war. Malthus's argument remained popular for decades, and his ominous forecasts are currently mirrored in various predictions that the human population will be unable to sustain itself in the future. Many researchers and scientists calculate that because the world's population could double to more than ten billion as early as the year 2050, increased human consumption and activity will rapidly deplete or exhaust the earth's vital natural resources. Others disagree, arguing that human activity is not critically reducing supplies of global resources. They contend that due to frequent discoveries of new reserves, known supplies of many resources are in fact increasing.

Some researchers blame industrial societies, particularly the United States, for extensive resource depletion. Dartmouth College environmental studies professor Donella Meadows states, "If everyone on Earth lived like the average North American and we utilized fully every productive acre (leaving no wilderness), we would need three Earths to support the present world population." According to these experts, humanity's growing impact on land and natural resources is straining the world's ability to support its increasing population. University of British Columbia planning professor William Rees calls this effect the "ecological footprint."

Many observers warn that humanity's ecological footprint is growing at a dangerous pace. Stanford University professor of population Paul R. Ehrlich and his wife, Stanford biologist Anne H. Ehrlich, maintain that the "explosion of human numbers has been combined with a four-fold increase in consumption per person.

The result is a twenty-fold escalation since 1850 of the pressure humanity places on its environment." The Ehrlichs are among those who contend that population increases will exert more pressure on land, soils, forests, water, and other resources. As Princeton University sociologist and demographer Charles F. Westoff writes, "Growing populations multiply whatever environmentally destructive behaviour is present."

Beginning in 1970, Meadows and others at the Massachusetts Institute of Technology administered a computer simulation model called World3 that studied such variables as population, pollution, and the use of energy and other resources. In their 1972 book *The Limits to Growth*, these researchers cautioned that humanity was fast approaching the limits—especially the environmental limits—to the rapid growth of civilization and its consumption of global resources. They maintained that if increases in population, industrialization, and resource depletion continued unabated, limits to growth would be reached early in the twenty-first century, causing drastic declines in energy use as well as food and industrial production.

The preface to their 1992 update, Beyond *the Limits to Growth,* notes that "the world has already overshot some of its limits, and if present trends remain unchanged, we face the virtually certain prospect of a global economic collapse."

However, other observers disagree with these predictions. They argue that although human consumption of global resources has increased, the supply of resources is not in jeopardy and remains abundant. These experts note that because of technological advances, more supplies of global resources are being discovered or conserved. Some maintain, for example, that raw materials such as lead, tin, wood, and zinc, which are used in manufacturing, are being conserved due to the increased use of other materials, including aluminum, glass, plastic, and rubber.

Also, new mining methods use bacteria, electricity, and foaming agents to recover copper, gold, and other minerals from low grade ores that would otherwise be discarded. Economist Julian L. Simon asserts that the prices of most resources are decreasing, suggesting that they are in ample supply. In Simon's words, "The real prices of food and of every other raw material are lower now than in earlier decades and centuries, indicating a trend of increased natural-resource availability rather than increased scarcity." Simon and others also contend that since the known supplies of many global resources are increasing, humanity will not be hindered by limits to growth. As Cato Institute economist Stephen Moore writes, "The introduction of new technologies and innovations, which make us more efficient in consuming and producing natural resources, has meant that the earth's resources have continually become less of a limit to growth over time rather than more so."

The downward trend in resource prices, Moore and others maintain, proves that resources are abundant and disproves the findings of the World3 model, which they claim did not use accurate data as input. Simon points out that the Club of Rome, an organization that sponsored the World3 model, later disavowed the Limits *to Growth* report for exaggerating the extent of resource depletion. Furthermore, according to *Eco-Scam* author Ronald Bailey and researchers Michael Sanera and Jane S. Shaw, the dire predictions of The *Limits to Growth* have not come true since the book's publication. Sanera and Shaw write, "Oil is plentiful and cheap.

The world did not run out of gold by 1981, or zinc by 1990, or petroleum by 1992, as the book predicted." Bailey adds, "America's population has risen 22% and its economy has grown by more than 58%." He notes that "humanity hasn't come close to running out of any mineral resource." Even if some resources do become more scarce over time, Sanera and Shaw assert, price increases will cause producers to seek cheaper substitute materials, thus maintaining consumers' access to products and services. In their words, "The resources that we use will change over time. Materials that were previously unknown or neglected will provide the services we want."

The debate over the effects of population growth on the availability of global resources is a main theme in *Global Resources: Opposing Viewpoints*, which poses arguments on resource scarcity in the following chapters: Are Global Resources Being Depleted? What Agricultural Policies Should Be Pursued? What Energy Sources Should Be Pursued? How Can Global Resources Be Protected? The contributors in this anthology examine the availability of and dependence on the world's vital natural resources.

Population Growth and Future Energy Consumption

At the UN conference on environmental and developmental issues in June 1992, it became clear that population growth and increasing resource consumption are closely linked with economic and social development. The previous chapters emphasised the fact that the industrial countries produce by far the greatest portion of greenhouse gas and are thus responsible for its accumulation in the atmosphere. For this reason, the developing countries should be given the chance to catch up on the development of the industrialised countries. At the Rio conference, it was the first time that this was officially confirmed and agreed upon.

The people of the developing countries suffer most from the consequences of the climate change, without contributing to it. We, living in the rich countries, are still worsening and destroying the basic conditions of existence in the third world by our way of life. This is particularly true with regard to some island states which are directly endangered by the rise of the sea level, but also for most of the other developing countries which are plagued by risk factors such as dry or half dry soil, water shortage or high population density in areas threatened by flooding.

The population of the poorer countries, due to the economic circumstances and to the lack of an institutionalised infrastructure, are to a higher degree defenceless against the consequences of drought, infectious decease, catastrophic floods and so on. Prof. Klaus Meyer-

Abich, once a member of the enquete commission of the German Bundestag on the protection of the atmosphere, rejects the opinion that the growing number of people in the developing countries overburdens the ecosystem of the earth by resuming "It would be the best development aid if we would stop harming the environment of the developing countries". Referring to te argument that the growing demand for fossil energy in the developing countries could only be satisfied by using nuclear energy in the industrialised countries, he says: "This argument serves only to justify the development in our countries by claiming its beneficiality for the developing countries while at the same time it blocks alternative solutions for our economy".

The overall aim must be to develop an alternative to the current way of running our economy, as the respected Wuppertal Institut in Germany has done, for instance, with the study "Zukunftsfähiges Deutschland (Sustainable Germany)" or as Prof. Ernst-Ulrich v. Weizsäcker, Amory B. Lovins and L. Hunter Lovins have presented with their book 'Faktor 4 (Factor 4)' [5.2] [5.3]. If we in the industrialised countries take in account not only the population growth in the developing countries but also their dynamic economic growth, then we can no longer entertain the illusion that we can just go on without changing anything. Although, in 1990, nearly 80% of the world's population lived in developing countries, their proportion of the world's energy consumption was only 1/3. This proportion will grow to over 50% according to the studies explained in detail below.

The current economic growth alone is causing a rapid rise of CO_2-emissions. This is due to the following factors (among others):

- People tend to use less 'traditional' fuel and more fossil fuel from the official market.
- The rise of the average personal income leads to an increase of consumer goods sales (such as refrigerators, air condition, cars and so on).
- Industries with high energy consumption are on the increase while subsistence farming is on the decline

The population growth is the second important factor which, in combination with the other factors described in the studies presented below, has an impact on the future energy use and by that on the CO_2-emissions. The global population has doubled in the period from 1950 to 1990, that is from 2.52 Billion to 5.28 Billion people in only forty years. During this period the increase of population growth was rising every year; in 1989 with 88.6 Millions an all-time peak was reached.

Although the growth rates are strongly variable (in 1990 it was only 1.69%), the total number of people is still rising in absolute numbers [5.4].

According to UN-scenarios (World Population Prospects 1950-2050) the world's population will increase further, despite falling birth rates. One reason for this is the age pyramid where younger generations are prevailing and the other reason is the rising life expectancy or decreasing mortality. This kind of dynamic influencing the population growth is called momentum by demographic experts. The momentum is so strong that it is hardly alterable [5.5].

The 'medium-growth' scenario, which is currently regarded as the most likely one, forecasts that the annual population growth will reach its highest value of 88.7 Million people already in 1998. However, in 2050 the population will still grow annually by 48.2 Millions and will have increased then by 86% compared to 1990. According to the 'high-growth' scenario, the increase is said to be 125%, whereas the 'low-growth' scenario expects the population to reach its maximum number of 7.97 Billion people in 2043 and predicts that it will start to decrease after that. The 'low-growth' scenario, however, is not seen as very likely to become reality [5.6].

Estimations about the future energy demand and the future CO_2-emissions are mainly based on the above mentioned assumptions about the population growth (mainly in the UN-scenarios) and the following factors:

- The global economic growth
- The rate at which innovational changes occur (e.g. more efficient use of energy)
- The rate at which new energy-saving technologies are implemented
- The relative availability and price of fossil and nuclear fuel vs. renewable energy sources (amount of known energy resources, future energy price)

It follows a presentation of the studies mentioned in the WRI report, which are: the World-Energy-Council study (WEC, prognosis until 2020), the study of the International Energy Agency (IEA, prognosis until 2010) and the US-Department-of-Energy study (DOE, prognosis until 2010). The results are summarised. Further information about the different prognoses can be found in the passage under the header 'Projecting Future Energy Use' sea box 12.2 of the WRI report [5.7]. All three prognoses predict a considerable increase of the energy consumption and of the CO_2-emissions over the next 20 to 30 years. In the WEC reference scenario the energy demand rises by 50% until 2020. The IEA and the DOE prognoses, which cover a shorter period, predict an increase by 34 to 44 per cent until 2010.

Similar findings show the prognoses of the International Institute for System Analysis (ILASA) in Laxenburg near Vienna and the scenario analyses by Wilfrid Bach (member of the enquete commissions of the 11th and 12th German Bundestag) [5.8]. The ILASA study forecasts, under the assumption of high economic growth, an increase of the energy consumption to 273% (current value=100 percent), for moderate economic growth to 220% and for a radically ecological scenario, which is regarded as unlikely, to 158%. The third scenario is to show mainly what would be technologically feasible in the direction of ecological innovations under extreme conditions [5.9].

Thinking about these prospects, we could be tempted to draw the conclusion that there is no way of solving the problems. However, this would be the worst kind of reaction and would help only those who profit from this development. Some economic experts claim that an active climate policy would allegedly cost appr. 850 billion DM, for Germany alone, of course connected with rising unemployment figures.

The WRI has made the interesting observation that the results of so-called bottom-up analyses , which are based on detailed lists of engineering costs for different technologies and on detailed assessments of energy consumption, are much more optimistic in regard to the costs and benefits of a change than the so-called top-down studies, which are preferred by the economic experts. The latter kind of analyses is based on macroeconomic figures which are generalised mean values extrapolated from past periods. With bottom-up studies the result is that the costs of a reduction of the emissions by 20%, below the value of 1990, would be negligible or even negative over a period of some decades. In the long-term perspective, reductions by 50% are possible without increasing the costs of the energy supply system as a whole, because some of the improvements will pay through their energy saving function alone [5.10]. In this context please test our Java-based simulation tool Energy Tool.

The development of wind and solar energy generation in Germany (tripling of applications for photovoltaic systems in 1996) gives rise to hope and shows that with persistence a change can be brought about. Many reputable research institutes, like the World Watch Institute or the National Renewable Energy Laboratory (NREL in Colorado), who have been in touch with the technological development for a long time, are convinced that the development on the energy market will enjoy a boom similar to the one in the telecommunications market [5.11] [5.12].

In addition, the WRI points out that the above mentioned studies are based on current trends of energy demand and do not consider the prospect of a more tangible course correction, united international efforts, for instance, to make a move towards renewable and other non-fossil energy sources. The clear signs of the significant and damaging effects caused by the man-made climate change could lead to a worldwide consensus and thus to a widespread support for a strengthened global convention on climate. By putting into practice such an agreement the availability of money for investment in alternative energy sources should improve considerably. This would turn around the whole energy system in the direction of a new climate-neutral technology, which is to a large degree available at present. Despite their lobbying of the fossil energy sources, the industry is preparing the ground for the day, when the renewable energy sources will replace the other sources. The WRI points out that the move away from fossil energy sources is necessary to avoid the dangerous risks of a climate change. Of the non-fossil forms of energy, wind and solar energy have the best long-term prospects.

Rapid Human Population Growth is Devouring Global Natural Resources

Each year, about 90 million new people join the human race. This is roughly equivalent to adding three Canadas or another Mexico to the world annually, a rate of growth that will swell human numbers from today's 5.6 billion to about 8.5 billion by 2025. These figures represent the fastest growth in human numbers ever recorded and raise many vital economic and environmental questions. Is our species reproducing so quickly that we are outpacing the Earth's ability to house and feed us? Is our demand for natural resources destroying the habitats that give us life? If 40 million acres of tropical forest—an area equivalent to twice the size of Austria—are being destroyed or grossly degraded every year, as satellite maps show, how will that affect us? If 27,000 species become extinct yearly because of human development, as some scientists believe, what will that mean for us? If nearly 2 billion people already lack adequate drinking water, a number likely to increase to 3.6 billion by the year 2000, how can all of us hope to survive?

The answers are hardly easy and go beyond simple demographics, since population works in conjunction with other factors to determine our total impact on resources. Modern technologies and improved efficiency in the use of resources can help to stretch the availability of limited resources. Consumption levels also exert considerable impact on our resource base. Population pressures work in conjunction with these other factors to determine, to a large extent, our total impact on resources. For example, although everyone contributes to resource waste, the world's bottom-billion poorest and top-billion richest do most of the environmental damage. Poverty compels the world's 1.2 billion bottom-most poor to misuse their environment and ravage resources, while lack of access to better technologies, credit, education, health care and family-planning condemns them to subsistence patterns that offer little chance for concern about their environment. This contrasts with the richest 1.3 billion, who exploit and consume disproportionate amounts of resources and generate disproportionate quantities of waste. One example is energy consumption.

Whereas the average Bangladeshi consumes commercial energy equivalent to three barrels of oil yearly, each American consumes an average of 55 barrels. Population growth in Bangladesh, one of the poorest nations, increased energy use there in 1990 by the equivalent of 8.7 million barrels, while U.S. population growth in the same year increased energy use by 110 million barrels. Of course, the U.S. population of 250 million is more than twice the size of the Bangladeshi population of 113 million, but even if the consumption figures are adjusted for the difference in size, the slower growing U.S. population still increases its energy consumption six or seven times faster yearly than does the more rapidly growing Bangladeshi population.

Human Numbers: the Crowd Swells

Population density varies by region but is a deceptive factor.

Many nations, from Europe to Africa, expand their land bases by importing food.

- Projected average yearly increase in human numbers for the next 40 years: 90 million
- Total world human population today: 5.6 billion
- Projected population in 2100 assuming reduced fertility: 11.2 billion
- Projected population in 2100 at current rate of fertility: 40 billion
- Percentage of total world population today living in developing nations: 78

In the future, the effects of population growth on natural resources will vary locally because growth occurs unevenly across the globe. Over the course of the 1990s, the Third World's population is likely to balloon by more than 900 million, while the population of the developed world will add a mere 56 million. Asia, with 3.4 billion people today, will have 3.7 billion by the turn of the century; Africa's population will increase from 700 million to 867 million; and Latin America's from 470 million to 538 million. By the year 2000, the Third World's total population is expected to be nearly 5 billion; only 1.3 billion people will reside in industrialized countries. The United Nations estimates that world population will near 11.2 billion by 2100. However, this figure is based on the assumption that growth rates will drop. If present rates continue, world population will stand at 10 billion by 2030 and 40 billion by 2110. The United Nations Population Fund estimates that to achieve the 11.2 billion projection, the number of couples using family planning services—such as modern contraceptives—in the developing world will have to rise to 567 million by the year 2000 and to 1.2 billion by 2025. In sub-Saharan Africa this means a 10-fold increase by 2025 in the number of people who use family planning. If these measures do not succeed, human population growth could blast the 11.2 billion figure clear out of the ball park.

Perhaps the most ominous aspect of today's unprecedented growth is its persistence despite falling annual population growth rates everywhere except in parts of Africa, the Middle East and South Asia. Annual global population growth stands at 1.6 percent, down from 2 percent in the early 1970s. Similarly, the total fertility rate (the average number of children a woman is likely to have) has dropped from a global average of six only three decades ago to slightly more than three today. Population continues to grow because of tremendous demographic momentum. China's annual growth rate, for example, is only 1.2 percent. However, the country's huge population base—1.2 billion people—translates this relatively small rate of growth into a net increase in China's population of around 15 million yearly. Clearly, any attempt to slow population growth is a decades-long process affected by advances in medicine, extended life spans and reduced infant, child and maternal mortality. The following pages survey the effects of human population growth on a wide range of natural resources.

Plants and Animals: the Shrinking Ark

Biologists have catalogued 1.7 million species and cannot even estimate how many species remain to be documented. The total could be 5 million, 30 million or even more. Yet, we are driving thousands of species yearly to extinction through thoughtless destruction of habitat. A survey conducted recently in Australia, Asia and the Americas by the International Union for Conservation of Nature and Natural Resources—The World Conservation Union (IUCN) found that loss of living space affected 76 percent of all mammal species. Expansion of settlements threatened 56 percent of mammal species, while expansion of ranching affected 33 percent. Logging and plantations affected 26 percent. IUCN has declared human population growth the number one cause of extinctions. The 10 nations with the worst habitat destruction house an average of 189 people per square kilometre (250 acres), while the 10 that retain the most original habitat stand at only 29 people per square kilometre. Future population growth poses a serious threat to wildlife habitat. Every new person needs space for housing, food, travel, work and other needs. Human needs vary widely from place to place, but a US survey found that the average person requires about 0.056 hectares (a hectare is a standard unit of land measurement equal to about 2.47 acres) of nonfarm land for daily living.

To this must be added land for food production. This varies with land quality and available technologies, but each newborn person probably will need at least 0.2 hectare of cropland unless food production per acre increases in the years ahead. This will require the conversion of more and more wildland into cropland. In East Asia, for example, the amount of irrigated, high-yield cropland per person is already near the 0.2 hectare limit. UN consultant and author Paul Harrison estimates, very conservatively, that each new person will need at least a quarter of a hectare. Thus, every billion people that we add to the planet in the years ahead will require 250 million hectares more of agricultural land. Most of this land will have to come from what is currently wildlife habitat. The UN's projected population of 11.2 billion by 2100 would require creation of roughly 20 million square kilometres (8 million sq. ml.) of new cropland—equivalent to more than 80 percent of all forest and woodland in developing countries today.

Plants and Animals: What we Protect

Using this tree as a symbol of the Earth's land shows that the 4.8 percent of the globe that lies in protected areas is a mere stump of the whole.

- Percentage of existing parks and reserves subject to agricultural encroachment and other human disruptions: 33

- Percentage of all species likely to become extinct within the next 30 years: 25
- Number of lives saved yearly in the United States by plant-derived anticancer drugs: 30,000
- Number of plant species used by Southeast Asian herbalists for medicinal purposes: 6,500
- Number of edible fruit species found in rainforests: 2,450.

Conversion of natural habitat for human use can even reduce the value of remaining wild areas for wildlife. When development chops wild lands into fragments, native species often decline simply because the small remnants do not meet their biological needs. For example, studies of U.S. forest birds indicate that species that prefer to nest in forest interiors are more subject to predation and lay fewer eggs when habitat fragmentation forces them to nest along forest edges. A study in southern California indicated that most canyons lose about half of native bird species dependent on chaparral habitat within 20 to 40 years after the canyons become isolated by development, even though the chaparral brush remains.

Biologist William Newmark's 1987 study of 14 Canadian and U.S. national parks showed that 13 of the parks had lost some of their mammal species, at least in part because the animals could not adapt to confinement within parks surrounded by developed land. Habitat loss in North America and in Latin American tropics has caused declines in many bird species that migrate between those regions. The Breeding Bird Survey, a volunteer group that tabulates nesting birds each June, found that 70 percent of neotropical migrant species monitored in the eastern United States declined from 1978 to 1987. So did 69 percent of monitored neotropical migrants that nest in prairie regions. Declining species include such familiar songbirds as veeries, wood thrushes, blackpoll warblers and rose-breasted grosbeaks. As human population growth continues to push development into wild areas, fragmentation will increase and its effects on wildlife survival will intensify.

Land Loss: A Food Crisis

Land degradation, a global problem, is becoming acute in much of the developing world. Population pressures and inappropriate farming practices contribute to soil impoverishment and erosion, rampant deforestation, overgrazing of common lands and misuse of agrochemicals. Worldwide, an estimated 1.2 billion hectares, an area about the size of China and India combined, have lost much of their agricultural productivity since 1945. Every year, farmers abandon about 70,000 square kilometres (27,000 sq. ml.) of farmland because soils are too degraded for crops.

Drylands, including grasslands that provide rich pastures for livestock, have been hardest hit. Although not as extensive as once thought, desertification—the ecological destruction that turns productive land into deserts—still threatens the Middle East and parts of Africa and Asia. Because of land degradation, large portions of the Sahel, including Burkina Faso, Chad, Mali, Mauritania, Niger and Senegal, can no longer feed their people. Although annual fluctuations in rainfall may interrupt the trend of cropland loss, the Sahel could suffer agricultural collapse within a decade. Sahelian croplands, as presently farmed, can support a maximum of 36 million people. In 1990 the rural population stood at an estimated 32 million and will exceed 40 million by the end of the decade even if annual population growth slows from the current 3 percent to 2 percent.

LAND: Farmland Diminishes

Though human numbers are growing, the amount of land suitable for agriculture is finite, and so hunger can grow faster than crops.

- Number of nations experiencing a decline in food production per capita during the 1980s: 75
- Number of farmers worldwide with too little land to meet subsistence needs for food and fuel: 200 million
- Number of people in those farmers' families: 1 billion
- Number of children who died in 1993 from nutrition related diseases: 10 million
- Current annual increase in human population in Sahelian Africa: 3 percent
- Estimated current annual increase in food production in Sahelian Africa: 2 percent

Since 1961, food production has matched world population growth in all developing regions except sub-Saharan Africa. In the early 1980s, the UN Food and Agriculture Organization (FAO) predicted that more than half of all developing nations examined in its study of carrying capacity (62 out of 115) may be unable to feed their projected populations by 2000 using current farming technology. Most of the 62 countries probably will be able to feed less than half of their projected population without expensive food imports.

As a direct result of population growth, especially in developing nations, the average amount of cropland per person is projected to decline from 0.28 hectares in 1990 to 0.17 by 2025. Three factors will determine whether food production can equal population growth:

1. New Croplands. Currently, the amount of new land put into production each year may equal the amount taken out of production for various reasons, such as erosion, salt deposits and water logging. Thus, the net annual gain in arable land, despite wide-spread habitat destruction to create it, may be zero.
2. New Water Sources. Agricultural demand for water is expected to double between 1970 and 2000. Already more than 70 percent of water withdrawals from rivers, underground reservoirs and other sources go to crop irrigation.
3. Agrochemical Use. Pesticides and fertilizers are boosting crop yields. However, in many areas agrochemicals are too expensive to use, while in other areas they are overused to prop up falling yields. Agrochemicals can pose health hazards, creating another expense for developing nations.

Forest: The Vanishing World

The quest for more crop and grazing land has sealed the fate of much of the world's tropical forests. Between 1971 and 1986, arable land expanded by 59 million hectares, while forests shrank by at least 125 million hectares. However, consultant Harrison estimates that during the same period, land used for settlements, roads, industries, office buildings and other development expanded by more than 50 million hectares as a result of growth in urban centres, reducing the amount of arable land in surrounding areas. Consequently, the amount of natural habitat wiped out to produce the 59-million-hectare net in arable land may have exceeded 100 million hectares.

Forests: Ending Forests Into Fuel

Wood accounts for a high percentage of total energy use in many nations. Every year, more than a billion people use wood faster than trees can grow.

- Number of people worldwide who depend on fulewood as primary energy source: more than 2 billion
- Percentage of original primary forest remaining in Haiti: 0
- Amount of remaining Ecuadorian forest to be cut by 2000: half

- Percentage of original tropical forest already destroyed in Bangladesh: 95 ...in India and Sri Lanka: almost 100 ... in Philippines: 80
- Percentage of all plant species found in tropical forests: 45

If current trends continue, most tropical forests will soon be destroyed or damaged beyond recovery. Of the 76 countries that presently encompass tropical forests, only four—Brazil, Guyana, Papua New Guinea and Zaire—are likely to retain major undamaged tracts by 2010, less than a generation away. Population pressure contributes to deforestation not only because of increased demand for cropland and living space but also because of increased demand for fuelwood, on which half of the world's people depend for heating and cooking. The majority of sub-Saharan Africa's population is dependent on fuelwood: 82 percent of all Nigerians, 70 percent of Kenyans, 80 percent of all Malagasies, 74 percent of Ghanaians, 93 percent of Ethiopians, 90 percent of Somalians and 81 percent of Sudanese.

By 1990, 100 million Third World residents lacked sufficient fuelwood to meet minimum daily energy requirements, and close to 1.3 billion were consuming wood faster than forest growth could replenish it. On average, consumption outpaces supply by 30 percent in sub-Saharan Africa as a whole, by 70 percent in the Sudan and India, by 150 percent in Ethiopia and by 200 percent in Niger.

If present trends continue, FAO predicts, another 1 billion people will be faced with critical fuelwood shortages by the end of the decade. Already, growing rings of desolation—land denuded for fuelwood or building materials—surround many African cities, such as Ouagadougou in Burkina Faso, Niamey in Niger and Dakar in Senegal. By 2000, the World Bank estimates, half to three-quarters of all West Africa's fuelwood consumption will be burned in towns and cities. According to the World Bank, remedying the fuelwood shortage will require planting 55 million hectares—an area nearly twice the size of Italy—with fast-growing trees at a rate of 2.7 million hectares a year, five times the present annual rate of 555,000 hectares.

Troubled Oceans: Disappearing Resources

Population and development pressures have been mounting in coastal areas worldwide for the past 30 years, triggering widespread resource degradation. Coastal fisheries are over exploited in much of Asia, Africa and parts of Latin America. In some cases—as in the Philippines, Indonesia, Malaysia, China, Japan, India, the west coast of South America, the Mediterranean and the Caribbean economically important fisheries have collapsed or are in severe decline.

"Nearly all Asian waters within 15 kilometres of land are considered over fished," says Ed Gomez, director of the Marine Science Institute at the University of the Philippines in Manila. Overfishing is not the sole cause of these declines. Mangroves and coral reefs— critical nurseries for many marine species and among the most productive of all ecosystems—are being plundered in the name of development. In 1990, a UN advisory panel, the Group of Experts on the Scientific Aspects of Marine Pollution (GESAMP), reported that coastal pollution worldwide had grown worse over the decade of the 1980s. Experts pointed to an overload of nutrients—mainly nitrogen and phosphorus from untreated or partially treated sewage, agricultural runoff and erosion—as the most serious coastal pollution problem. Human activities may be responsible for as much as 35 million metric tons of nitrogen and up to 3.75 million metric tons of phosphorus flowing into coastal waters every year. Even such huge amounts could be dissolved in the open ocean, but most of the pollution stays in shallow coastal waters where it causes massive algal blooms and depletes oxygen levels, harming marine life near the shores.

Oceans: Rushing to the Sea

The 4 billion people who live near coasts today will jump to 6.4 billion by 2025, increasing ocean pollution and other marine problems.

- Number of people worldwide living on coasts in 1990: 3.6 billion
- Projected number of people worldwide who will live on coasts in 2025: 6.4 billion
- Percentage of original coastal mangrove swamps, important to the breeding of commercial fish and shellfish, that remain worldwide: 50
- Number of the world's 17 major fishing areas that have reached or exceeded natural limits: 17
- Percentage decline in coral reefs worldwide since World War II: 50

Although the world still possesses an estimated 240,000 square kilometres (93,000 sq. mi.) of mangrove swamps—coastal forests that serve as breeding grounds and nurseries for many commercially important fish and shell-fish species—this represents only about half the original amount. Clear-cutting for timber, fuelwood and wood chips; conversion to fish and shellfish ponds; and expansion of urban areas and croplands have claimed millions of hectares globally. For example, of the Philippine's original mangrove area—estimated at 500,000 to 1 million hectares—only 100,000 hectares remain: 80 to 90 percent are gone.

Some 600,000 square kilometres (230,000 sq. milt) of coral reefs survive in the world's tropical seas. Unfortunately, these species-rich ecosystems are suffering widespread decline. Clive Wilkinson, a coral reef specialist working at the Australian Institute of Marine Science, estimates that fully 10 percent of the world's reefs have already been degraded "beyond recognition." Thirty percent are in critical condition and will be lost completely in 10 to 20 years, while another 30 percent are threatened in and will be lost in 20 to 40 years. Only 30 percent, located away from human development or otherwise too remote to be exploited, are in stable condition. Throughout much of the world, coastal zones are overdeveloped, overcrowded and over exploited. Already nearly two-thirds of the world's population—some 3.6 billion people—live along coasts or within 150 kilometres (100 ml.) of one. Within three decades, 75 percent, or 6.4 billion, will reside in coastal areas—nearly a billion more people than the current global population.

In the United States, 54 percent of all Americans live in 772 coastal counties adjacent to marine coasts or the Great Lakes. Between 1960 and 1990, coastal population density increased from 275 to nearly 400 people per square kilometre. By 2025, nearly 75 percent of all Americans will live in coastal counties, with population density doubling in areas such as southern California and Florida. Similarly, nearly 780 million of China's 1.2 billion people—almost 67 percent—live in 14 southeast and coastal provinces and two coastal municipalities, Shanghai and Tianjin. Along much of China's coastline, population densities average more than 600 per square kilometre. In Shanghai they exceed 2,000 per square kilometre. During the past few years, as many as 100 million Chinese have moved from poorer provinces in central and western regions to coastal areas in search of better economic opportunities. More ominously, population growth is expected to accelerate in the nation's 14 newly created economic free zones and five special economic zones, all of them coastal.

Water: Distribution Woes

Nearly 75 percent of the world's fresh water is locked in glaciers and icecaps, with virtually all the rest underground. Only about 0.01 percent of the world's total water is easily available for human use. Even this tiny amount would be sufficient to meet all the world's needs if it were distributed evenly. However, the world is divided into water "haves" and "have note." In the Middle East, north Asia, northwestern Mexico, most of Africa, much of the western United States, parts of Chile and Argentina and nearly all of Australia, people need more water than can be sustainably supplied.

Water: the Thirst Grows

Water availability per person is dropping, Already, some 2 billion people live with water constraints each year.

- Percentage of the world's water that is freshwater: 3
- Percentage of the world's freshwater that is easily accessible as surface water: 1
- Percentage of easily accessible freshwater that comes from rivers and marshes: 13
- Percentage of easily accessible freshwater that comes from lakes: 87
- Number of nations whose water use exceeds 100 percent of their renewable supplies: 9
- Percentage of its renewable water supplies that Libya uses yearly: 374
- Years required for Libya to double it s population: 20.4

As the world's human population increases, the amount of water per person decreases. The United Nations Educational, Scientific and Cultural Organization (UNESCO) estimates that the amount of fresh water available per person has shrunk from more than 33,000 cubic metres (1.2 million cu. ft.) per year in 1850 to only 8,500 cubic metres (300,000 cu. ft.) today. Of course, this is a crude, general figure. But because of population growth alone, water demand in more than half the world's countries by 2000 is likely to be twice what it was as recently as 1971.

Already some 2 billion people in 80 countries must live with water constraints for all or part of the year. By the end of the 1990s, Egypt will have only two-thirds as much water for each of its inhabitants as it has today, and Kenya only half as much. By then, six of East Africa's seven nations and all five nations on the south rim of the Mediterranean will face severe shortages. In 1990, 20 nations suffered water scarcity, with less than 1,000 cubic metres (35,000 cu. ft.) of water per person, according to a study by Population Action International.

Another eight experienced occasional water stress. The 28 nations represent 335 million people. By 2025, some 48 nations will suffer shortages, involving some 3 billion residents, according to the study. China—although not listed as water short because of the heavy amount of rain that falls in its southern region—has, nevertheless, exceeded its sustainable water resources. According to Qu Geping, China's Environment Minister, the country can supply water sustainably to only 650 million people, not the current population of 1.2 billion. In other words, China is supporting twice as many people as its water resources can reasonably sustain without drawing down groundwater supplies and overusing surface waters.

Fossil Fuels: Energy Breakdown

Human society runs on energy, principally fossil fuels such as oil, gas and coal. These three account for 90 percent of global commercial energy production. Nuclear power, hydro-electricity and other sustainable resources provide the rest. The industrialized nations, with less than a quarter of the world's people, burn about 70 percent of all fossil fuels. The United States alone consumes about a quarter of the world's commercial energy, and the former Soviet Union about a fifth. In terms of per capita consumption patterns, Canada burns more fuel than any other nation—in 1987 the equivalent of 9 metric tons of oil per person—followed by Norway at 8.9 metric tons of oil per person and the United States at 7.3. By contrast, developing nations on average use the equivalent of only about half a metric ton of oil per person yearly.

Known oil reserves should meet current levels of consumption for another 41 years, up from an estimated 31 years in 1970 thanks to better energy efficiency and conservation measures, along with new oil fields brought into production. Natural gas reserves should meet current demand for 60 more years, up from 38 years in 1970. Coal reserves should be good for another 200 years.

But our addiction to fossil fuels has resulted in chronic, sometimes catastrophic, pollution of the atmosphere, in some cases far beyond what natural systems or man-made structures can tolerate. A noxious atmospheric cocktail of chemical pollutants is primarily responsible for the death and decline of thousands of hectares of European forests. Acid rain— caused by a combination of nitrogen and sulfur dioxides released from fossil-fuel combustion—has eaten away at priceless monuments and buildings throughout Europe and North America, causing billions of dollars in damage.

Fossil Fuels: Who's Doing What With Oil?

- Percentage of the world's population that resides in industrialized nations: 25

- Percentage of annual global fossil-fuel production used by industrialized nations: 70
- Nation with the highest per capita consumption of fuels: Canada
- Average amount of fuels used per Canadian, expressed in metric tons of oil: 9
- Average amount of fossil fuels used yearly per person in the developing nations, expressed in metric tons of oil: 0.5.

Urban air contains a hazardous mix of pollutants everything from sulfur dioxide and reactive hydrocarbons to heavy metals and organic compounds. Smog alerts are now commonplace in many cities with heavy traffic. In Mexico City, for example, smog levels exceeded World Health Organization standards on all but 11 days in 1991. Breathing the city's air is said to be as damaging as smoking two packs of cigarettes a day, and half the city's children are born with enough lead in their blood to hinder their development.

The only way to stretch fossil fuel reserves and reduce pollution levels is to conserve energy and use it much more efficiently than we do now. Some progress has been made, but the benefits of energy conservation have been realized in only a few industrialized countries. Recent history has shown what can happen. In the decade following the first oil shock, per capita energy consumption fell by 5 percent in the member states of the Organization for Economic Cooperation and Development (OECD)—consisting of the industrialized countries of Western Europe and North America, plus Japan, Australia and New Zealand—while their per capita gross domestic product grew by a third. Buildings in the OECD countries use a quarter less energy now than they did before 1973, while the energy efficiency of industry has improved by a third. Worldwide, cars now get 25 percent more kilometres per gallon than they did in 1973. In all, increased efficiency since 1973 has saved the industrialized nations $250 billion in energy costs. Even more savings could be realized through concerted efforts to conserve energy and improve efficiency. Three relatively simple, cost effective measures could be introduced immediately: 1) making compact fluorescent lamps generally available in homes and offices; 2) tightening up building codes to require better insulation against cold and heat; and 3) requiring lean-burn engines, which get up to 80 kilometres per gallon (50 mpg), in all new compact cars. These three "technical fixes" could save billions of dollars in energy costs.

7

Types and Patterns of Settlements

Elements of Settlement

Generally speaking, a settlement consists of two visible elements: (i) the man who is the dynamic one and is wholly responsible for the construction of the second (ii) the static forms. Obviously, size, shape, from, layout, types and patterns–all are elements of a settlement. While the first element is the subject matter of population geography, in particular, the forms of houses and settlements as a whole are important elements of settlement. In this chapter, two distinct elements, namely, types and patterns, will be discussed. The components of these elements like house, street, enclosure etc., are equally important and will be explained in the sequel in next few chapters. The two elements of type and pattern are intricately woven but visible, hence, identifiable. Likewise, other attributes of settlement are also distinguishable on comparison. The type of size, shape or layout is discernible always in relation to different types of settlements in existence with various degrees of variations on the basis of certain norms. These norms vary according to landscape—physical as well cultural (i.e., small, big, amorphous)—with certain directions or fixed sites or forms in the first world or other worlds. That is why, the terms assigned to these elements convey relative meanings as well as connotation, *i.e.*, size and shape of an English and Ethiopian or Indian settlement or even form of a farmstead or homestead in U.S.A. or in Indian northern *teraizone* and *chak* farmsteads in the Ganga plain. The number and magnitude of habitations also vary as do the appearance. Thus, the elements of settlement, as geographical terms used universally, convey various conceptual meanings and significance to a particular group of people living in various environments. A compact settlement of a country may be just equal to a hamlet of ancient country or a big size settlement of New World may be a small, tiny settlement along a road in India.

Difference Between Type and Pattern

These terms find place in geographical literature, particularly in rural settlement geography, conveying various meanings, sometimes as synonymous, at others interchangeable and yet others as one being element/part of the other. But, actually, these are neither of them. Let us see a few examples. Einch and Trewartha *et. al.* refer to two primary types of settlements: (a) the isolated or dispersed and (b) the nucleated. Hudson says that the major patterns in rural areas, then, are either (a) nucleated, or (b) dispersed. There are similar references, treatments and explanations regarding types and patterns of settlements by other geographers in India like Enayat Ahmed and R.L. Singh, to name a few.

Pattern of settlement has been defined by Emrys Jones, as the relationship between one house or building and another and to isolate this relationship he refers to a large-scale map. He thinks that often pattern in unrelated to site and site may have little or no bearing on pattern. But Finch and Trewarthy *el. al.* attribute the contrasts in the arrangement of streets and houses, *i.e.*, patterns to the site as well as historical causes. Thus, two identifying factors are clear: (1) pattern refers to geometric form and shape of the settlement which may be of different types; and (2) the latter refers to relationship of number of dwellings and number of sites. It is the analysis of patterns which brings before us varous classified types of settlements with varous shapes and forms. The intra-settlement analysis of inter-dwelling distance clarifies the occupance of village territory on one or more than one sites. This provides the picture of nucleation or dispersion, hence, types. But when we refer to a certain form of settlement depicting a particular shape, a distinct pattern gets a name according to geometrical attributes, *i.e.*, elongated, linear, block, L-shaped etc. Pattern also refers to two dimensional geometrical arrangement of rural settlements in an erea. This arrangement exposes itself through the relationship of the rural settlements to each other and the adjacent physio-cultural landscape or topographic features. This pattern clearly indicates comparison among several settlements and identification of one, *i.e.*, linear along road, valley or fan pattern along foothills etc. But, it is different from the type and pattern observed in the form of individual settlement dealt with in sequel. The two patterns–geometric and non-geometric–are easily discernible on a map drawn or airphoto taken for/of a wider area.

Classification of Settlement Types and Patterns

Let us have a few examples of classifications of types first. D.C. Money, in his *Introduction to Human Geography,* broadly classifies as: (1) the single large nucleated village, (2) hamlets scattered throughout the countryside, and (3) single home-steads. Enayat Ahmed gives four types: (1) compact, (2) cluster and hamlet type, (3) fragmented or hamleted, and (4) dispersed settlement. R.L. Singh discerns four main types : (1) compact settlements, (2) semi-compact or hamleted cluster, (3) semi-sprinkled or fragmented or hamleted settlements, and (4) sprinkled or dispersed type. Most of the settlement geographers have classified the types according to their regional distribution paterns of such habitations on the basis of theoretical, empirical and associational considerations. In the Indian context, the term signifies the characteristic groupings of rural dwellings in that well-defined parcel of the ground which is known as 'mauza'. But, in a regional framework, the term denoted the relationship between settlements within space. Thus, types are to be recognized on a large-scale map through the distribution of houses on one or more sites in a defined village territory whether on record or national. On a small-scale map inter-settlement spacing and number of sites of a named settlement would help in identifying the types. Often the inter-site or inter-settlement space is occupied by other land-uses, *i.e.*, agriculture, orchard, wasteland, water bodies etc.

Theoretically, the two extreme types of groupings of the rural settlements are: (i) the isolated farmsteads or dispersed dwellings in which the single family residence unit is the distinctive nucleus occupying its own farm, and (ii) nucleated settlement in which all the dwellings are clustered almost in the centre of the village lands. Between these two extremes there are gradations. We can classify them in four categories as shown in the map on the basis of nucleation and dispersion as well as their dominant occupation of a particular area:

(1) *Semi-compact type settlements* are common features on plateau or plains according to environmental constraints as well as cultural considerations. These reflect outgrowth of later periods by the people of diverse castes during settling process, sometimes as a separate grouping by aboriginals and low caste people in the neighbourhoed of the main residential unit. This type also reflects modification of the compact type because here dwellings are not very closely knitted and huddled together at one common site. Also, it covers more area than the former; the hamlets occupy new sites near the periphery of the village boundary mostly the common jungle or grazing land.

(2) *Hamleted settlements:* In such villages, the entire territory exhibits hamlets spread with Narmada valley, Nimar upland, Great and Little deserts, paddy lands in Bihar, Uttar Pradesh, Vindhyan plateau, western Uttar Pradesh in particular and several other cultivated parts in India in general. In such villages or 'mauzas', all the dwellings of *abadi* or settlement areconcentrated in one central site. The fertile soil extending through homogeneous and sometimes undulating plains attracted people since early historical times to live in groups and follow primitive type of agriculture. The existin formreflects now aggregation of such agricultural cultivators and other dependents living reciprocally under *jajmani* system and enjoying the benefits of community life. Such settlements, however, range from a cluster of thirty to hundreds of dwellings of different forms, size and functions with various types of arrangements and patterns dealt with in the sequel inintervening fields and the main or central settlement is either conspicuously absent or has a feeble influence upon others. Often the main or original site is not easily distinguishable. In such settlements, morphological diversity is rarely found. In some areas, hamlets in number cross the number of castes varying from 5 to 20. Clan and caste ties are loosened but family ties become more strengthened. The sense of cohesion and unity expressed in all day-to-day behaviour in compact settlements are absent in conspicuous. Also, they are not at par with the compact ones with regard to other varied aspects of community life, such as common rejoicing on the occasion of fairs, festivals, cermonies, weddings, worhips, *keertans* (chanting of songs), dramas etc. The visible, concrete objects or morphological details do not exist, *i.e.*, streets, open space, community centres, schools, amenities, temples, *dih* (common worship-place for a clan or village settlers). Mostly, such settlements are found either in later occupance or fertile soil tracts or due to tribal racial characteristics (of Gonds in Madhya Pradesh), *e.g.*, in West Bengal, eastern Uttar Pradesh, Madhya Pradesh and coastal plains. They unincorporated hamlets of U.S.A. are a combination of rural and urban functions with a population ranging from 20 to 150 inhabitants. They contain post office, church, school, general store, cheese factory, feed mill, tavern, filling station, garage, etc. The residents of these hamlets mostly are non-farmers and some are farmstead dwellings.

(3) *Dispersed settlement:* These are commonly found in tribal areas covering the central part of India, eastern and southern Rajasthan, Himalayan slopes in India and land with dissected and uneven topography in several world tracts. Homesteads or farmsteads of U.S.A.

and Canada or *terai* areas in India belong to this group. Here, dwellings belonging to one family or nucleus family occupy one site situated in his cultivated field. The whole (*mauza*) village territory throughout its margins receives scattered dwellings. Individualism, sentiments of living freely, custom of marriage relations are conducive to such rural settlements. Private ownership of land and its occupance go side by side. But, such isolated dwellings lack the sense of neighbourhood and communal inter-dependence. This type, however, is not original but secondary type of occupance in the process or humanization of the earth. Modern society too is affected to follow suit due to availability of facilities, resources, security and ambition to achieve one's aim individually.

Causes of Diverse Type of Rural Settlements

Most of the studies in settlement geography repeat the same two factors—physical and cultural— as responsible for various types of agglomerations and dispersions. A few modern studies have drawn attention towards more significant role played by culture, tradition and clan organizations. But, environmental determinists' emphasis upon various physical factors is not without weight or explanation. Empirical studies done in various areas would reveal one or the other factors more significant. Valid generalizations applicable universally are rather impossible. One has to be cautious about spatio-temporal dimensions while dealing with causes of agglomera-tions or dispersion in a country or even a macro region. Both, old and new world regions have historical as well as archaeological evidences of big compact agglomerations as referred to earlier. Aurousseau, in the study, *The Arrangement of Rural Settlements,* observed that the definite grouping of rural populations is a conscious human response to, rather than an actual physiographic control by a number of factors in each region, chief amongst which were: the type of pursuit, nature of groundwater supply, rainfall, surface water, soil, size of landholdings, space economy, local physiographic conditions and the topography of the region. These, in short, may be categorized as (i) physical, and (ii) cultural factors which determine the type of rural settlements separately or by their interactions and simultaneous inerplay.

Physical Factors for Compact Settlements

The practice of living in compact settlements was fostered among newly settled communities (*e.g.*, the Neolithic cultivators of ancient Egypt and China, and the early anglo-saxon immigrants into Roman

Britain) by a necessity of dealing effectively with a somewhat hostile environment, *e.g.*, a forested or marshy landscape, and by the advantage of organizing a permanent system of cultivation (Hudson, 1976: 64). The physical factors for compact settlements are as under:

Distributional Pattern of Settlements in Nimarupland:

1. The compact farm village is the basic unit of settlement in eastern and southern Aisa. Such settlements are found in great river valley plains and 'will be found', in words of Demangeon, "as an ancient feature, chiefly, on lands which were fertile from the beginning. Similarly, Blache concludes that "clustered village is indigenous in districts where the arable area is continuous, admitting of uniform and extensive exploitation". Uniformity of relief and fertility of soil attracted the early settlers, who started community life and aggregation of cultivators and other caste members resulted into compact habitations as shown in Figures 2.4A and 2.8.
2. Wherever sparsely populated hilly tract meets the plain surface of plateau or plane surface of plain, big compact villages come up.
3. Similarly, dry points upon the bluffs of the river valleys support big settlements.
4. Suitable water table, easy sinking of water wells, storing of water in several parts are conducive to big agglomerations. Springs or sources of water also attract human groups to concentrate and form compact settlements. Interfluves of rivers, free from ravines, easily support such villages.
5. In some parts, likewise, the collective building of dams are irrigation channels for the storage and distribution of rain water and the construction of tanks for artificial irrigation have promoted the evolution of compact villages.

Cultural Factors

The following are the cultural factors responsible for the establishment of compact settlements:

1) Man tends of necessity to gravitate towards his fellowmen. Of all animals, he is the most gregarious and the greater the number collected in a given space, the greater is the attractive force there exerted, as is seen to be the case with the great cities of the ancient world. Forest clearing, cultivation of land and related activities centralized at one place and agricultural

cooperation and practices of the past as well as present have been conducive to compact settlements. Necessity for cooperation in the regulation and control of water, digging of wells, upkeep of certain public works and preparation of the environment to make it favourable to crops—such things mean consolidation. The village dwellers of the great plains, plateaux of the world, since hoary past, followed agricultural practices based on cooperation leading to the establishment of compact villages. Likewise, "for the first hundred years and more of its history rural New England was of village dwelling farmers" but changed later on due to technical advance.

2) Fragmentation of holdings and strip cultivation present disadvantage to the village dweller which are best counterbalanced by nucleation where farmer avails all the amenities of close, warm, communal life. Blache rightly remarks that "concentration of living quarters is necessitated by the diversity of parcels to be cultivated, because their only common meeting ground is the village, whither all paths lead." Similar view has been expressed by Mukerjee in similar terms: "All paths and tracks across the fields, which for each cultivator lie scattered like autumn leaves, lead to the village that is meeting ground of all" Obviously, the villager, in compact village, lives in the centre which minimizes his economic distance.

3) Rajput clans, *inter alia,* in the process of occupance, have helped the settlements to grow into compact habitations enclosed by mud walls, ditch or around a fortress during early days. To these were attracted groups of other people like priests, menilas and artisans who aided in maintaining the solidarity, and self-sufficiency of the rural organization.

4) The reciprocal social relationships under the *jajmani* system have tended to maintain compactness since long. Among others, regarding socio-cultural factors, Enayat Ahmed states: "The social gathering in the centre of the village usually under some shady tree or near the temple, the mutual rejoicings on festivals, the gathering of neighbours after the days work near the well in summer and round the fire in winter when tales are told and talks of friends and crops exchanged; all these have contributed their influence in the direction of compact settlement.

5) Among economic factors, one cannot ignore the money lending system. Big cultivators or village *mahajan* (money lender) exercises centripetal force for settlers.

6) Unemployed or semi-employed labourers engage themselves in the subsidiary occupations which can easily flourish in such village. Similarly, a host of intermediaries like petty traders find it convenient to supply articles of everyday life and purchase grains in times of need in compact villages.
7) Land system also associated the landlord and cultivator well in compact villages.
8) Religious centres along rivers, near springs also attract agglomerations around them. Temples in the middle of such big settlements still signify their historical role, *i.e.*, Vindhyachal, Chitrakut, Pushker etc.
9) Some villages grow as compact settlements due to definite political bias or administrative decision, *i.e.*, Manpur (Indore) during the British rule, Mandu by Muslims and others of Hindu period, Tefki in Ethiopia with Italian stronghold.
10) Defence plays significant role in agglomerations. Its examples are walled villages of the Hansa tribes in northern Nigeria, acropolis villages in the Mediterranean and others in Algeria, Kenya and Mormon villages of U.S.A. The internecine war, robbery, *thug* menaces and looting during the period of anarchy, particularly in Central India, compelled the people to live in closed and compact sites, still present in several parts. The presence of outer wall, ditch, *garhi* and the usual practice of erecting *khala* (enclosure) and huddled together houses exhibit the need of defence in the past and their continued use during present rural landscape.
11) Hall, rightly observes that "the compact village form (haufendorf) is well-adapted to the mode of life of a paddy area." Various operations linked with paddy cultivation generate such centripetal force.
12) Mukerjee's remark that "the seasonal idleness of the peasant, especially marked in the rice region, contributes to the development of a large variety of cottage industries which can thrive only in compact settlements." Besides, cottage industry flourishes well in agglomerations as visualized in carpet industry, *i.e.*, in big villages, such as Khamaria, Ghosia etc.
13) During old days, new site was rarely selected to live separately due to being inauspicious till it was approved of by a group of settlers after getting confirmation from the priests.

14) In modern agricultural system of USSR, Israel (Kibbutzim), China etc., collective farms are conducive to compact settlements.
15) During medieval period, open field system of farming required communal field labour which favoured agglomeration in western countries.

Factors Responsible for Dispersion

Though dispersed settlement unit is taken to be granted as synonymous with the farmstead, its main characteristic is the nucleus family along with isolation and privacy. Various factors, such as environmental, socio-economic as well as socio-psychological are responsible for such dispersion. This has its own economic advantages and social disadvantages attached with the living pattern.

Physical Factors

The reasons for disperse type of settlements seem to be different in different regions and no logical explanation of universal application may be given. However, some common factors as given below are clearly visible:

1) A number European writers have observed that dispersion appears to increase in direct proportion to the raggedness of the land surface. Blache related such scattered dwellings to the dissected relief. In Malwa region, one finds a proportionate increase in dispersion closely related to the extent of fertile land. So, the scattered 'tapro'(homestead) of tribals is visualized along a river, a slope, on a hill top, a spur or wherever he could play his hand on plough. The poor soil strewn with boulders enhances dispersion to such an extent that one dwelling is enough for several acres. Gradation from a homestead of Bhil or Korku to hamleted *dhanas* of the Gonds well illustrates the influence of land upon concentration of dwellings.
2) In the areas of harsh climate and sterile soils, such as high mountainous lands of the Himalayas, dispersion is common according to supporting capacity of land, forest and pasture.
3) High water table uniformly available in plains attracts settlers to form homesteads or hamlets with close dwellings, *e.g.*, in Bengal, Belgium (with jutish land holding system), irrigated areas of Spain.
4) In New world, the vast fertile lowlands have extensive farming land to support isolated farmer, *e.g.*, in U.S.A. and Canada.

5) Floods in river flood plains provide only seasonal agricultural opportunities. Temporary or shifting type of dispersed settlements grow in such areas. On higher ground permanent type of huts mark the land according to landownership, *e.g.*, in the Ganga and Ghaghara river flood plains, such settlements are found throughout the plain.

Cultural Factors

Varied cultural factors related with land tenure, type of agriculture, individual initiative, peaceful conditions, clan affinities, and racial system have separately or jointly been responsible for various gradations in settlement dispersion ranging from a hut to a hamlet. These are as follows :

1) The land tenure system changed to a great extent in the mid-nineteenth century in India and with the decline of feudalism later on, private landownership favoured outgrowth of hamlets and isolated dwellings. Tenants of Jagirdars were also bound to live near the field they cultivated. The land dedicated to a *sadhu* (a saint) results in *Math* type settlement. Grants of lands by *Zamindars* (land-lords) as charity also attracted people to form separate dwelling on such sites. After *zamindari* abolition the drift appears to be away from the compact village towards farm dwelling and centripetal forces are loosening hold due to change in social order. In areas of consolidation of holdings farmers are coming out of compact village *abadi* (settlement) and occupying their own *chaks* (plots). There are examples of such isolated farms and settlements in England, Germany, Sweden and Denmark too. Among areas in Britain having individual ownership, fruit farms and market gardens represent dispersed settlement pattern. The trend is also visible in peasants of Egypt, Fiji, Mexico, Israel, Ethiopia etc.
2) Where cultivable land is divided into too small fields to permit plough cultivation, hoe is the alternative used by sowing which needs intensive labour. People living in such fields do form dispersed settlements. Tribal, hilly and mountainous areas, having terraced slope cultivation, such as Himalayan valley slopes, Ethiopian highlands, also present such isolated habitations. Also, where the existing peasantry is poor, illiterate and unskilled in intensive farms of agriculture and lacks mechanical equipment, it is without question essential to locate the farmsteads on the holding.

3) Individual initiative also plays its role in the selection and formation of isolated settlements in newly developing areas, on newly purchased or possessed plots/sites either for living, better agriculture, mining, forestry or some business. It may also be due to desire to get away from religious or ethnic persecution.
4) Due to peaceful conditions prevailing during modern times, open country isolated living is increasing. In Italy, newly planned areas with small holdings have disperse type of new habitations. This is the trend in other parts of the world where irrigational facilities, security, eradication of disease are improved by now.
5) Clan affinities also make the closer, kindred to live at one place quite separate from other. Blache quotes Richthofen regarding clan characteristic of Chinese who divided into clans live in little hamlets, with manners and customs differing from those of plains.
6) The type of economy and racial characteristics have determined the dispersion of settlements in tribal areas. Still, privacy of life and polygamy, two concurrent causes, have led them to live separately in scattered dwellings. Residing in his *tapro* (habitation), a Bhil feels himself safe and keeps a close eye on his wives staying at the house or working in the field in the neighbourhood. Security of crops from wild animals and birds and also theft, so common a feature in hilly Central India, compels them to make their huts separate at a central place closely related to the contour of the terrain. They can also construct their huts within some days out of woods and try to be as near as possible to their cultivated fields. Superstitions and ignorance also play their part in keeping them aloof from other members. Such is the case with other, several, tribals spreading over the world.
7) Colonization of available agricultural land following industrial revolution in Europe has been conducive to disperse type of settlements, *i.e.*, in Danube plains on the open flattish grasslands (Puszta). Poland, Czechoslovakia and Hungary all show such trends. After the second World War, Japan saw the same show.
8) In areas of pastoralism and transhumance, dispersed dwellings are common. Herders in Switzerland, Austria and Norway make dispersed chalets (Almhutte) or saeter huts. Seas-onal huts of Sawannah and Steppes' pastorals are other examples.

9) New forest clearings or reclamation and occupance of user margin land have, since medieval period, encouraged dispersion.
10) Newly constructed rail-road network has also attracted the villagers to come out along the road or near railway station to erect shops, *dhabas,* resting/halting places for trucks along highways, and later on permanent dwellings resulting into separate hamlets.
11) Rural market (*hat*) villages have also encouraged the establishment of separate dwellings and hamlets near the hat site or fair site. The fair sites are occupied by a shopkeeper to serve the casual traveler, or a separate hamlet of priests.
12) Caste system has also been conductive to the dispersion during recent times. Separate hamlets of Kachhi, Koli, Ghosi, Ahir, Bhils and some others of low agricultural class and service class like Chamar, Balai, sweeper and other scheduled castes and tribes, have been developed outside the main village as a satellite of the latter. *Banjaras* (wanderers), *Lauhpite* (ironsmiths) and *Patharkatta* (stone cutters) live in separate dwellings away from the main residen-tial units. *Chamars* live generally at the outskirts of the villages or sometimes even entirely segregated from it and possessing its own tanks, wells and boundary Gods.
13) The headquarters of community development blocks or tribal welfare blocks and their subsidiary affiliations have also contributed to new dispersions in the vicinity of villages or towns. Similarly, big farms, ginning and spinning factories have also encouraged new *bastis* in their neighbourhood.

Other Types

We saw in Chapter 1 some general criteria based settlements. But, all varied form cannot be explained on the basis of functional types alone. Site is the most significant factor in developing certain patterns which are discussed below. A few sites are divided on the basis of physical phenomena which prove to be more attractive factors in settling process while in others cultural factors become determining, or controlling ones. Since all sites have topographic locations, it is simply more convincing to present them with generalized categories of *physiographic* and *cultural.*

Physiographic Sites

All the physiographic sites are further discernible according to their relations to the environmental features: (1) hydrographic, (2) geomorphic, and (3) vegetational.

Hydrographic

Man breaths and exists but he survives only when he drinks and eats. Water, therefore, is the sole and the most determining factor in occupance. Water containing features also serve as means of livelihood, communication, defence as barriers, cultivation through irrigation as well as climate ameliorating device. Among many minor and major factors affecting hydrographic features, a few more significant are water table depth, portability of water, its volume, seasonal fluctuations, accessibility, skill of inhabitants in making use of water from different sources and nature of reservoir, spring, or tank and stream banks.

(a) *Tanks* have played a major role in attracting rural habitations since hoary past as the water for drinking for man and his cattle was in itself an attracting force. In northern India, 'Chandravedi' and 'Suryavedi' tanks are used to decide the alignment of settlements. In hilly or undulating parts, these tanks, mostly constructed by throwing embankments on small rivers, are widely scattered on plateaus and big compact villages stick to them almost every where. Construction of tanks as means of water, *inter alia,* is considered to be a step leading one to salvation. Similarly, lakes attract and give shape to settlements along the banks.

(b) *Springs* available in mountainous, hilly or plateau regions due to geological formations providing flow of natural water have given rise to several settlements rather, have in-fluenced the social organization of sites. Artesian wells in many parts of the world, and in *terai* zone of India, have been centri-petal force for human habitation. 'Ukala' (spring) in the Mahi-Chambal divide or springs of the Siwaliks are other examples which attracted settlers since antiquity.

(c) *River Side* or wet point settlements as big compact rural or urban agglomerations mark the landscape, be it along the Ganga, Volga, Thames, Nile, Mississippi, Danube or Yangtze. Small streams too sometimes attract big human nucleation. Various elongated, linear and nucleated block patterns are discernible in different landscapes.

(d) *Canal Side* settlements of modern times show elongated or linear pattern. New sites are at the source or the road-crossings where hamlets are taking the shape of market centres.

(e) *Well-settlements* are the original havitation. Most of the old settlement surround the wells giving semi-circular or rectangular layout. Even, number of well sites determine the site of settlements especially for various caste people in India. Tubewells belonging to government or private cultivator also emerge as attractive force for new development of farmsteads and hamlets.

To these 'water point' or 'wet point' settlements may be added other surrounding 'oases' in deserts. It is also remarkable that ownership of means of water, its control, use, distribution and restricted supply play their specific, definitive role in shaping the settlements. The dominant group or clan occupies space closer to the site and others away from them.

Geomorphic

In the process of such selection, he keeps in mind the following aspects:

(a) Suitability of available land for occupance for both settlement and primary production, *i.e.*, agriculture, forestry, mining, fishing etc.

(b) Suitability of size of the site in a territory.

(c) Contour relations according to local slope.

(d) Strategic situation regarding overall defence.

(e) Approach and accessibility linkages in relation to pathways, roads, other settlements, water and other landuses.

It is obvious from Figures 2.11 to 2.13 that different habitations show diversity in form and size closely related to site which in itself reveals fundamental diversity. Let us see with examples.

(a) *Narrow valleys* of small rivers bestowed with fertile black or alluvial soils give birth to compact settlements on Malwa plateau region like Shahgarh and Binaika (Sagar district.), Bardo in Dhar, Segaon and Un in Nimar and Kalwari, Dhodra Mau, Sopani (Betul) etc., and semi-compact villages on Betual plateau. Ensconced with hills and hill spurs, these settlements have been, in later periods, connected by routes sometimes rails, roads or age-old footpaths.

(b) *Fort settlements* on hills, river sides scatter throughout the world reflecting compulsion of site selection for the purpose of administration and defence, *i.e.*, Tefki in Ethiopia and Hopi settlements (Pueblos) on mesas in south-western U.S.A. and Castle villages of England. The incessant internecine wars, a common feature of political history of Malwa region, compelled the settlers and their chiefs to establish fortresses as strong-holds throughout the region on suitable sites, the examples being Bijagarh, Ramgarh, (Khargone district), Dhadgaon (Dhulia), Makrai (Hoshangabad), Khimlasa, Bashhari (Sagar), Burhi Chanderi, Isagarh (Guna), Asir (Betul), Malhargaon (Vidisha) and Asirgarh (Khandwa).

(c) *Ferry point settlements* are of common occurrence along the rivers. Nemawar in Dewas, Handia and Babri-Babri (Hoshangabad) are suitable examples.

(d) *Dry-Point settlements* like Babai and Sangkhera in Hoshangabad lie on the land above flood level almost one kilometer away from river banks. Big rivers have also such sites along narrow banks as well as vast flood plain.

(e) *Double ferry point:* Some of the rivers have developed meanders and the land between the bends served as the best defensive site in early historical period. Eron, rich in inscriptions, lies on such a site of double ferry point.

(f) *River confluence* sites have, in several parts, been inhabited in the form of compact settlements; its examples being Pirotha, Madankheri (Vidisha), Aonri (Hoshangabad), Singaoda (Ujjain).

(g) *Levee* settlements have developed on the high banks or levees almost free from floods along big meandering rivers like Ganga, Ghaghara, Narmada, Chambal, Betwa etc. A few of them include Godgawn, Pathari Khurd, Behgaon (Khargone), Mardana, Bakawan (Barwaha, Khargone), Ghata Billod (Dhar), Nemawar (Dewas), Handia (Hoshangabad) and Dharampuri (Dhar)—all of compact type.

(h) Contact points of *break of slope* or slope-foot sites have given rise to several big compact villages; examples being Garhola (Sagar), Bagaud (Dhargone), Manpur (Indore), Bargoan in Khandwa in Malwa region, in the Siwalik hills zone settled by Kanets in lower Himalayas and in other areas on such junction points.

(i) *Terrace site* settlements are occupied by mostly Gujars in the Siwalik hills and the Dun and in lesser Himalayan zone by Kanets. They enjoy the benefit of proximity of water, flat cultivable terrain good for means of transport etc., as well as for grazing. Volcanic mount terraces provide such sites up to last dividing rest line, *i.e.*, Zuquolla Mounts in Ethiopia where settlements scatter surrounding the cone slope. Woods and easily available cultivable slopes provide sustenance.

(j) *Alluvial fan* sites have attracted people since historical times. Often many converging routes merge in one main road or street towards the apex of the alluvial fans. The three segments—upper, middle and lower— are observed as occupied by various groups of people in the Himalayan *terai* belt.

(k) *Natural basin* settlements are commonly found in the little desert region of Rajasthan. Surrounded by sand ridges, they are located with radial layout where converge many foot paths of the area.

(l) *Amphitheatrical basin crest site* settlements occupy the space a little below the water divide, the typical example being Nashal.

(m) *Ravined upland sites* have two diverse types: (a) edge sites having settlements younger than the ravines, and (b) interior sites having settlements older than the edge settlements and ravines.

(n) *Stream islands* in big rivers serve as good settlement sites, *i.e.*, Mokalpur and Gobaraha in Varanasi amidst Ganga channels.

Such types of sites are further to be named as *hill settlements* having hilly physiographic characteristics at the base, hence separate treatment. It is rightly remarked that with its self-evident disadvantages for agriculture and life in a peaceful countryside and its aesthetic recommendations, the origin, history and survival of the hill village offer intriguing problems.

A careful study of topographical sheets and keen observations in field make it possible to categorize sites of hill settlements as discussed below:

(i) *Parallel to contour site:* Such settlements spread on hill slopes almost parallel to contour as regards their housing, street plan etc. Tora and Bori Wali are examples.

(ii) *Irregular to contour site:* Some settlements occupy such sites due to fundamental diversity in physical form. Besia (Sagar) is the best example. Jujharpani in Udaipura (Raisen) represents a similar instance. Tribals in the Satpura and Vindhya hills present several such examples due particularly to their racial characteristics of occupying separate sites on different heights.

(iii) *Close knit cluster or crest site:* These settlements occupy some available level surface above the slope and below the steep sides. Bikrampur in Mungaoli (Guna) and Sanchi (Raisen) citable examples.

(iv) *High valley site:* Such settlements occupy small river basins on high divides of the Satpuras. Korkus and Barelas inhabit the trace, examples being Ramkola in Sendhwa (Khargone) and Dongaria (Raisen).

(v) *Saddle site:* These settlements occupy a saddle between two hills presenting a defensive site. Budho (Sagar) is the best example. The Aravalli out-crops region has many radial and elongated settlements of such gap sites. Such sites are in abundance in the lesser Himalayan region.

(vi) *Summit sites.* These are better suited where water is available and woods supply fuel and hunting ground. Khurmabad in Sendhwa (Khargone) and Chargawan in Udaipura (Raisen) are good examples.

(vii) *Ride top sites :* These are occupied by people during the process of settlement starting from slope foot after clearing the wood. Jagthar in Banda (Sagar) and Gadra in Betul and Mandu in Dhar are examples.

(Viii) *Lower ridge site or dyke sites.* These are often inhabited by people forming compact to semi-compact settlements along with the cultivated land below. The examples are Chainpura and Patpiri in Udaipura (Raisen) and Wail and Dedula of Manawar in Dhar.

It would be pertinent to mention here itself that the siting and distributional pattern of these settlements present a lot of disadvantages: steep approach and consequent difficulties of transporting loads to the villages and of reaching it on foot from the main road; the remoteness from the main arteries of trade and social life; scarcity of water supply; costly construction of wells and failure of this source of supply in period of drought; thin soil cover and rapid depletion on high steep slopes; lack of enough fertile lands; the general poverty of agriculture; exposure to wind and weather; and dangers of animals. Defence and religious factors in early historic and medieval period have played major role in siting and distribution and continuation of these villages. Invasions from outside compelled the aboriginals, like other parts of the world, to shift to hilly areas and occupy some fertile tracts, clear the woods and live upon the forest resources. But, now most of the rural settlements, with some exceptions, lie within the agricultural zone of altitude isolated and dispersed. Medieval fortresses are mostly deserted and inhabitants have shifted down to the small river basins. Some fort settlements on high summits, once developed into towns, lie ruined only to attract some tourists and archaeologists at present.

Vegetational

Removal of forests started since proto-historical times and humanization and occupance of suitable forests sites mentioned in epics speak about the settlement process on forest sites. Along with occupance, forest preservation seems to have been the motto of forest settlers who even worshipped trees of varied species. This shows the affection of settlers towards life sustaining qualities of forests. On one hand, they possess the ambivalent attitude of fear and mystical reverence on the other, forests are regarded as an integral element of primordial nature or even the seat of Hundu Gods and Goddesses. So, the culture trait of preservation continued since past still survives in spite of the technological exploitaion. Of the varied site types, two have spatial, territorial origin and spread.

(i) *Forest edge sites* are in the areas where margins are cleared and inhavited. This may be near a spring or stream on level plain or no spurs. Such sites scatter near all types of protected or reserved forests. These lands provided easy access to woods for wood product and grazing ground and piece of tract available for construction of house, cultivation and wood-cutting. *Terai* and Mirzapur in Uttar Pradesh, and Jhabua (Malwa) in Madhya Pradesh present various examples.

(ii) *Forest core sites* are mostly occupied after cutting by government agencies for convenience of administration or by tribals who naturally like to live away from the civilized part of the land. Such examples are available in forest areas of tropical zones occupied by the Pygmies, Negritos and other old primitive tribals. Newly developed areas also exhibit such sites now being changed into high hamlets. Old *ashramas* are better examples to be named.

Cultural Sites

The man-made landscape presents many forms showing associations during the occupance of a particular area. Settlements occupy such sites which later on are so much deeply interlinked that it becomes difficult to tell which preceded what. Roads, railways, canals, dams, reservoirs, hydle projects, hydle sub-stations, factory point, wells, tanks, temples etc., all seem to have attracted settlers and settlements. A few of these cultural features have already been discussed. Now we emphasize the general cultural features easily discernible on the cadastral and large scale topographical maps.

(i) *Roads:* Many ancient routes in oriental world are associated with large settlements, a few of them converted into urban centres like Ujjain, Vidisha, Mathura etc. The pilgrim routes also exhibit settlements still existing in changed form; whether it be silk route of traders or others or pedestrians, they are proof of being antecedent to settlements. The ancient Ram-Janaki Road extending from Ayodhya to Janakpur (Bihar), Parikrama Road surrounding Ayodhya, Kashi and other *teerthas* present clear-cut examples of such sites. Even Shahi Road (administrative highways) of medieval period too are antece-dent to newer settlement, *i.e.* Muratganj, Jangiganj, Mirzamurad etc., along Grand-Trank Road. Halting places of old pilgrim routes are other examples. *Sarai* (inns) along routes are many in number, *i.e.* Khojwa in Varanasi, and Kanjari Sarai in Moradabad.

(ii) *Canal sites* are newer phenomena and attract settlers due to facilities of water, transport road and transportation line. Many settlements clung to such sites and are developing into market centres. Defence site has also been a centripetal force to settlers.

(iii) *Canal road* crossings are other cultural features to act as sites.

(iv) *Road river crossings* present good sites showing interaction of various factors remarkably stamped on the arrangement of dwellings, layout plan, development of roads themselves in relation to water features.

(v) *Road side halt spots :* Some newly originated and established halt spots along highways are direct results of road and means of transport, *i.e.*, truck and bus in particular. Pack-track site settlements are other examples.

(vi) *Forts :* In most cases constructed for defence such sites exhibit good settlements in hilly, plateau and plain areas too. Mostly they served as administrative centres. Bhar castles (small forts or fortress) now in ruined form as big *teela* (hill) are scattered throughout the Ganga plain. Tefqee in Ethiopia presents an example of Italian occupance of the site.

(vii) *Miscellaneous religious sites :* Besides temples of Gods and Goddesses, several other sites related to hero (converted into deity), *majars,* saints' church etc., Get sanction from society as sacred places where tanks, *dharmshala* (resting place), school are provided, well-linked with settlements. These sites later on develop into hamlets. *Chhatri and satii* site settlements also deve-lop at village settlement level as a separate hamlet.

Layout Plan/Pattern of Settlements

The external shape of the morphological structure of settlements reveals some geometrical form as a result of definite layout of houses, streets, open spaces etc. in relation to the field. This form is pattern defined as, relationship of one dwelling to another, sometimes irrespective of site. This relationship of dwellings presents, distinct form of the village which in itself is a natural growth determined by physical and cultural setting of the region. These, comprising various factors, find treatment in the sequel.

Ancient

Before going into detail about the pattern of the present villages, we may have passing reference to the ancient rural settlements recognized by the Buddhist, Jain and Pauranika literatures. The Jain texts speak about Uttanamallakakara (looking like an open bowl) in *Avanmukha* (circular in pattern), *Khanda* (semi-circular), *Patalika* (avenue pattern), *Valabhi* (settlement with the trees planted at the four corners) and *Ruckak* (with uneven ground ringed with trees) *(Brihatkalpasutrabhasya* 1103, 1104, 1105, 1106*).*

Mansara Shilpshastra and *Arthashastra* have description about rural settlement plans which are not perceptible at present in their true form; based on the description and illustrations of Acharya and Havel these are treated below.

Dandaka was rectangular or square and possessed a rampart of the same shape; *sarvatobhadra,* having oblong or square plan—the temple of Brahma, Vishnu and Shiva being located in the centre and inhabited by the Brahmins and religious aesthetic; *padmaka* was lotus shaped; *svastika* resembled the mystic figure of Svastika; *prastara* was either square or oblong in shape; *karmuka,* semi-circular or semi-elliptical like bow; *nandyavarta* circular; and *chaturmukh,* having four gates extending east to west. These plans have, however, been obliterated, modified, during the long period of history and only relics are visualized in the form of fortresses or walled villages. The patterns visible in the field, on the large-scale maps, cadastral maps and referred to in records present little conscious planning of rural settlements. Yet, we find an arrangement in the internal structural elements as well as external outlines of the villages. The compact villages so conspicuously found in the middle Ganga valley, in the Malwa region and elsewhere, "present a definite layout and an unmistakable connection between the configuration of the site, surface water (river, tank, pond, well), the nature of soil, cultivation, groves and the shapes of the fields." These patterns are closely related to cart tracks, roads, mosques and temples, the cultural elements and also to the physical environment of the dwellings like site. Caste communities based on *jajmani* system play their own part in occupying separate sectors and so do the vertical differences in house system based upon caste, prestige and status of villager. Impact of defence, a significant element to determine the shape and size of villages in the past, is still visualized in several rural settlements in many part of the world. Let us see these patterns one by one.

Rectangular or Squared Plan

The ancient village plans, discussed earlier, reveal that this plan is the heritage of the past. These are easily adaptable on level plains under plough culture. It is easier to plough in rectangular plots and these were maintained to keep close relation with the orientation of dwellings having squared or rectangular rooms. In Japan and China respectively, the *Jori* and *Han den* systems of land measure involve the partitioning and repartitioning of the land into square units which is related to the rectangular form settlements. The *bigha* system of land measure seems to be the end-product of these orientations and ploughing system. The arrangement of paths and houses find maximum place in compact villages of such plan. Like *bigha,* the traditional furrow long (furlong) became 220 yards, the traditional width of ridge 22 yards, thus evolved the common land measure of an acre 484 square yards, the area of the usual unit of ploughing the strip.

This rectangular plan is conspicuously found in proper Malwa plateau, Nimar upland and in the Narmada valley plain around Maheshwar. These rectangular villages may be of natural growth or regular square villages occupying the four squares on a crossing, varying in size according to the attractive or restrictive forces of the site. Guljhara, Piplod Khurd and Khurda, treated elsewhere, present distinct morphological structure.

Chess Board Plan

A rough grid plane is visible in some of the villages in the Narmada valley where two main lanes intersect each other at the centre. Other small lanes go to interior houses parallel to the former main lanes. In between these lanes, houses are arranged in sectors or castes. Wells are found in one corner of lane-crossing sometimes serving a ward or the sector but open for all castes people. In these villages, high caste Brahmins or Rajputs occupy the central position and lower castes inhabit the marginal areas. The central parts of Dharar and Manpur villages present such plan.

Radial Plan

In such a village, a number of streets and lanes converge on its centre, the nucleus occupied by Patel's or landlord's *garhi* (big house) or a market place or some temples of *Shiva or Hanuman* (the Hindu

Gods). Most of these villages are old in origin representing the ancient aggregation of maximum possible houses under the protection of *garhi*. The well situated in the centre also serves the villagers.

Dopple-Dorfer Pattern

Villages separated by roads, streets, small rivulets or ponds present double or sometimes treble nucleation, particularly in the level of the Narmada valley and in northern plateau region of Malwa. Settlements like Bhugore and Bhilkheri (Shujalpur) and Datana-Matana (Ujjain) seem to have grown by colonisation upon the edge of the other. Other examples are Damkhera and Bardia Surta, Batholi Tajpura (Maheshwar), Dival-Gujaria Khera (Khargone), Rampura-Gadaria-Rupadeh (Seoni-Malwa) and Nimach-Malona, Barkala-Charkhera (Harda).

Strassendorfer

Some villages working as rural markets are linked with the neighbouring towns by road and lie on both sides of roads or streets and present street village plan. Sometimes houses arranged in line along an open space resemble same pattern particularly, found in Gond inhabited areas of Betul. Such pattern is visualized in the Narmada valley as well as on Nimar upland.

Linear Plan (Reihendorfer)

Some settlements develop in one direction like kellendorfer or strassendorfer and include Dickinsons' marschhufendorfer (marsh village), waldhufendorfer (forest villages), thukolonien and gutskolonien (estate settlements). Attractive forces encourage linear growth and restrictive elements of marsh, forest or highland prevent expansion in other sides and linear plan extends along the track or pathway leading to ferry point or big village.

Double Linear (Angerdorfer)

In the Narmada valley plain of Hoshangabad, some villages occupy high ground spreading in one direction in two lines separated by cart tracks or open space leading to field and forest.

Elongated Plan

Drypoint villages develop along the high level surface restricted by floods or dissected topography form two sides and form elongated shape. Sometimes houses aligned along the stream for the advantage of water front present such forms. Matkuli Mongra (Sohagpur), Hari

Dhana (Betul) and others in the Narmada valley along the river represent well-developed elongated plan. Morphological structure of Matkuli village treated elsewhere gives spatial expansion of settlements in between river and *nala*.

Hollow Pattern

An open or unbuilt space, a pond, high ground or *satti* (structure, platform, temple in the memory of a pious lady) or temple or big banyan or *peepal* tree occupying the central place in a settlement of compact form resembles such plan visualized in many parts of the world, here exemplified by Kajalkheri (Hoshangabad), Dalchi (Barwaha), Piranpur (Mungoli), and Barauda in Jaora (Ratlam).

L-Shaped Pattern

Sometimes at the junction of a main road and a minor street or track, two rectangular blocks of houses meet at right angles. The smaller block represents new growth due to attractive forces applying in one side greater force and restrictive forces fixing them to extend in one direction. Chatarkhera (Hoshangabad), Churia (Betul), Kodhur (Khandwa) and Dogaha Kalan in Khurai and others in the Narmada valley in Udaipura and Hoshangabad along the river represent such plan.

T-Shaped Plan

In some villages, a smaller limb extends towards cultivated fields at an angle to give the L- shape a new form resembling T. Such a limb also develops from a main rectangular or elongated form of village into T-shape following the terrain. Sita Dongari etc., are citable examples.

Semi-Circular Plan

These settlements develop along the bend of streams and the crescent shape of meanders in semi-circular form separated by streets as exemplified by Dolaria, Semri (Hoshangabad), Barkachh Kalan (Bareli) and Maniar in Ballia in Uttar Pradesh.

Oval Pattern

Sometimes restrictive forces determine the extent of some villages to take oval shape with houses huddled together to occupy maximum available space particularly found in the Narmada valley and on Nimar upland.

Triangular Plan

Sometimes sites or villages provide peculiar triangular shape, the main block forming the base and other extensions growing towards the apex as shown in Figure. 2.25 K_1-K_2.

Ditch Walled

Defence has played significant role for constructing walls and ditches around villages of compact form, especially in Guna and Sagar districts, showing distinct forms.

Horse-Shoe Pattern

On the arcuate bends of river meanders, a special form of settlement is visualized which is named as horse-shoe plan village like Bamhangaon Kalan and Chitawad. Some oblong villages are found along the higher levees and oxbow lakes or the abandoned channels or the rivers.

Polygonal Pattern

Many old big and compact villages both on the plateau and in the Narmada valley represent distinct geometrical form of hexagon, octagon and polygon indicating aggregation of dwellings of diverse castes on the fertile soil.

Amorphous Pattern

Most of the villages, grown amidst irregular physical surrounding, with hamlets having dispersion and having no definite pattern under a single nomenclature, hence amorphous pattern seems best they deserve. Amorphous is the best form in interior countryside where every direction to the field is street/pathway is rightly stated. Udaigir, Mandu, and Aser villages treated elsewhere present similar morphological structure.

Green Villages

Dudley Stamp recorded many village greens in England which originated in forest clearings. They protected animals and resembled Bantu *Kraals* and other enclosures in settlements in Africa. These also acted as pastoral centres, social centres, market centres, defensive centres etc. They may be recognized by the shape of their green.

Planned Village Pattern

A few 'model' villages are planned to get definite shape. These are also called 'garden' villages in England mostly for providing residence to industrial employees. New model villages/settlements in India organized by non-government organizations as well as government colonies represent planned pattern. The *Kolkhozy* of the former U.S.S.R. presents another types of layout plan for agricultural organizations. The communal settlements of Israel and Coliery settlements in mining areas show planned character in shape. New ideal villages are coming up on Indian landscape with various amenities and institutional structures depicting planned layout.

Sample Villages

Now we can visualize some of these patterns with the help of structural details of the following villages :

Guljhara: Cultivator's Village in the Narmada Valley

Guljhara exhibits rectangular plan with few exceptions of additional growth along the highway of recent origin which is bound to take D-shape along the Maheshwar road in near future. The community structure presents sectorwise spatial occupations. Bhils form a separate hamlet near the forest (60 in number), only one Muslim household lies by the road. Brahmins and cultivators occupy the core of the village, businessmen, are long the road and agricultural and service class people on peripheral areas each separated by *kuchcha* lanes and a few concrete streets. The ginning and pressing mills of cotton in extreme south are distinct morphological features. Mostly engaged in agricultural operations, villagers depend also on manufacturing, household industry and a few on trade and transport. Cash cropping and manufacturing will soon change the morphological conditions of the villages in the south.

Piplod Khurd: A Nimar Upland Village

The village (21^0 48'N–76^0 17' E, Population 2,973) lies on the Nimar upland about 17km south of Khandwa along the metalled road running to Burhanpur. A *nala,* tributary to the Abna river, flows in the north along the village land boundary. It derives its name from the Piploda State, the counterpart village Piplod Khas lying about 30 km in the east. Like Dharar village of Malwa plateau, this village was also preoccupied by aboriginals who were relegated by the state grantees to the marginal areas. It is a compact rectangular village, a typical settlement of the Nimar upland. The *garhi* (landlord's palace) named as *bari* and *chhoti* reminds us about the two clan members round whose dwellings aggregated other Rajputs of closer kindred or from relations or others as helpers and dependents.

The village is now electrified and flour mill and pumping sets are coming up as innovations. With 3,133 acres of total, 2,869 acres of cultivated land devoted to *jowar,* cotton, groundnut, wheat and others in order of importance, a few orchards of orange, lemon and papaya, about 100 acres of forest and 50 acres under fallow land, the village exhibits a true rural landscape of the region.

Khurda: A Mixed Type Missionary Village

Situated in a depression between hills of the Vindhyas, drained by the headwaters of the Ajnar river, the village (21°23'N–75°39'E; Population 1,233) lies 1.5 km south-west of Khurdi, a road bus terminus, 8 km from Manpur, the market village. A *kachcha*-cum-concrete road joins the village with Khurdi. Three hamlets of Christians, Gujars and Bhils have grown at intervals having cultivated fields in the neighbourhood surrounded by forested hills on the boundary. The missionary sector is well-planned having residential quarters, health centre, schools, hostel, church, tubewell and wells within easy reach by streets and roads. Gujar houses assemble haphazardly varying in space, size and shape with temples in the north. Bhils occupy separate space quite different in outlook and layout. Two houses of businessmen are later additions.

Dharar: An Ancient Village

The village (23°15' N—75°12'E, Population 3,975) is a squared compact settlement located on the Mahi-Maleni divide, 11 km south-east of Ratlam on Ratlam-Badnawar road. The village was originated by some Hindus about 1,900 years ago as is evident from Mahakaleshwar temple of 89 *Vikram Samvat* but its real growth in the present form came after Rajput occupation in the seventeenth century, as a Jagir village, under the Ratlam chief Ratan Singh. It was a tehsil headquarters till 1974 when Ratlam usurped its place. Dharar is a corrupt form of Dhadamar named after a grand victory against invaders during the historical period.

The village, as a revenue unit, consists of six other hamlets based upon castes like Bhil, Kolambi and Balai, far apart from the main nucleus. One is concerned here with this central settlement presenting a chessboard plan, the main road and street running from the highway to the Tejaji temple. Other streets run at right angle connected by zigzag lanes which divide caste sections. *Hanuman Mandir* (the *garhi*) lies in the centre and the core of the village around it is occupied by the Brahmins and Kshatriyas. A detached aggregation along the main road depicts signs of new dispersion. It is also remarkable that Bhils, the original settlers, have been relegated to one corner separated by lanes.

Manpur: An Administrative and Market Village

Manpur village (22^0 25'N—75^0 37'E, Population 3,939) lies along the National Highway 3,21 km south of Mhow and 44 km from Indore, on the plateau at a point whence the Vindhyan scarp breaks its height and level surface ends into rugged hilly terrain. Though originally established by Man Singh, whose ruined 'Bhavan' still lies there, it got impetus during the British rule as a centre of the Agency, Manpur, being a separate British territory, governing the strategical location and as tehsil headquarters, recently shifted to Mhow. Surrounded by hills, the nearest being a spur of the great knot of the main Vindhyas, in the south-east corner of the map whose lower part is occupied by Agency House of the past, the village morphology reflects the impact of historico-culturo economic transformations.

Datana: A Mixed Type Village of Malwa Proper

Lying in the fertile valley of the Kshipra river, the village ($23^0$12'N—$75^0$47' E, Population 1,079) is situated along the metalled road running from Ujjain to Dewas, 9 km distant from the historical capital of Avanti, Ujjain—the seat of Mahakal whence spread the Aryan culture of the past having its clear impact on the rural landscape. The dopple-dorfer village along with Matana separated by a *nala* originating from a big tank, appears to owe its origin to the feudal grant system signifying 'duttam' (given over) to some Jagirdar whose descent has now lost his genealogy. The morphological expressions of the settlement exhibit occupance of the site by Rajputs and other cultivators including Muslims either through purchase of the land or as revenue makers of later periods. The small *nala* bisects it into halves as does the *kachacha* road in the northern section. Mostly engaged in agricultural operations, a few employed in Ujjain, the villagers are not unaffected by cash-nexus society of the city or *shahar* as they call it.

Matkuli: A New Village

Matkuli (22^0 32'N—78^0 29'E, Population 1,803) lies on the crossroad of metalled roads joining Pipariya and Panchmarhi and the other running to Chhindwaa, on a plateau surrounded by forested hills of the Satpuras in Sohagpur tehsil (Hoshangabad), 23 km from Pipariya and 29 km north of Panchmarhi on the bank of the Denwa river. It derives its name from *Meth-Kuli* (inhabited by contractors and labours) engaged in forest clearing and road construction during the last century.

Primarily occupied by Gond Thakurs, it was inhabited by other caste people on the basis of purchase of land by enterprises or revenue makers. As usual, caste sectors separated by lanes, pathways or some common place spread in elongated form. General outlook varies and so the size, space and height of the house.

Mandu: Village of Political Origin

The village (22°20'N—75°25'E, Est. 1986, Pop. 2,808) occupies now the ruined fort of Mandu (2270' or 667 meters), 36 km south of Dhar, on the southern scarp-bend of the Vindhyas. Mandu is a corrupt form of *Mandap Durga* (looking like canopy) or Mandavgarh, a stronghold from the earliest days. Farishta refers to traditions which tell about its origin by Anand Deo Basis (A.D. 531-574) but it is true that it remained a scene of seize and battle between the chiefs of Gujarat and Malwa, and Muslims and Parmars. Mandu is closely related to Hoshangshah and almost synonymous with Baz Bahadur and his highly talented musician consort Rupmati. The forest around the village remained often very thick; its best days have, however gone. The archaeological department now looks after the ruins of the old capital and village panchyat runs the rural work.

The village is now occupied by cultivators, shopkeepers, tongamen, agricultural labour class, stock raisers and few others depending upon the rourists and limited trade.

Aser: A Forest Village Reminding Past

Situated on the lower slopes of the famous Asergarh hills, occupied by ruined fort of the same name along the road running from Khandwa to Burhanpur, 48 km from the former and 18 km from the latter, in Burhanpur tahsil, the village is a typical forest village of mixed caste.

Udaigir

It derives its name from the Udaigir caves having Jain and Hindus statues. It seems that the old village was demolished by bigot Muslims and the village flourished later on during the British rule. Inhabitants are mostly cultivators, stock raisers or herders and agricultural labourers. *Kachhi* is the dominating caste which is followed by *Gaderia*.

8

Location of Economic Activities and Spatial Organization of Economies

A Simplified Model of Spatial Organization of Economic Activities

The space economy is real, but to understand its fundamental aspects we will make it unreal by assuming away much of the reality that gives it its chaotic nature. This is a standard tactic in economics, but the reader must be cautious to relax the assumptions before determining the actual outcome of a particular spatial economic relation in the real world. Some of the assumptions we make to simplify reality will pertain to the land itself, others to the inhabitants of that land.

Land Assumptions

- Completely flat and homogeneous in every respect—an isotropic (having equal physical properties in all directions) plain
- No barriers to movement across our isotropic plain—movement can occur in all directions with equal ease
- Only one type of transportation
- Transportation costs—the costs of overcoming the friction of distance—are exactly proportional to distance
- Costs 2X more to travel 200 miles than it does to travel 100 miles
- Limitless...unbounded—so that real boundary complexities can be ignored

Population Assumptions

- Spread perfectly evenly over the plain—density the same everywhere

- Each of these people is identical—demands and preferences are the same
- Same financial resources
- Spends money same way
- Each is fully aware of all possible behavioural alternatives—perfect knowledge
- Each acts in a totally rational way—the desire to optimize
- Each producer aims for largest possible profit
- Each consumer aims to satisfy needs as cheaply as possible
- This world is a perfectly competitive market
- Large number of producers, a single one of which is unable to excessively influence the market solution

Spatial Organization of Production of One Good

- Production can be established at home because all materials are available everywhere at same cost
- Market for the good is the point where it is produced, people come there to purchase that good
- What is the market area for that good
- Depends on the real price that has to be paid to procure the good
- Price at point of sale—market price, AND
- Cost of travelling to and from that point
- The latter is the more important of these two in determining market area size
- Example:
- Market price for sausage is $1.50/lb.
- Customers have $6.00/wk to buy sausage
- Those customers right next to sausage shop get 4 lbs. of sausage
- Those needing to travel to the butcher get less, because they have to use some of their $6.00 in paying the cost of travelling to the butcher.
- The farther away from point of sale (POS), the fewer sausage they can buy
- If travel costs = $.10/mile for a return trip, then a person living 15 miles from POS must spend $1.50 to get there, leaving only $4.50 left to buy sausage...so they can only purchase 3 lbs.

- As distance increases, real price also increases
- At 30 miles only 2 lbs. can be purchased, at 45 miles only 1 lb., at 60 miles there is no money left to buy sausages when they reach POS.
- Anyone living beyond 45 miles from POS will not be making the trip...This Distance Represents The *Range* Of That Good
- If the producer wants to remain in business, then there is a minimum amount of sausage that he/she must sell to cover basic costs and yield some profit
- If that weekly return is $105 then 70 customers must buy one pound of sausage each (or some similar combination)...only a few of them, in our isotropic plain, will live next to POS, the rest will be displaced some distance from POS
- The area around POS that encompasses enough customers to sell the weekly minimum (in this case 30 miles given the equal spacing assumption) Is Called The *Threshold* Of That Particular Good
- The THRESHOLD of a good must not extend beyond the RANGE of that good, or losses will be incurred
- Customers located outside the range of the single producer of sausage, represent unserved demand and, thus, market entry opportunities to other sausage makers...so others will locate outside of the range of the established producer so as to eliminate the cost of competition
- In our isotropic plain, producers will arrange themselves according to the range of the goods they produce...producer B will locate at least twice the range from producer A
- And so on...until the area is saturated (all demand is served)
- As a matter of additional fact, the distance between the threshold and range of each producer equals excessive profits...therefore, more market entry opportunities
- So the more producers will enter squeezing the locations between producers until all are separated at threshold distance, not range
- Producer A will be located twice the threshold distance from producer B
- *The result is a "compact, uniform lattice of production centers, each serving hexagonal market areas (circles, when squished*

together leave unserved "interstitial" spaces between them, hexagons don't) of identical size, equivalent to the threshold size for that good."

What Happens when other goods are Introduced into our Isotropic Plain?

The same principles would apply no matter the service or good in question...BUT thresholds and ranges will differ from one good or service to another according to:

- Basic price (including relative transport costs)
- Frequency with which they are demanded
- Low order goods (small threshold, small range)
- High order goods (large threshold, large range)

Size of hexagonal market area networks will vary according to good order

- Low order goods = smaller hexagons
- High order goods = larger hexagons

High order goods will be available at few locations across the isotropic plain...low order goods available at many locations

Moreover, the locations at which these different types of goods can be acquired will tend to cluster together (to be explained by Economies of Agglomeration later) into CENTRAL PLACES

The primary function of Central Places (towns, cities, etc.) is to provide its surrounding population with goods and services

- The relative importance of each central place depends on both the number and the order of goods and services it provides
- A central place on a particular level in the hierarchy of central places provides not only goods and services that are specific to its highest order level, but also all other goods and services of lower order

Within a ranked hierarchy of ten available goods...the highest order good will be available in only one central place, for example, whereas the lowest order goods would be available in that same central place as well as numerous smaller places according, again to total demand and size of threshold value for that particular good.

Each level in the hierarchy is also characterized by equal distances between centers on that hierarchical level

- All "A" centers (higher order) are the same distance from each other, each "B" center is equidistant from other "B" centers,

AND B-level distances are less than A-level distances...and so on down the central place hierarchy

Central Place Theory was particularly rigorous in its formative stages from mid-1800s to mid-1900s. The rigid spatial patterns suggested by Christaller, underwent several modifications to allow for the distortion of reality, but the essential components described above remain. Two other useful principles refer to the distortion of the hexagons as traffic routes and differences in population distribution are allowed to change over space:

- Hexagons will tend to "elongate" in the direction of any linear transportation route intersecting its area
- Hexagons of the same good order will be larger in spaces with a sparser population density

Spatial Organization of Agricultural Production

Because agriculture tends to use large units of land, how those large units of land are used becomes the organizing principle for agricultural production.

Given the hierarchy of demand across a particular space—like our isotropic plain—how will the production of agricultural goods be organized spatially?

- In general, different units of land will be devoted to the uses that can achieve the highest return per unit of land, as allocated by ECONOMIC RENT
- ECONOMIC RENT is the surplus income that can be obtained from one unit of land above what can be obtained from an inferior unit of land
- Measured against land at the margin, or limit, of cultivation
- Marginal land is just capable of producing a return large enough to cover the cost of bringing it into production
- ECONOMIC RENT is a measure of the level of return that the market at large (consisting of all potential bidders for land) would expect a particular piece of land to produce...a measure of the advantage, as the bidders see it, of one piece of land over another.
- In our isotropic plain, the only advantage that one piece of land can have over another piece of land is its location in relation to the market for agricultural products...for this reason we can refer to ECONOMIC RENT as LOCATION RENT.

Spatial Organization of One Agricultural Product

Where land is located relative to the market is the critical factor in determining the net advantage that one piece of land has over another.

- The greatest advantage accrues to that land nearest the market

LR = Y(m-c) – Ytd

LR = Location Rent

Y = yield (quantity produced per unit land)

"m" = market price per unit product

"c" = production cost per unit product

"t" = transport rate per unit distance

"d" = distance of the unit of land from the market

Location rent decreases as distance from market increases

Total transport costs increase as distance from market increases

Given the above formula, at some distance from the market the farmer's net return will be completely obliterated by the costs of transporting the product to the market—at that point the "ceiling rent" will be encountered and location of that agricultural product will no longer be feasible.

Imaginary Milk Producer Example

Y = 100 gallons per acre

"m" = $5.00 per gallon

"c" = $3.00 per gallon

"t" = $0.05 per mile

At the market the value of the milk will be:

LR = 100 ($5 - $3) – 100 (0.05 X 0) = $200

Following this pattern and incrementally increasing "d" we reach LR = $0 at 40 miles

- No milk will be produced beyond 40 miles form the market unless yields, prices, production costs, or transport rates change.

Spatial Organization of Several Agricultural Products

The basic principle *for each product* will remain the same.

- Each product will be identified by its particular "bid-rent curve."
- A comparison of these curves for each land use will determine the ceiling-rent of each.

- The one with the highest ceiling-rent at the given distance will be able to procure the land for that use.

The prevailing pattern will be a series of circles concentric on the market for those products, arranged by the bid-rent curves for each particular land use.

- This is referred to as an *Economic Optima-Limits Model*

The actual arrangement of agricultural land uses predicted by this model will be distorted by *Physical Optima-Limits* criteria—some crops just won't grow in some places, and will grow best when certain physical attributes are present in the landscape.

Economic Activities around the World

Economic activities around the world are deeply integrated and interconnected in a global system of trade, production, and consumption. Global markets have developed as a result of liberal trade policies that have reshaped where and how goods and services are produced, and who consumes them. In this conceptual framework for the *Global Economy* module, you will be introduced to geographic concepts and theories that can help you understand how economic activities are organized spatially and integrated across scales from the local to the global, and what this means for people, places, and environments in different regions of the world. Geographers study the spatial activities of economies at different scales. In the global economy, these activities include patterns of international trade, the flow of information through communication networks, regional flows of capital and resources, and the spatial distribution of labour. Increasingly, economic processes and patterns are affected by *globalization* – a process by which "events, activities, and decisions in one part of the world can have significant consequences for communities in distant parts of the globe".

One way to begin to understand the global economy is to classify the activities that produce goods and services that are consumed by people worldwide. These activities can be divided into four sectors:

1. *Primary sector* activities are concerned with the direct extraction of materials from the earth's surface, generally through agriculture, mining, fishing, and forestry.
2. *Secondary sector* activities include industries that process, transform, and assemble raw materials into products like cars, computers, and clothing.
3. *Tertiary sector* activities involve the provision of goods and services to people in exchange for payment. Examples of service providers include banks, universities, and retail shops.

4. Finally, there is a *quaternary sector* of activities related to the management of data and information.

Geographic Dimensions of the Global Economy

According to Dicken (2007), the global economy can be conceived as horizontal areas of investment, production and consumption that have become vertically integrated across extensive geographical scales (from local to regional to territorial to global). In this system, geographic patterns of economic investment, production, and consumption are shaped by state governments as well as by supranational (e.g., World Trade Organization) and regional (e.g., NAFTA) financial groupings through environmental regulations, taxes, labour laws, and other policies.

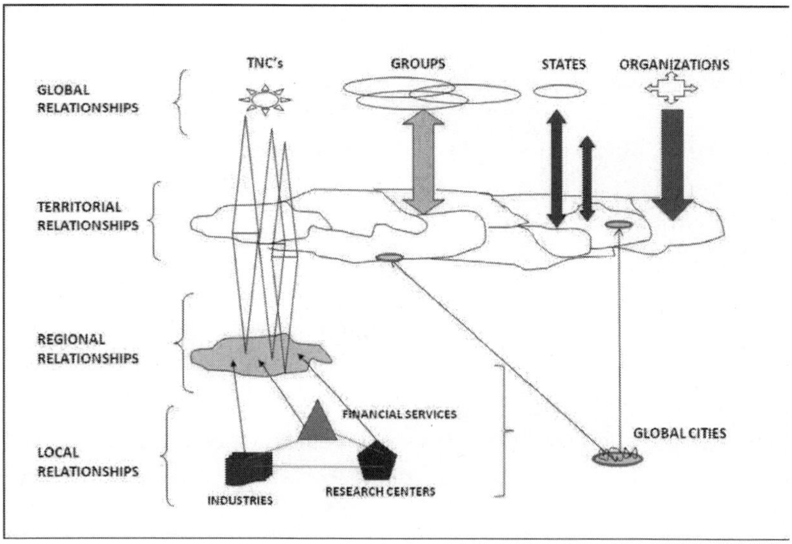

As you continue reading this conceptual framework, keep in mind Sayer and Walker's distinction between industries, enterprises, and workplaces. *Industry* describes a section of the economy associated with the exploitation of a renewable or non-renewable resource; it can also refer to any of a large variety of services (e.g., health care, transportation, finance, insurance). An *enterprise* – a company, firm or corporation – is the locus of economic decision-making and control. Enterprises own resources, employ workers, organize production, and make contracts. Enterprises can be as large as Transnational Corporations (TNCs) or as small as a local store. *Workplaces* are factories, farms, shops, offices, and all kinds of mobile and temporary sites. They are places of production where labour is organized into some sort of productive activity. A dairy factory, for example, requires substantial investment in the form of equipment and buildings, the hiring of a sizable workforce, and the purchase of raw materials and a range of other consumable items.

Competitive Advantage and Industrial Location

The formation, expansion, or contraction of a given industry depends on decisions made by enterprises. Indeed, enterprises are profit driven and regularly evaluate their activities in terms of production costs and marketing strategies (e.g., "Which is the most profitable way to distribute and sell a particular good or service?" "How can we get our product to the market at a lower price than our competitors?").

Today, decisions made by many enterprise — especially those known as transnational corporations — must take into account global *and* local conditions such as the existing balance between supply and demand, the cost of credit, expected return rates (profits), labour costs, and overall production costs at a given location or in multiple locations.

How do enterprises in different industries decide where to locate their firms and manufacturing plants? In some cases, it is purely an idiosyncratic decision, related to the chief executive's preferences or where a family business was started. More often than not, however, it is a carefully thought out decision that involves the consideration of numerous factors all related to how to best generate competitive advantage. Michael Porter proposed a Theory of Competitive Advantage (1990) that views factor conditions, demand conditions, related and supporting industries, and firm structure, strategy, and rivalry as being key components of a firm's ability to develop competitive advantage. Firms that amass more favourable conditions in each of these areas are more likely to have competitive advantage. Additionally, factors such as government regulations and chance weigh on the ability of the firm to achieve competitive advantage. Without competitive advantage, it will be difficult for the firm or industry to be successful in the long term.

The Importance of Place in the Global Economy

Geographers are interested in the effects of trade policies promoting economic liberalization on local economies as well as how the conditions and activities in local places shape the processes of the global economy. Not only economic factors play a role in the decisions made by a particular enterprise. Non-economic factors – those that cannot be directly measured nor incorporated in the production cost – can also play a major role.

Indeed, economic activity is socially and culturally situated in places. These factors include, but are not limited to: business climate, political environment, educational attainment of the population, governmental competence, quality of life, and existing social capital. If a firm has similar production costs and a rate of capital return in two locations, choosing where to invest might involve an array of considerations such as: where do we encounter a more stable and trustworthy political system? Where is the firm more likely to find more skilled and responsible workers? What is the quality of life in each location?

As you may have guessed from reading about competitive advantage earlier, Porter's theory is inherently geographic. Factor conditions, demand conditions, related and supporting industries, and even firm structure, strategy, and rivalry all happen in a place. The government and chance circumstances of that place then also can impact the firm or industry. For that reason, it is not surprising that one of the applications of Porter's research has been the development of industry clusters to drive economic development and competitive advantage.

Think about it for a moment: Are there not places we automatically associate with the types of industry located there?. Detroit and automobiles, Hollywood and entertainment, Wall Street and finance, Silicon Valley and computers, and the list goes on. Firms who want to be considered a key player in a certain industry need to locate in these places to access knowledge and resources. Economies of scale are developed for a particular industry in a cluster. A labour pool that is properly skilled for the types of jobs necessary will situate itself near the cluster. Firms with similar infrastructure needs can share the costs of development and maintenance. All of this allows firms to reduce their fixed costs and increase their competitive advantage.

Think about it in more simple term: You want to open a lemonade stand. Your neighbour has an ice tea stand. If the two of you locate near to each other, you can share the costs of supplying both stands with water and other raw materials that are necessary to manufacture the final product. Employees who have been trained to work in the ice tea stand are just as qualified to work in the lemonade stand, so you do not need to search elsewhere for labour. Perhaps the two stands can then draw in a related business, like a cookie stand to complement your services and make the cluster more attractive to sophisticated consumers seeking a variety of products and therefore all the businesses will be more competitive.

Social capital has become an important concept to assess the importance of clustering. According to Putnam, social capital refers to the collective value of all "social networks" and the inclinations that arise from these networks to do things for each other. Social capital is a key component to building and maintaining democracy and free markets because these social and cultural relations serve to reduce uncertainty among local economic actors by providing tacit or collective knowledge, and by encouraging confidence and risk sharing. Amin and Thrift have further developed this line of thought in their concept of institutional thickness. Some economic theorists are skeptical of the importance of intangible factors such as social capital in a place, arguing the focus on a place's culture and social networks is a distraction from the "production of things" in those places. In any case, we live in a world that is constantly remaking itself. Enterprises are in a constant struggle to find new frontiers for investment, while at the same time abandoning other locations that have proven too costly or unprofitable.

The Global Economy and Interdependence

The global economy is nowadays a very complex system linking people and places through the trade and flow of goods, services, and information. Since the 1950s, the scope and reach of national economies expanded, leading to an increase in the number of exports produced for trade.

There are several elements that are responsible for the expansion of the global economy during the past several decades: new information technologies, reduction of transportation costs, the formation of economic blocs such as the North American Free Trade Association (NAFTA), and the reforms implemented by states and financial organizations in the 1980s aimed at liberalizing the world economy.

The importance, extent, and sheer economic scale of these spatial changes, most notably during the 1970s and 1980s, took many governments and industrial enterprises by surprise. Many governments struggled to react in the face of the industrial and labour relocations that took place and to recognize that the foundations of the new economy were no longer locally or nationally based, but were now global. Likewise, private firms had to adapt by restructuring their production systems to consider the most effective and efficient means of doing business in a global market.

One of the hallmark characteristics of the global economy is the concept of interdependence. Economic globalization is linking places around the world through activities such as production, trade, and consumption. As national economies become increasingly integrated through global trade, the economic growth of any given nation becomes increasingly dependent upon the economic welfare of its trade partners. Activities such as the choice of clothes you buy have a direct impact on the lives of people working in the nations that produce those goods. As Giddens put it, we now live in a world characterized by an "intensification of worldwide social relations (linking) distant realities in such a way that local events are shaped by events occurring many miles away, and vice versa".

With globalization, competition occurs between nations having different standards for worker pay, health insurance, and labour regulations. Corporations are able to benefit from lower labour costs found in developing regions, thanks to free-trade agreements and a new international division of labour. A worker in a high-wage country is thus increasingly struggling in the face of competition from workers in low-wage countries. Entire sectors of employment in developed countries are now subject to this growing international competition, and unemployment has crippled many localities. The outcome has been an international division of labour in all sectors of the economy. In particular, manufacturing is increasingly being contracted out to lower-cost locations, which are often found in developing countries with no minimum wage and few environmental regulations.

A good example of international division of labour can be found in the clothes-making industry. What was once a staple industry in most developed Western economies has now been relocated to developing countries in Central America, Eastern Europe, North Africa, Asia, and elsewhere.

This change has prompted some observers to ask questions that lie at the heart of the globalization debate: Are large retailers in the United States and Europe exploiting workers who are paid low wages in some developing regions? Is globalization placing developing countries on a road to a more advanced economy that will pay higher wages in the future?

Global Value Chains

A powerful way to analyze the global economy – and especially global industries – is through the use of the global value chains perspective. In this approach, industries are described as a sequence of discrete stages of production, or nodes. Products move between these nodes, each representing the sequential conversion of raw materials into final goods for consumption. These nodes and flows are the basic building blocks of the global value chains framework.

The value-chain sequence from raw materials through the various, distinct stages of procurement, transformation, marketing, distribution and sales may be applied to any industry. While nodes describe logical stages in an industry, they tend to have distinct geographic properties and may be quite different from other nodes in the same industry. Furthermore, each node has a different set of technologies and labour requirements, and often a distinctive type of enterprise. Thus the chain describes an industry's technology, its enterprises, its workplaces and its geographies.

Foreign direct investment (FDI) adds to the complexity of industry value chains. Dicken (2007, 36) explains the two types of FDI as: "when a firm from one country buys a controlling investment in a firm in another country, or where a firm sets up a branch or subsidiary in another country." Albuquerque et al. (2003, 2) emphasize that "foreign direct investment is the fastest growing form of international capital flows and the most important form of private international financing for emerging market economies." Inward flows of FDI are particularly important in the mining sectors of less economically developed countries. However, FDI are also concentrated in some other sectors of the economy.

The "New" Economic Geography of Globalization

According to Ritzer, globalization theory implies a shift away from a focus on the nation-state, and towards a concern with transnational processes such as global "networks" and global "flows". Globalization can be thought of as the worldwide diffusion of practices, expansion of cultural relations across continents, organization of social life on a global scale, and growth of a shared global consciousness.

Although "globalization" is not synonymous with "global economy", the two concepts are related. In particular, a lot of attention has been placed on the relationship between globalization and a variety of social problems like poverty, economic inequality, environmental degradation, and consumerism, among others. In this context "anti-globalization" protests in opposition to multi-national corporations and the powers exercised through trade agreements has emerged, as exemplified by the anti-World Trade Organization (WTO) protests in Seattle in 1999.

Globalization is implicated in the generation of a new "geography of centrality" that is reshaping traditional divides of the world between the rich developed countries and poor underdeveloped countries. Researchers have identified the emergence of new global hierarchies of cities (Beaverstock, Smith and Taylor 1999). For example, the Globalization and World City Study Group and Network (GaWC) re-published their roster of leading world cities (e.g., London, New York, Tokyo, Frankfurt, Milan, Singapore, Chicago, Paris) with new indicators identifying these cities as the most influential urban centers over global flows of products, services, and information. World cities such as these have become centers of power in the global economy.

Conclusion

This conceptual framework for the *Global Economy* module introduced you to some of the ideas and theories that geographers use to interpret the spatial organization of the global economy. As you proceed to the module's case studies, you will examine two of the main forces of the global economy – international trade and multinational corporations – and consider evidence of the global economy's impacts on human developments and natural environments.

Levels of economic development and human welfare can vary greatly between countries, ranging from advanced economies with high standards of living to developing countries where the basic needs of the majority of the population are not being met. Understanding the reasons for this disparity lies at the heart of economic geography. Some scholars believe that economic globalization benefits everyone by expanding markets, promoting efficiency in production, creating jobs, and lowering the prices of goods. Other scholars disagree with that premise, and argue that economic globalization is creating a world in which wealth and power is heavily concentrated in a few privileged regions and also in the hands of a few individuals. These issues will be analyzed in greater detail as you proceed through the case studies.

Global Economy Case Studies

The *Global Economy* module currently offers four geographical case studies built on the ideas and theories presented in this conceptual framework:

1. *Case study: How does the dairy industry operate in the global economy?* The story of the dairy industry in New Zealand demonstrates how industrial restructuring, state regulations, and transnational corporations shape patterns of economic

globalization. Beginning with New Zealand's colonial history, this case study illustrates the importance of the dairy industry to the New Zealand economy and its emergence in the global economy.

2. *Case study: How does wine reach the global market?* Wine has a long history as a commodity in international trade. In recent decades, Chile's wine industry has transformed into a major force in the world market. This case study examines how the geographic characteristics of the Chilean wine industry have changed over time, and explains the factors responsible for the high quality and competitiveness of Chilean wine in the international marketplace.
3. *Case study: What is the impact of foreign direct investment on the mining industry?* Economic liberalization policies and global market integration have opened up mining operations in Central and South America to the influence of foreign direct investment (FDI). Extractive industries account for the bulk of inward FDI of many low-income, mineral-rich countries (UNCTAD, 2007a). In turn, many transnational corporations (TNCs) have established large-scale mining operations in Chile, Peru, Colombia, and Argentina, and other countries. This case study explores the details of these developments and their impact on people and natural environments.
4. *Case study: Where are new forms of manufacturing promoting economic development?* The machine tool industry is an important indicator of a national economy's manufacturing strength. This case study investigates global patterns of machine tool production, consumption, and trade. Relationships among partial clustering, downriver industries, and regional economic development provide the basis for understanding the machine tool industry in the global economy.

In the last few years there has been a dramatic increase in research on economic geography — that is, on where economic activity occurs and why. This surge of interest has been driven to some extent by real-world concerns — the field has been given a big boost in particular by plans to unify the European market, and the attempt to understand how this deeper integration will work by comparing international economics within Europe with interregional economics within the United States. But economic geography has always been important; if it has been notably neglected by the economics profession, this is not because economists have been uninterested in the subject, but because they have regarded it as intractable. Their new willingness to work on economic geography comes from their sense that new tools — in particular, modelling tricks that have been developed to analyze industrial organization, international trade, and economic growth — have removed crucial technical barriers, and transformed a once inhospitable field into fertile ground for theorists.

The basic problem with doing theory in economic geography has always been the observation that any sensible story about regional and urban development must hinge crucially on the role of increasing returns. Suppose that we really lived in the constant-returns world that is still assumed in much economic theory. Then it would be hard to understand why the economy is not characterized by "backyard capitalism", in which each household or small group produces most items for itself. There would, admittedly, be some unevenness in population density and some trade between locations because of the variation in the natural environment: land differs in fertility, while differences in soil, climate, and resources mean that no one locality would produce all goods even under constant returns. Nonetheless, the dramatic spatial unevenness of the real economy — the disparities between densely populated manufacturing belts and thinly populated farm belts, between congested cities and desolate rural areas; the spectacular concentration of particular industries in Silicon Valleys and Hollywoods — is surely the result not of inherent differences between locations but of some set of cumulative processes, necessarily involving some form of increasing returns, whereby geographic concentration can be self-reinforcing.

Unfortunately, increasing returns have always posed difficulties for economic theorists. Except under very special circumstances they lead to a breakdown of perfect competition; even if this problem can somehow be finished, they pose problems for the existence and uniqueness of equilibria. For the theorist determined to make some headway in understanding the location of economic activity, these difficulties have not been insurmountable. For example, one can, like much of urban economics, simply take the existence of cities (or central business districts within cities) as a given, and trace out the consequences for land rents and land use; this is the basis of the famous von Thünen model, which has given rise to a rich and productive literature. Or one can, like urban systems theorists, represent increasing returns in a somewhat black-box way as localized production externalities; this approach sidesteps some important questions, but opens the door to a powerfully insightful analysis of others. Still, until a few years ago these efforts remained peripheral to the main body of economic theory, to such an extent that most textbooks in economic principles still contain literally no reference to the existence or role of cities and other geographic concentrations of economic activity.

What has happened in the last few years is the emergence of a "new economic geography" that is the fourth wave of the increasing returns revolution in economics. The revolution began in the 1970s, in the field of industrial organization, when theorists began for the first time to develop tractable models of competition in the presence of increasing returns; in particular, Dixit and Stiglitz (1977) developed a formalization of Chamberlin's concept of monopolistic competition that, while admittedly a very special case, has turned into the workhorse of theoretical modelling in a number of fields. Beginning at the end of the 1970s, the analytical tools of the new industrial organization theory were applied by a number of theorists to international trade; a few years later the same tools were applied to technological change and economic growth. In each case it was, of course, necessary to do much more than mechanically apply the Dixit-Stiglitz model to the subject at hand: new concepts needed to be developed, and at first there was a proliferation of seemingly inconsistent models and approaches, in which each author appeared to be inventing his or her own private language and notation. In time, however, it became clear in each case that a core set of useful insights had emerged; indeed, in retrospect it is remarkable how tightly integrated, how classical in feel, both the "new trade" and "new growth" theory have turned out to be.

That is, an exuberant and initially exhilarating growth of theory has reached the point at which it has become difficult to see the forest for the trees; and yet there is, if one looks for it, a strong element of commonality among many if not all the analyses. The integration of new trade and new growth theory was, we believe, powerfully aided by the appearance of judiciously timed monographs that endeavoured to synthesize each field into a coherent whole: Helpman and Krugman's *Market Structure and Foreign Trade* (1985), and Grossman and Helpman's *Innovation and Growth in the World Economy* (1991).

Linkages and Circular Causation

We would argue that the defining issue of economic geography is the need to explain concentrations of population and/or economic activity — the distinction between manufacturing belt and farm belt, the existence of cities, the role of industry clusters. Broadly speaking, it is clear that all these concentrations form and survive because of some form of agglomeration economies, in which spatial concentration itself creates the favourable economic environment that supports further or continued concentration. But the main thrust of the new geography literature has been to get inside that particular black box, and derive the self-reinforcing character of spatial concentration from more fundamental considerations. The point is not just that positing agglomeration economies seems a bit like assuming one's conclusion — as a sarcastic physicist remarked after hearing one presentation on increasing returns, "So you're telling us that agglomerations form because of agglomeration economies". The larger point is that by modelling the sources of increasing returns to spatial concentration, we are able to learn something about how and when these returns may change — and then explore how the economy's behaviour will change with them.

How should the returns to spatial concentration be modelled? More than a century ago Alfred Marshall suggested a threefold classification. In modern terminology, he argued that industrial districts arise because of knowledge spillovers ("the mysteries of the trade become no mysteries, but are as it were in the air"), the advantages of thick markets for specialized skills, and the backward and forward linkages associated with large local markets. While all three of Marshall's forces are clearly operating in the real world, the new geography models have generally downplayed the first two, essentially because they remain hard to model in any explicit way. Instead, they have focussed on the role of linkages.

The linkage story is easy to tell if one is willing to be a bit vague about the details. Producers, so the story goes, want to choose locations that (i) have good access to large markets and (ii) have good access to supplies of goods that they or their workers require. However, a place that for whatever reason already has a concentration of producers will tend to offer a large market (because of the demand generated by the producers and their workers) and a good supply of inputs and consumer goods (made by the producers already there). These two advantages correspond precisely to the "backward linkages" and "forward linkages" of development theory. Because of these linkages, a spatial concentration of production, once established, may tend to persist — and a small difference in the initial economic size of two otherwise equivalent locations may tend to grow over time.

Discussions of linkage-based spatial concentration that embody more or less this story have been familiar to regional scientists for many years. And provided that one is prepared to be strategically sloppy about details, it is possible to jump straight from such stories into heuristic models that are quite useful both for quick-and-dirty discussions of real-world issues and as guides to the results of more careful modelling. Such loose-jointed modelling is under-appreciated in economics; we try to give it its due.

Nonetheless, there are certain questions that traditional discussions of linkages and economic geography do not address, yet become crucial once one tries to get beyond the simplest stories. Most important of these is the nature of competition. Linkage stories only work if there are increasing returns in production at the level of the individual firm — otherwise the firm would not concentrate production where the market is largest, but rather establish a separate facility to serve each market. But if there are increasing returns, competition must be imperfect; how do firms compete and set prices? Models like the base-multiplier story are also sloppy about budget constraints — it is unclear where all the money comes from or where it goes. And in any story in which transportation costs play a crucial role — as they must in linkage stories about location, because otherwise why does location matter? — one must worry about how the resources used in transportation fit into the picture. The key enabling technology for the new economic geography has been the development of a basic approach that deals in a consistent, if more than a bit artificial, way with these problems — together with an angle of approach that allows theorists to cut through what might at first sight seem be intractably complex problems of analysis.

Industry

Industry is the production of an economic good or service within an economy. Industry is often classified into three sectors: primary or extractive, secondary or manufacturing, and tertiary or services. Some authors add quaternary (knowledge) or even quinary (culture and research) sectors.

Industries can be classified on the basis of raw materials, size and ownership and time.

- *Raw Materials:* Industries may be agriculture based, Marine based, Mineral based, Forest based....
- *Size:* It refers to the amount of capital invested, number of people employed and the volume of production.
- *Ownership:* Industries can be classified into private sector, state owned or public sector, joint sector and co-operative sector

Industry in the sense of manufacturing became a key sector of production and labour in European and North American countries during the Industrial Revolution, which upset previous mercantile and feudal economies through many successive rapid advances in technology, such as the steel and coal production. It is aided by technological advances, and has continued to develop into new types and sectors to this day. Industrial countries then assumed a capitalist economic policy. Railroads and steam-powered ships began speedily establishing links with previously unreachable world markets, enabling private companies to develop to then-unheard of size and wealth. Following the Industrial Revolution, perhaps a third of the world's economic output is derived from manufacturing industries—more than agriculture's share. Many developed countries and many developing/ semi-developed countries (People's Republic of China, India etc.) depend significantly on industry. Industries, the countries they reside in, and the economies of those countries are interlinked in a complex web of interdependence.

Industry is divided into four sectors. They are:

Sector	***Efinition***
Primary	This involves the extraction of resources directly from the Earth, this includes farming, mining and logging. They do not process the products at all. They send it off to factories to make a profit.
Secondary	This group is involved in the processing products from primary industries. This includes all factories—those that refine metals, produce furniture, or pack farm products such as meat.
Tertiary	This group is involved in the provision of services. They include teachers, managers and other service providers.
Quaternary	This group is involved in the research of science and technology. They include scientists.
Quinary Sector	Some consider there to be a branch of the quaternary sector called the quinary sector, which includes the highest levels of decision making in a society or economy. This sector would include the top executives or officials in such fields as government, science, universities, nonprofit, healthcare, culture, and the media.

An Australian source relates that the quinary sector in Australia refers to domestic activities such as those performed by stay-at-home parents or homemakers. These activities are typically not measured by monetary amounts but it is important to recognize these activities in contribution to the economy.

As a country develops people move away from the primary sector to secondary and then to tertiary.

There are many other different kinds of industries, and often organized into different classes or sectors by a variety of industrial classifications.

Industry classification systems used by the government commonly divide industry into three sectors: agriculture, manufacturing, and services. The primary sector of industry is agriculture, mining and raw material extraction. The secondary sector of industry is manufacturing. The tertiary sector of industry is service production. Sometimes, one talks about a quaternary sector of industry, consisting of intellectual services such as research and development (R&D). Market-based classification systems such as the Global Industry Classification Standard and the Industry Classification Benchmark are used in finance and market research. These classification systems commonly divide industries according to similar functions and markets and identify businesses producing related products.

Industries can also be identified by product: chemical industry, petroleum industry, automotive industry, electronic industry, meatpacking industry, hospitality industry, food industry, fish industry, software industry, paper industry, entertainment industry, semiconductor industry, cultural industry, poverty industry

- labour-intensive industry - capital-intensive industry
- light industry - heavy industry

Industrial Development

The industrial revolution led to the development of factories for large-scale production, with consequent changes in society. Originally the factories were steam-powered, but later transitioned to electricity once an electrical grid was developed. The mechanized assembly line was introduced to assemble parts in a repeatable fashion, with individual workers performing specific steps during the process. This led to significant increases in efficiency, lowering the cost of the end process. Later automation was increasingly used to replace human operators. This process has accelerated with the development of the computer and the robot.

Deindustrialisation

Historically certain manufacturing industries have gone into a decline due to various economic factors, including the development of replacement technology or the loss of competitive advantage. An example of the former is the decline in carriage manufacturing when the automobile was mass-produced.

A recent trend has been the migration of prosperous, industrialized nations toward a post-industrial society. This is manifested by an increase in the service sector at the expense of manufacturing, and the development of an information-based economy, the so-called informational revolution. In a post-industrial society, manufacturing is relocated to economically more favourable locations through a process of off-shoring.

The major difficulty for people looking to measure manufacturing industries outputs and economic effect is finding a measurement which is stable historically. Traditionally, success has been measured in the number of jobs created. The lowering of employee numbers in the manufacturing sector has been assumed to be caused by a decline in the competitiveness of the sector although much has been caused by the introduction of the lean manufacturing process. Eventually, this will lead to competing product lines being managed by one of two people, as is already the case in the cigarette manufacturing industry.

Related to this change is the upgrading of the quality of the product being manufactured. While it is easy to produce a low tech, low skill product, the ability to manufacture high quality products is limited to companies with a high skilled staff.

Society

An industrial society can be defined in many ways. Today, industry is an important part of most societies and nations. A government must have some kind of industrial policy, regulating industrial placement, industrial pollution, financing and industrial labour.

Industrial Labour

In an industrial society, industry employs a major part of the population. This occurs typically in the manufacturing sector. A labour union is an organization of workers who have banded together to achieve common goals in key areas such as wages, hours, and working conditions. The trade union, through its leadership, bargains with the employer on behalf of union members (rank and file members) and negotiates labour contracts with employers. This movement first rose among industrial workers.

War

The industrial revolution changed warfare, with mass-produced weaponry and supplies, machine-powered transportation, mobilization, the total war concept and weapons of mass destruction. Early instances of industrial warfare were the Crimean War and the American Civil War, but its full potential showed during the world wars.

ISIC

ISIC (Rev.4) stands for International Standard Industrial Classification of all economic activities, the most complete and systematic industrial classification made by United Nations Statistics Division.

ISIC is a standard classification of economic activities arranged so that entities can be classified according to the activity they carry out. The categories of ISIC at the most detailed level (classes) are delineated according to what is, in most countries, the customary combination of activities described in statistical units, and considers the relative importance of the activities included in these classes.

While ISIC Rev.4 continues to use criteria such as input, output and use of the products produced, more emphasis has been given to the character of the production process in defining and delineating ISIC classes.

Developed Country

A developed country or "more developed country" (MDC), is a sovereign state that has a highly developed economy and advanced technological infrastructure relative to other less developed nations. Most commonly the criteria for evaluating the degree of economic development are gross domestic product (GDP), the per capita income, level of industrialization, amount of widespread infrastructure and general standard of living. Which criteria are to be used and which countries can be classified as being developed are subjects of debate.

Developed countries have post-industrial economies, meaning the service sector provides more wealth than the industrial sector. They are contrasted with developing countries, which are in the process of industrialization, or undeveloped countries, which are pre-industrial and almost entirely agrarian. According to the International Monetary Fund, advanced economies comprise 65.8% of global nominal GDP and

52.1% of global GDP (PPP) in 2010. In 2011, the ten largest advanced economies by either nominal GDP or GDP (PPP) are the United States, Germany, France, the United Kingdom, Japan, Italy, Canada, Spain and South Korea.

Similar Terms

Terms similar to "developed country" include "advanced country", "industrialized country", ""more developed country" (MDC), "more economically developed country" (MEDC), "Global North country", "first world country", and "post-industrial country". The term industrialized country may be somewhat ambiguous, as industrialization is an ongoing process that is hard to define. The term MEDC is one used by modern geographers to specifically describe the status of the countries referred to: more economically developed. The first industrialized country was the United Kingdom, followed by Belgium. Later it spread further to Germany, United States, France and other Western European countries. According to some economists such as Jeffrey Sachs, however, the current divide between the developed and developing world is largely a phenomenon of the 20th century.

Definition and Criteria

Economic criteria have tended to dominate discussions. One such criterion is income per capita; countries with high gross domestic product (GDP) per capita would thus be described as developed countries. Another economic criterion is industrialization; countries in which the tertiary and quaternary sectors of industry dominate would thus be described as developed. More recently another measure, the Human Development Index (HDI), which combines an economic measure, national income, with other measures, indices for life expectancy and education has become prominent. This criterion would define developed countries as those with a very high (HDI) rating. However, many anomalies exist when determining "developed" status by whichever measure is used.

Kofi Annan, former Secretary-General of the United Nations, defined a developed country as follows: "A developed country is one that allows all its citizens to enjoy a free and healthy life in a safe environment." But according to the United Nations Statistics Division, There is no established convention for the designation of "developed" and "developing" countries or areas in the United Nations system.

And it Notes That

The designations "developed" and "developing" are intended for statistical convenience and do not necessarily express a judgement about the stage reached by a particular country or area in the development process.

The UN also Notes

"In common practice, Japan in Asia, Canada and the United States in Northern America, Australia and New Zealand in Oceania, and Europe are considered "developed" regions or areas. In international trade statistics, the Southern African Customs Union is also treated as a developed region and Israel as a developed country; countries emerging from the former Yugoslavia are treated as developing countries; and countries of Central Europe and of the Commonwealth of Independent States (Russian Federation, Ukraine, Belarus, and Central Asia; code 172) in Europe are not included under either developed or developing regions."

Human Development Index (HDI)

The UN HDI is a statistical measure that gauges a country's level of human development. While there is a strong correlation between having a high HDI score and a prosperous economy, the UN points out that the HDI accounts for more than income or productivity. Unlike GDP per capita or per capita income, the HDI takes into account how income is turned "into education and health opportunities and therefore into higher levels of human development."

Since 1990, Norway (2001–2006, 2009–2011), Japan (1990–91 and 1993), Canada (1992 and 1994–2000) and Iceland (2007–08) have had the highest HDI score. The top 47 countries have scores ranging from 0.793 in Barbados to 0.955 in Norway.

Many countries listed by IMF or CIA as "advanced" (as of 2009), possess an HDI over 0.788 (as of 2010). Many countries possessing an HDI of 0.788 and over (as of 2010), are also listed by IMF or CIA as "advanced" (as of 2009). Thus, many "advanced economies" (as of 2009) are characterized by an HDI score of 0.9 or higher (as of 2007).

The latest index was released on 14 March 2013 and covers the period up to 2012. The following are the 47 countries in the top quartile - having an HDI above 0.8, and classified as possessing a "Very high human development".

Note: The green arrows (Δ), red arrows (∇), and blue dashes (–) represent changes in rank when compared to the 2011 data – published in the 2011 report.

1. Norway 0.955 ()
2. Australia 0.938 ()

3. United States 0.937 (1)
4. Netherlands 0.921 (1)
5. Germany 0.920 (4)
6. New Zealand 0.919 (1)
7. Ireland 0.916 ()
8. Sweden 0.916 (3)
9. Switzerland 0.913 (2)
10. Japan 0.912 (2)
11. Canada 0.911 (5)
12. South Korea 0.909 (3)
13. Hong Kong 0.906 ()
14. Iceland 0.906 ()
15. Denmark 0.901 (1)
16. Israel 0.900 (1)
17. Belgium 0.897 (1)
18. Austria 0.895 (1)
19. Singapore 0.895 (7)
20. France 0.893 ()
21. Finland 0.892 (1)
22. Slovenia 0.892 ()
23. Spain 0.885 ()
24. Liechtenstein 0.883 (16)
25. Italy 0.881 (1)
26. Luxembourg 0.875 (1)
27. United Kingdom 0.875 (1)
28. Czech Republic 0.873 (1)
29. Greece 0.860 ()
30. Brunei 0.855 (1)
31. Cyprus 0.848 (1)
32. Malta 0.847 (4)
33. Andorra 0.846 (1)
34. Estonia 0.846 ()
35. Slovakia 0.840 ()
36. Qatar 0.834 (1)

37. Hungary 0.831 (1)
38. Barbados 0.825 (9)
39. Poland 0.821 ()
40. Chile 0.819 (4)
41. Lithuania 0.818 (1)
42. United Arab Emirates 0.818 (12)
43. Portugal 0.816 (2)
44. Latvia 0.814 (1)
45. Argentina 0.811 ()
46. Seychelles 0.806 (6)
47. Croatia 0.805 (1)

Average Disposable Wage of OECD Members

Rank	*Country*	*Disposable 2011*	*$Disposable growth*	*$Compulsory deduction*	*Gross $ 2011*
1	United States	42,050	242	22.8%	54,450
2	Ireland	41,170	531	18.9%	50,764
3	Luxembourg	37,997	-1,477	28.1%	52,847
4	Switzerland	35,471	-57	29.4%	50,242
5	Australia	34,952	835	22.3%	44,983
6	United Kingdom	33,513	-1,272	25.1%	44,743
7	Canada	32,662	-648	22.7%	42,253
8	Norway	31,101	913	29.3%	43,990
9	South Korea	31,051	1,341	12.3%	35,406
10	Netherlands	29,269	-544	37.8%	47,056
11	Austria	29,008	-177	33.4%	43,555
12	Sweden	28,301	480	25.0%	37,734
13	Denmark	27,974	-335	38.6%	45,560
14	Japan	27,763	724	21.0%	35,143
15	France	27,452	93	28.0%	38,128
16	Spain	26,856	-466	21.9%	34,387
17	Finland	25,747	146	29.8%	36,676
18	Belgium	25,642	25	42.2%	44,364
19	Israel	24,225	147	18.9%	28,804
20	Germany	24,174	379	39.9%	40,223

Contd...

Rank	Country	Disposable $ 2011	Disposable $ growth	Compulsory deduction	Gross $ 2011
21	Italy	23,194	-562	30.8%	33,517
22	Greece	21,352	-2,039	18.8%	26,295
23	Portugal	17,170	-2,044	24.5%	22,742
24	Czech Republic	15,115	-191	23.0%	19,630
25	Slovakia	14,701	-328	22.9%	19,068
26	Poland	14,390	116	28.3%	20,069
27	Estonia	13,737	-444	20.7%	17,323
28	Hungary	12,843	52	35.0%	19,437

While GDP per capita is often used to measure how developed a country is, it includes components that do not contribute to a citizen's standard of living. GDP per capita may increase while real incomes for the majority decline. However, measuring only wages and salaries gives a more accurate picture of a country's standard of living. Unlike the gross wage, which can be a misleading indicator of the well-being of a citizen since it does not represent the full amount of money the worker will be left to consume on goods or services, the disposable wage excludes compulsory deductions such as income tax, municipal tax, provincial/ state income tax, social security (pension plan, medicare) and compulsory insurance. The list below has compulsory deductions applied with rates obtained from the OECD Tax Database, which assumes that the citizen is single with no children, with an income level 100% of the average wage. All monetary values are based on the OECD's purchasing power parity exchange rates. Note that the OECD does not publish data for some countries and hence they are not listed.

Other lists of Developed Countries

Only three institutions have produced lists of "developed countries". The three institutions and their lists are the UN list (shown above), the CIA list and the FTSE Group's list, whose list is not included because its association of developed countries with countries with both high incomes and developed markets is not deemed as directly relevant here. However many institutions have created lists which are sometimes referred to when people are discussing developed countries. The International Monetary Fund (IMF) identifies 35 "advanced economies", The OECD, also widely known as the "developed countries club" has

34 members. The World Bank identifies 66 "high income countries". The EIU's Quality-of-life survey and a list of countries with welfare states are also included here. The criteria for using all these lists and for countries' inclusion on these lists are often not properly spelt out, and several of these lists are based on old data.

Developing Country

A developing country, also called a less-developed country (LDC), is a nation with a low living standard, underdeveloped industrial base, and low Human Development Index (HDI) relative to other countries. There is no universal, agreed-upon criteria for what makes a country developing versus developed and which countries fit these two categories, although there are general reference points such as the size of a nation's GDP compared to other nations. Countries with more advanced economies than other developing nations but that have not yet demonstrated signs of a developed country, are often categorized under the term *newly industrialized countries.*

Kofi Annan, former Secretary General of the United Nations, defined a developed country as follows. "A developed country is one that allows all its citizens to enjoy a free and healthy life in a safe environment." But according to the United Nations Statistics Division,

There is no established convention for the designation of "developed" and "developing" countries or areas in the United Nations system.

The UN Also Notes

In common practice, Japan in Asia, Canada and the United States in northern America, Australia and New Zealand in Oceania, and Europe, are considered "developed" regions or areas. In international trade statistics, the Southern African Customs Union is also treated as a developed region and Israel as a developed country; countries emerging from the former Yugoslavia are treated as developing countries; and countries of eastern Europe and of the Commonwealth of Independent States (code 172) in Europe are not included under either developed or developing regions.

On the other hand, according to the classification from International Monetary Fund (IMF) before April 2004, all countries of Eastern Europe (including Central European countries that still belongs to the "Eastern Europe Group" in the UN institutions) as well as the former Soviet Union (USSR) countries in Central Asia (Kazakhstan, Uzbekistan, Kyrgyzstan, Tajikistan and Turkmenistan) and Mongolia, were not included under either developed or developing regions, but rather were referred to as "countries in transition"; however they are now widely regarded (in the international reports) as "developing countries".

The IMF uses a flexible classification system that considers "(1) per capita income level, (2) export diversification—so oil exporters that have high per capita GDP would not make the advanced classification because around 70% of its exports are oil, and (3) degree of integration into the global financial system."

The World Bank classifies countries into four income groups. These are set each year on July 1. Economies were divided according to 2011 GNI per capita using the following ranges of income:

- Low income countries had GNI per capita of US$1,026 or less.
- Lower middle income countries had GNI per capita between US$1,026 and US$4,036.
- Upper middle income countries had GNI per capita between US$4,036 and US$12,476.
- High income countries had GNI above US$12,476.

The World Bank classifies all low- and middle-income countries as developing but notes, "The use of the term is convenient; it is not intended to imply that all economies in the group are experiencing similar development or that other economies have reached a preferred or final stage of development. Classification by income does not necessarily reflect development status."

Measure and Concept of Development

The development of a country is measured with statistical indexes such as income per capita (per person) (gross domestic product), life expectancy, the rate of literacy, et cetera. The UN has developed the Human Development Index (HDI), a compound indicator of the above statistics, to gauge the level of human development for countries where data is available.

Developing countries are, in general, countries that have not achieved a significant degree of industrialization relative to their populations, and have, in most cases, a medium to low standard of living. There is a strong correlation between low income and high population growth.

The terms utilized when discussing developing countries refer to the intent and to the constructs of those who utilize these terms. Other terms sometimes used are less developed countries (LDCs), least economically developed countries (LEDCs), "underdeveloped nations" or Third World nations, and "non-industrialized nations". Conversely, developed countries, most economically developed countries (MEDCs), First World nations and "industrialized nations" are the opposite end of the spectrum.

To moderate the euphemistic aspect of the word *developing*, international organizations have started to use the term less economically developed country (LEDCs) for the poorest nations—which can, in no sense, be regarded as developing. That is, LEDCs are the poorest subset of LDCs. This may moderate against a belief that the standard of living across the entire developing world is the same. The concept of the developing nation is found, under one term or another, in numerous theoretical systems having diverse orientations — for example, theories of decolonization, liberation theology, Marxism, anti-imperialism, and political economy. Another important indicator is the sectoral changes that have occurred since the stage of development of the country. On an average, countries with a 50% contribution from the Secondary sector of Manufacturing have grown substantially.

The "BRIC" countries, Brazil, Russia, India, and China are difficult to categorize because of their rapid economic development in recent years. However, they are still not developed countries.

Criticism of the Term 'Developing Country'

There is criticism of the use of the term 'developing country'. The term implies inferiority of a 'developing country' or 'undeveloped country' compared to a *developed country*, which many countries dislike.

It assumes a desire to 'develop' along the traditional 'Western' model of economic development, which a few countries, such as Cuba and Bhutan, choose not to follow.

The term 'developing' implies mobility and does not acknowledge that development may be in decline or static in some countries, particularly in southern African states worst affected by HIV/AIDS. In such cases, the term *developing country* may be considered a euphemism. The term implies homogeneity between such countries, which vary widely. The term also implies homogeneity within such countries when wealth (and health) of the most and least affluent groups varies widely. Similarly, the term 'developed country' incorrectly implies a lack of continuing economic development/growth in more-developed countries.

In general, development entails a modern infrastructure (both physical and institutional), and a move away from low value added sectors such as agriculture and natural resource extraction. Developed countries, in comparison, usually have economic systems based on continuous, self-sustaining economic growth in the tertiary sector of the economy and quaternary sector of the economy and high material standards of living. However, there are notable exceptions, as some countries considered developed have a significant component of primary industries in their national economies, e.g., Norway, Canada, Australia.

The USA and Western Europe have a very important agricultural sector, and are major players in international agricultural markets. Also, natural resource extraction can be a very profitable industry (high value added), e.g., oil extraction.

An alternative measurement of that has been suggested is that of Gross national happiness. Measuring the actual satisfaction of people as opposed to how money orientated a country is.

List of Developing Economies

The following are considered developing economies according to the International Monetary Fund's World Economic Outlook Report, April 2012 and World Bank data.

Typology and Names of Countries

Countries are often loosely placed into four categories of development. Each category includes the countries listed in their respective article. The term "developing nation" is not a label to assign a specific, similar type of problem.

1. Newly industrialized countries (NICs) are nations with economies more advanced and developed than those in the developing world, but not yet with the full signs of a developed country. NIC is a category between developed and developing countries. It includes Brazil, China, India, Indonesia, Malaysia, Mexico, Philippines, South Africa, Thailand and Turkey.
2. The Advanced Emerging Markets are: Brazil, Hungary, Malaysia, Mexico, Poland, South Africa, Taiwan and Turkey.
3. Countries with long-term civil war or large-scale breakdown of rule of law ("failed states") (e.g. Democratic Republic of Congo, Afghanistan, Somalia) or non-development-oriented dictatorship (North Korea, Myanmar and Zimbabwe).
4. Some developing countries such as Antigua and Barbuda, Bahamas, Barbados, Brunei, Equatorial Guinea, Trinidad and

Tobago and the Arab states of the Persian Gulf have been classified as "Developed countries" by the World Bank.

Least Developed Country

Least developed country (LDC) is a country which, according to the United Nations, exhibits the lowest indicators of socioeconomic development, with the lowest Human Development Index ratings of all countries in the world. The concept of LDCs originated in the late 1960s and the first group of LDCs was listed by the UN in its resolution 2768 (XXVI) of 18 November 1971. A country is classified as a Least Developed Country if it meets three criteria:

- Poverty (three-year average GNI per capita of less than US $905, which must exceed $1,086 to leave the list)
- Human resource weakness (based on indicators of nutrition, health, education and adult literacy) and
- economic vulnerability (based on instability of agricultural production, instability of exports of goods and services, economic importance of non-traditional activities, merchandise export concentration, handicap of economic smallness, and the percentage of population displaced by natural disasters)

LDC criteria are reviewed every three years by the Committee for Development Policy (CDP) of the UN Economic and Social Council (ECOSOC). Countries may "graduate" out of the LDC classification when indicators exceed these criteria. The United Nations Office of the High Representative for the Least Developed Countries, Landlocked Developing Countries and Small Island Developing States (UN-OHRLLS) coordinates UN support and provides advocacy services for Least Developed Countries. The classification (as of 1 January 2011) applies to 48 countries. Since the LDC category was initiated, only three countries have graduated to *developing country* status. The first country to graduate from LDC status was Botswana in 1994. The second country was Cape Verde, in 2007. Maldives became the third country to graduate to *developing country* status on 1 January 2011. In 2011 the UN suggested that Equatorial Guinea, Samoa, Tuvalu, and Vanuatu are among the candidates for promotion from LDC status. At the UN's fourth conference on LDCs held in May 2011, delegates endorsed a goal targeting the promotion of at least half the current LDC countries within the next ten years.

Usage and Abbreviations

Least developed countries can be distinguished from developing countries, "less developed countries", "lesser developed countries", or other terms for countries in the so-called "Third World". Although many contemporary scholars argue that "Third World" is outdated, irrelevant or inaccurate, others may use the term "Fourth World" in reference to least developed countries (although Fourth World is also used to refer to stateless ethnic groups). The term "less economically developed country" (LEDC) is also used today.

However, in order to avoid confusion between "least developed country" and or LEDC "less economically developed country" (which may both be abbreviated as LDC), and to avoid confusion with landlocked developing country (which can be abbreviated as LLDC), "developing country" is generally used in preference to "less developed country". Least developed countries suffer conditions of extreme poverty, ongoing and widespread conflict (including civil war or ethnic clashes), extensive political corruption, and lack political and social stability. The form of government in such countries is often authoritarian in nature, and may comprise a dictatorship, warlordism, or a kleptocracy. AIDS is a major issue in many of these countries. The majority of LDCs are in Sub-Saharan Africa.

Note, however, that the above characteristics generally do not apply to LDCs located in Oceania. Kiribati, Samoa, Tuvalu, and Vanuatu are politically stable democracies, and lack any form of civil or ethnic strife. Nor are they strongly affected by AIDS. Although they have small economies, often dependent on monocultures, the population generally does not suffer from extreme poverty, thanks to an enduring subsistence sector in the economy. The Solomon Islands is the only Oceanian LDC currently affected by political instability and ethnic tension. In 2006, the United Nations recommended that Samoa be graduated from LDC status. The Samoan government disagreed, however in 2007 the UN Economic and Social Council endorsed the recommendation, setting Samoa's graduation date for 31 December 2010. Following the tsunami that hit Samoa in 2009, Samoa's graduation was deferred until January 2014. During the last United Nations review in 2009, the UN defined LDCs as countries meeting three criteria, one of which was a three-year average estimate of gross national income (GNI) per capita of less than US $905. Countries with populations over 75 million are excluded.

UN Conferences on the Least Developed Countries

The first conference - in Paris, 1981. The second conference - in Paris, 1991. The third conference - in Brussels, 2001. There have been four United Nations conferences on LDCs, the most recent being held 9–13 May 2011 in Istanbul.

Fourth UN Conference on LDCs (UN LDC-IV)

The Fourth UN Conference on Least Developed Countries (LDC-IV) was held in Istanbul, Turkey, 9–13 May 2011. It was attended by Ban Ki-Moon, the head of the UN, and close to 50 prime ministers and heads of state. The conference endorsed the goal of raising half the existing Least developed countries out of the LDC category by 2022. As with the Seoul Development Consensus drawn up in 2010, there was a strong emphases on boosting productive capability and physical infrastructure, with several NGO's not pleased with the emphases placed on the private sector.

Role of Civil Society

In the process of increasing awareness towards the needs of the LDCs, the importance of the inputs and contributions of the members of the Civil Society were first acknowledged during the NGO Forum held in parallel to the third UN Conference on Least Developed Countries in Brussels in 2001.

The importance of civil society and its contributions has also been recognised in the UNGA Resolution 63/227. Post LDC III, civil society actors have been actively engaged and involved in the UN Decision making processes concerning LDCs.

They have also been involved in the implementation and follow-up, monitoring and review of the progress made by LDCs and the success of the implementation of the BPoA. For LDC IV, the UN-OHRLLS has entrusted LDC Watch, a global network of LDC Civil Society Organizations (CSOs), with taking the lead in coordinating the civil society track.

LDC Watch has organised civil society consultations at various levels. At the regional level, in partnership with the UN-OHRLLS and relevant UN agencies, the following three consultations have been organised:

1. Africa LDC Civil Society Assembly on 4–5 March 2010, Addis Ababa (Ethiopia) in the lead-up to the official regional review in Africa
2. Pacific LDC Civil Society Assembly on 3–6 August 2010, Port Vila (Vanuatu) in parallel to the forty-first official Pacific Islands Forum
3. Asia LDC Civil Society Assembly on 22–23 November 2010, Bangkok (Thailand)

These consultations were organised to critically assess the progress made by LDCs in the ten years since the adoption of the Brussels Programme of Action and with the intention of influencing the outcome of LDC IV.

As the LDC Governments and their development partners prepare to gather together for UNLDC IV, members of Civil Society are also preparing to meet during the Civil Society Forum which is going to be held in parallel to the official conference. UN-OHRLLS has mandated LDC Watch as the lead Civil Society Organization to coordinate the Civil Society track towards the LDC-IV conference.

The Forum will open two days before the official conference begins and will continue till the end of the conference. It will bring together NGOs from all the LDCs, as well as representatives from the civil society at all levels including women's movements, youth movements, trade unions, peasant federations, media personnel and human rights defenders.

Trade and LDCs

Issues surrounding global trade regulations and LDCs have gained a lot of media and policy attention thanks to the recently collapsed Doha Round of World Trade Organization (WTO) negotiations being termed a development round. During the WTO's Hong Kong Ministerial, it was agreed that LDCs could see 100 percent duty-free, quota-free access to U.S. markets if the round were completed. But analysis of the deal by NGOs found that the text of the proposed LDC deal had substantial loopholes that might make the offer less than the full 100 percent access, and could even erase some current duty-free access of LDCs to rich country markets. Dissatisfaction with these loopholes led some economists to call for a reworking of the Hong Kong deal.

Dr. Chiedu Osakwe, as of 2001 the Director, Technical Cooperation Division at the Secretariat of the WTO, and adviser to the Director-General on developing country matters, was appointed as the WTO Special Coordinator for the Least Developed Countries beginning in 1999. He worked closely with the five other agencies that together with the WTO constitute the Integrated Framework of action for the Least Developed Countries. They addressed issues of market access, special and differential treatment provisions for developing countries, participation of developing countries in the multilateral trading system, and development questions, especially the interests of developing countries in competition policy.

Current LDCs

The List of "least developed countries" according to the United Nations with some that are categorised into the Landlocked developing countries and the Small Island Developing States :

Africa (34 Countries)

- Angola
- Benin
- Burkina Faso
- Burundi
- Central African Republic
- Chad
- Comoros
- Democratic Republic of the Congo
- Djibouti
- Equatorial Guinea
- Eritrea
- Ethiopia
- Gambia
- Guinea
- Guinea-Bissau
- Lesotho
- Liberia
- Madagascar
- Malawi
- Mali
- Mauritania
- Mozambique
- Niger
- Rwanda
- São Tomé and Príncipe
- Senegal
- Sierra Leone
- Somalia
- South Sudan

- Sudan
- Togo
- Tanzania
- Uganda
- Zambia

Asia-Pacific (14 Countries)

- Afghanistan
- Bhutan
- Bangladesh
- Cambodia
- East Timor
- Kiribati
- Laos
- Myanmar
- Nepal
- Samoa
- Solomon Islands
- Tuvalu
- Vanuatu
- Yemen

Americas (1 Country)

- Haiti

9

Classification of Industries

Industry is the production of an economic good or service within an economy. Industry is often classified into three sectors: primary or extractive, secondary or manufacturing, and tertiary or services. Some authors add quaternary (knowledge) or even quinary (culture and research) sectors.

Industries can be classified on the basis of raw materials, size and ownership and time.

- Raw Materials: Industries may be agriculture based, Marine based, Mineral based, Forest based....
- Size: It refers to the amount of capital invested, number of people employed and the volume of production.
- Ownership: Industries can be classified into private sector, state owned or public sector, joint sector and co-operative sector

Light Industry

Light industry is usually less capital intensive than heavy industry, and is more consumer-oriented than business-oriented (i.e., most light industry products are produced for end users rather than as intermediates for use by other industries). Light industry facilities typically have less environmental impact than those associated with heavy industry, and zoning laws are more likely to permit light industry near residential areas. It is the production of small consumer goods. One economic definition states that light industry is a "manufacturing activity that uses moderate amounts of partially processed materials to produce items of relatively high value per unit weight". Examples of light industries include the manufacturing of clothes, shoes, furniture, consumer electronics and home appliances. Conversely, ship building would fall under heavy industry.

Characteristics

Light industries require only a small amount of raw materials, area and power. The value of the goods are low and they are easy to transport. The number of products is high. While light industry typically causes relatively little pollution, particularly when compared to heavy industries, some light industry can cause significant pollution or risk of contamination. Electronics manufacturing, itself often a light industry, can create potentially harmful levels of lead or chemical wastes in soil due to improper handling of solder and waste products (such as cleaning and degreasing agents used in manufacture).

Heavy Industry

Heavy industry does not have a single fixed meaning as compared to light industry. It can mean production of products which are either heavy in weight or in the processes leading to their production. In general, it is a popular term used within the name of many Japanese and Korean firms, meaning 'construction' for big projects. Example projects include the construction of large buildings, chemical plants, the H-IIA rocket and also includes the production of construction equipment such as cranes and bulldozers. Alternatively, heavy industry projects can be generalized as more capital intensive or as requiring greater or more advanced resources, facilities or management.

Many East Asian companies rely on heavy industry as part of their overall economy. Amongst Japanese and Korean firms with "heavy industry" in their names, many are also manufacturers of aerospace products and defence armaments, along with being defence contractors to their respective countries' governments such as Japan's Fuji Heavy Industries and Korea's Hyundai Rotem, a joint project of Hyundai Heavy Industries and Daewoo Heavy Industries.

Heavy industry is also sometimes a special designation in local zoning laws.

Manufacturing

Manufacturing is the production of goods for use or sale using labour and machines, tools, chemical and biological processing, or formulation. The term may refer to a range of human activity, from handicraft to high tech, but is most commonly applied to industrial production, in which raw materials are transformed into finished goods on a large scale. Such finished goods may be used for manufacturing other, more complex products, such as aircraft, household appliances or automobiles, or sold to wholesalers, who in turn sell them to retailers, who then sell them to end users – the "consumers".

Manufacturing takes turns under all types of economic systems. In a free market economy, manufacturing is usually directed toward the mass production of products for sale to consumers at a profit. In a collectivist economy, manufacturing is more frequently directed by the state to supply a centrally planned economy. In mixed market economies, manufacturing occurs under some degree of government regulation.

Modern manufacturing includes all intermediate processes required for the production and integration of a product's components. Some industries, such as semiconductor and steel manufacturers use the term *fabrication* instead.

The manufacturing sector is closely connected with engineering and industrial design. Examples of major manufacturers in North America include General Motors Corporation, General Electric, and Pfizer. Examples in Europe include Volkswagen Group, Siemens, and Michelin. Examples in Asia include Toyota, Samsung, and Bridgestone.

History and Development

- In its earliest form, manufacturing was usually carried out by a single skilled artisan with assistants. Training was by apprenticeship. In much of the pre-industrial world the guild system protected the privileges and trade secrets of urban artisans.
- Before the Industrial Revolution, most manufacturing occurred in rural areas, where household-based manufacturing served as a supplemental subsistence strategy to agriculture (and continues to do so in places). Entrepreneurs organized a number of manufacturing households into a single enterprise through the putting-out system.
- Toll manufacturing is an arrangement whereby a first firm with specialized equipment processes raw materials or semi-finished goods for a second firm.

Manufacturing systems: changes in methods of manufacturing

- Craft or Guild system
- Agile manufacturing
- American system of manufacturing
- English system of manufacturing
- Fabrication
- Flexible manufacturing
- Just In Time manufacturing
- Lean manufacturing
- Mass customization
- Mass production
- Ownership
- Packaging and labelling
- Prefabrication
- Putting-out system
- Rapid manufacturing
- Reconfigurable manufacturing system
- Soviet collectivism in manufacturing

Industrial Policy

Economics of Manufacturing

According to some economists, manufacturing is a wealth-producing sector of an economy, whereas a service sector tends to be wealth-consuming. Emerging technologies have provided some new growth in advanced manufacturing employment opportunities in the Manufacturing Belt in the United States. Manufacturing provides important material support for national infrastructure and for national defence.

On the other hand, most manufacturing may involve significant social and environmental costs. The clean-up costs of hazardous waste, for example, may outweigh the benefits of a product that creates it. Hazardous materials may expose workers to health risks.

Developed countries regulate manufacturing activity with labour laws and environmental laws. Across the globe, manufacturers can be subject to regulations and pollution taxes to offset the environmental costs of manufacturing activities.

Labour Unions and craft guilds have played a historic role in the negotiation of worker rights and wages. Environment laws and labour protections that are available in developed nations may not be available in the third world.

Tort law and product liability impose additional costs on manufacturing. These are significant dynamics in the on-going process, occurring over the last few decades, of manufacture-based industries relocating operations to "developing-world" economies where the costs of production are significantly lower than in "developed-world" economies. Manufacturing may require huge amounts of fossil fuels. Automobile construction requires, on average, 20 barrels of oil.

Manufacturing and Investment

Surveys and analyses of trends and issues in manufacturing and investment around the world focus on such things as:

- the nature and sources of the considerable variations that occur cross-nationally in levels of manufacturing and wider industrial-economic growth;
- competitiveness; and
- attractiveness to foreign direct.

In addition to general overviews, researchers have examined the features and factors affecting particular key aspects of manufacturing development. They have compared production and investment in a range of Western and non-Western countries and presented case studies of growth and performance in important individual industries and market-economic sectors.

On June 26, 2009, Jeff Immelt, the CEO of General Electric, called for the United States to increase its manufacturing base employment to 20% of the workforce, commenting that the U.S. has outsourced too much in some areas and can no longer rely on the financial sector and consumer spending to drive demand. Further, while U.S. manufacturing performs well compared to the rest of the U.S. economy, research shows that it performs poorly compared to manufacturing in other high-wage countries.

A total of 3.2 million – one in six U.S. manufacturing jobs – have disappeared between 2000 and 2007. In the UK, EEF the manufacturers organisation has led calls for the UK economy to be rebalanced to rely less on financial services and has actively promoted the manufa-cturing agenda.

Standard Industrial Classification

The Standard Industrial Classification (abbreviated SIC) is a system for classifying industries by a four-digit code. Established in the United States in 1937, it is used by government agencies to classify industry areas. The SIC system is also used by agencies in other countries, e.g., by the United Kingdom's Companies House.

In the United States the SIC code is being supplanted by the six-digit North American Industry Classification System (NAICS code), which was released in 1997; however certain government departments and agencies, such as the U.S. Securities and Exchange Commission (SEC), still use the SIC codes.

The SIC codes can be grouped into progressively broader industry classifications: industry group, major group, and division. The first 3 digits of the SIC code indicate the industry group, and the first two digits indicate the major group. Each division encompasses a range of SIC codes. From 0100 till 0999 is the division Agriculture, Forestry and Fishing, from 1000 till 1499 is the division Mining, from 1500 till 1799 is Construction, 1800 to 1999 is not used, from 2000 till 3999 is the division Manufacturing, from 4000 till 4999 is the division Transportation, Communications, Electric, Gas and Sanitary service, from 5000 till 5199 is the division Wholesale Trade, from 5200 till 5999 is the division Retail Trade, from 6000 till 6799 is the division Finance, Insurance and Real Estate, from 7000 till 8999 is the division Services and from 9100 till 9729 is the division Public Administration. The codes that start with 99 are Nonclassifiable. To look at a particular example of the hierarchy, SIC code 2024 (ice cream and frozen desserts) belongs to industry group 202 (dairy products), which is part of major group 20 (food and kindred products), which belongs to the division of manufacturing.

The following table is from the SEC's website, which allows searching for companies by SIC code in its database of filings. The acronym NEC stands for "not elsewhere classified".

SIC Code	*Industry*
0100	Agricultural Production-Crops
0200	Agricultural Prod-Livestock & Animal Specialties
0700	Agricultural Services
0800	Forestry
0900	Fishing, Hunting and Trapping

Contd...

SIC Code	***Industry***
1000	Metal Mining
1040	Gold and Silver Ores
1090	Miscellaneous Metal Ores
1220	Bituminous Coal & Lignite Mining
1221	Bituminous Coal & Lignite Surface Mining
1311	Crude Petroleum & Natural Gas
1381	Drilling Oil & Gas Wells
1382	Oil & Gas Field Exploration Services
1389	Oil & Gas Field Services, NEC
1400	Mining & Quarrying of Nonmetallic Minerals (No Fuels)
1520	General Bldg Contractors - Residential Bldgs
1531	Operative Builders
1540	General Bldg Contractors - Nonresidential Bldgs
1600	Heavy Construction Other Than Bldg Const - Contractors
1623	Water, Sewer, Pipeline, Comm & Power Line Construction
1700	Construction - Special Trade Contractors
1731	Electrical Work
2000	Food and Kindred Products
2011	Meat Packing Plants
2013	Sausages & Other Prepared Meat Products
2015	Poultry Slaughtering and Processing
2020	Dairy Products
2024	Ice Cream & Frozen Desserts
2030	Canned, Frozen & Preserved Fruit, Veg & Food Specialties
2033	Canned, Fruits, Veg, Preserves, Jams & Jellies
2040	Grain Mill Products
2050	Bakery Products
2052	Cookies & Crackers
2060	Sugar & Confectionery Products
2070	Fats & Oils
2080	Beverages
2082	Malt Beverages
2086	Bottled & Canned Soft Drinks & Carbonated Waters
2090	Miscellaneous Food Preparations & Kindred Products

Contd...

SIC Code	***Industry***
2092	Prepared Fresh or Frozen Fish & Seafood
2100	Tobacco Products
2111	Cigarettes
2200	Textile Mill Products
2211	Broadwoven Fabric Mills, Cotton
2221	Broadwoven Fabric Mills, Man Made Fibre & Silk
2250	Knitting Mills
2253	Knit Outerwear Mills
2273	Carpets & Rugs
2300	Apparel & Other Finished Prods of Fabrics & Similar Matl
2320	Men's & Boys' Furnishings, Work Clothing, & Allied Garments
2330	Women's, Misses', and Juniors Outerwear
2340	Women's, Misses', Children's & Infant's Undergarments
2390	Miscellaneous Fabricated Textile Products
2400	Lumber & Wood Products (No Furniture)
2421	Sawmills & Planing Mills, General
2430	Millwood, Veneer, Plywood, & Structural Wood Members
2451	Mobile Homes
2452	Prefabricated Wood Bldgs & Components
2510	Household Furniture
2511	Wood Household Furniture, (No Upholstered)
2520	Office Furniture
2522	Office Furniture (No Wood)
2531	Public Bldg & Related Furniture
2540	Partitions, Shelvg, Lockers, & office & Store Fixtures
2590	Miscellaneous Furniture & Fixtures
2600	Papers & Allied Products
2611	Pulp Mills
2621	Paper Mills
2631	Paperboard Mills
2650	Paperboard Containers & Boxes
2670	Converted Paper & Paperboard Prods (No Containers/Boxes)
2673	Plastics, Foil & Coated Paper Bags
2711	Newspapers: Publishing or Publishing & Printing

Contd...

SIC Code	***Industry***
2721	Periodicals: Publishing or Publishing & Printing
2731	Books: Publishing or Publishing & Printing
2732	Book Printing
2741	Miscellaneous Publishing
2750	Commercial Printing
2761	Manifold Business Forms
2771	Greeting Cards
2780	Blankbooks, Looseleaf Binders & Bookbinding & Related Work
2790	Service Industries For The Printing Trade
2800	Chemicals & Allied Products
2810	Industrial Inorganic Chemicals
2820	Plastic Material, Synth Resin/Rubber, Cellulos (No Glass)
2821	Plastic Materials, Synth Resins & Nonvulcan Elastomers
2833	Medicinal Chemicals & Botanical Products
2834	Pharmaceutical Preparations
2835	In Vitro & In Vivo Diagnostic Substances
2836	Biological Products, (No Diagnostic Substances)
2840	Soap, Detergents, Cleaning Preparations, Perfumes, Cosmetics
2842	Speciality Cleaning, Polishing and Sanitation Preparations
2844	Perfumes, Cosmetics & Other Toilet Preparations
2851	Paints, Varnishes, Lacquers, Enamels & Allied Prods
2860	Industrial Organic Chemicals
2870	Agricultural Chemicals
2890	Miscellaneous Chemical Products
2891	Adhesives & Sealants
2911	Petroleum Refining
2950	Asphalt Paving & Roofing Materials
2990	Miscellaneous Products of Petroleum & Coal
3011	Tires & Inner Tubes
3021	Rubber & Plastics Footwear
3050	Gaskets, Packg & Sealg Devices & Rubber & Plastics Hose
3060	Fabricated Rubber Products, NEC
3080	Miscellaneous Plastics Products

Contd...

SIC Code	***Industry***
3081	Unsupported Plastics Film & Sheet
3086	Plastics Foam Products
3089	Plastics Products, NEC
3100	Leather & Leather Products
3140	Footwear, (No Rubber)
3211	Flat Glass
3220	Glass & Glassware, Pressed or Blown
3221	Glass Containers
3231	Glass Products, Made of Purchased Glass
3241	Cement, Hydraulic
3250	Structural Clay Products
3260	Pottery & Related Products
3270	Concrete, Gypsum & Plaster Products
3272	Concrete Products, Except Block & Brick
3281	Cut Stone & Stone Products
3290	Abrasive, Asbestos & Misc Nonmetallic Mineral Prods
3310	Steel Works, Blast Furnaces & Rolling & Finishing Mills
3312	Steel Works, Blast Furnaces & Rolling Mills (Coke Ovens)
3317	Steel Pipe & Tubes
3320	Iron & Steel Foundries
3330	Primary Smelting & Refining of Nonferrous Metals
3334	Primary Production of Aluminium
3341	Secondary Smelting & Refining of Nonferrous Metals
3350	Rolling Drawing & Extruding of Nonferrous Metals
3357	Drawing & Insulating of Nonferrous Wire
3360	Nonferrous Foundries (Castings)
3390	Miscellaneous Primary Metal Products
3411	Metal Cans
3412	Metal Shipping Barrels, Drums, Kegs & Pails
3420	Cutlery, Handtools & General Hardware
3430	Heating Equip, Except Elec & Warm Air; & Plumbing Fixtures
3433	Heating Equipment, Except Electric & Warm Air Furnaces
3440	Fabricated Structural Metal Products

Contd...

SIC Code	***Industry***
3442	Metal Doors, Sash, Frames, Moldings & Trim
3443	Fabricated Plate Work (Boiler Shops)
3444	Sheet Metal Work
3448	Prefabricated Metal Buildings & Components
3451	Screw Machine Products
3452	Bolts, Nuts, Screws, Rivets & Washers
3460	Metal Forgings & Stampings
3470	Coating, Engraving & Allied Services
3480	Ordnance & Accessories, (No Vehicles/Guided Missiles)
3490	Miscellaneous Fabricated Metal Products
3510	Engines & Turbines
3523	Farm Machinery & Equipment
3524	Lawn & Garden Tractors & Home Lawn & Gardens Equip
3530	Construction, Mining & Materials Handling Machinery & Equip
3531	Construction Machinery & Equip
3532	Mining Machinery & Equip (No Oil & Gas Field Mach & Equip)
3533	Oil & Gas Field Machinery & Equipment
3537	Industrial Trucks, Tractors, Trailers & Stackers
3540	Metalworkg Machinery & Equipment
3541	Machine Tools, Metal Cutting Types
3550	Special Industry Machinery (No Metalworking Machinery)
3555	Printing Trades Machinery & Equipment
3559	Special Industry Machinery, NEC
3560	General Industrial Machinery & Equipment
3561	Pumps & Pumping Equipment
3562	Ball & Roller Bearings
3564	Industrial & Commercial Fans & Blowers & Air Purifying Equip
3567	Industrial Process Furnaces & Ovens
3569	General Industrial Machinery & Equipment, NEC
3570	Computer & office Equipment
3571	Electronic Computers
3572	Computer Storage Devices
3575	Computer Terminals

Contd...

SIC Code	***Industry***
3576	Computer Communications Equipment
3577	Computer Peripheral Equipment, NEC
3578	Calculating & Accounting Machines (No Electronic Computers)
3579	Office Machines, NEC
3580	Refrigeration & Service Industry Machinery
3585	Air-Cond & Warm Air Heatg Equip & Comm & Indl Refrig Equip
3590	Misc Industrial & Commercial Machinery & Equipment
3600	Electronic & Other Electrical Equipment (No Computer Equip)
3612	Power, Distribution & Speciality Transformers
3613	Switchgear & Switchboard Apparatus
3620	Electrical Industrial Apparatus
3621	Motors & Generators
3630	Household Appliances
3634	Electric Housewares & Fans
3640	Electric Lighting & Wiring Equipment
3651	Household Audio & Video Equipment
3652	Phonograph Records & Prerecorded Audio Tapes & Disks
3661	Telephone & Telegraph Apparatus
3663	Radio & TV Broadcasting & Communications Equipment
3669	Communications Equipment, NEC
3670	Electronic Components & Accessories
3672	Printed Circuit Boards
3674	Semiconductors & Related Devices
3677	Electronic Coils, Transformers & Other Inductors
3678	Electronic Connectors
3679	Electronic Components, NEC
3690	Miscellaneous Electrical Machinery, Equipment & Supplies
3695	Magnetic & Optical Recording Media
3711	Motor Vehicles & Passenger Car Bodies
3713	Truck & Bus Bodies
3714	Motor Vehicle Parts & Accessories
3715	Truck Trailers
3716	Motor Homes

Contd...

SIC Code	***Industry***
3720	Aircraft & Parts
3721	Aircraft
3724	Aircraft Engines & Engine Parts
3728	Aircraft Parts & Auxiliary Equipment, NEC
3730	Ship & Boat Building & Repairing
3743	Railroad Equipment
3751	Motorcycles, Bicycles & Parts
3760	Guided Missiles & Space Vehicles & Parts
3790	Miscellaneous Transportation Equipment
3812	Search, Detection, Navigation, Guidance, Aeronautical Sys
3821	Laboratory Apparatus & Furniture
3822	Auto Controls For Regulating Residential & Comml Environments
3823	Industrial Instruments For Measurement, Display, and Control
3824	Totalizing Fluid Meters & Counting Devices
3825	Instruments For Meas & Testing of Electricity & Elec Signals
3826	Laboratory Analytical Instruments
3827	Optical Instruments & Lenses
3829	Measuring & Controlling Devices, NEC
3841	Surgical & Medical Instruments & Apparatus
3842	Orthopedic, Prosthetic & Surgical Appliances & Supplies
3843	Dental Equipment & Supplies
3844	X-Ray Apparatus & Tubes & Related Irradiation Apparatus
3845	Electromedical & Electrotherapeutic Apparatus
3851	Ophthalmic Goods
3861	Photographic Equipment & Supplies
3873	Watches, Clocks, Clockwork Operated Devices/Parts
3910	Jewellery, Silverware & Plated Ware
3911	Jewellery, Precious Metal
3931	Musical Instruments
3942	Dolls & Stuffed Toys
3944	Games, Toys & Children's Vehicles (No Dolls & Bicycles)
3949	Sporting & Athletic Goods, NEC
3950	Pens, Pencils & Other Artists' Materials

Contd...

SIC Code	*Industry*
3960	Costume Jewellery & Novelties
3990	Miscellaneous Manufacturing Industries
4011	Railroads, Line-Haul Operating
4013	Railroad Switching & Terminal Establishments
4100	Local & Suburban Transit & Interurban Hwy Passenger Trans
4210	Trucking & Courier Services (No Air)
4213	Trucking (No Local)
4220	Public Warehousing & Storage
4231	Terminal Maintenance Facilities For Motor Freight Transport
4400	Water Transportation
4412	Deep Sea Foreign Transportation of Freight
4512	Air Transportation, Scheduled
4513	Air Courier Services
4522	Air Transportation, Nonscheduled
4581	Airports, Flying Fields & Airport Terminal Services
4610	Pipe Lines (No Natural Gas)
4700	Transportation Services
4731	Arrangement of Transportation of Freight & Cargo
4812	Radiotelephone Communications
4813	Telephone Communications (No Radiotelephone)
4822	Telegraph & Other Message Communications
4832	Radio Broadcasting Stations
4833	Television Broadcasting Stations
4841	Cable & Other Pay Television Services
4899	Communications Services, NEC
4900	Electric, Gas & Sanitary Services
4911	Electric Services
4922	Natural Gas Transmission
4923	Natural Gas Transmission & Distribution
4924	Natural Gas Distribution
4931	Electric & Other Services Combined
4932	Gas & Other Services Combined
4941	Water Supply

Contd...

SIC Code	*Industry*
4950	Sanitary Services
4953	Refuse Systems
4955	Hazardous Waste Management
4961	Steam & Air-Conditioning Supply
4991	Co-generation Services & Small Power Producers
5000	Wholesale-Durable Goods
5010	Wholesale-Motor Vehicles & Motor Vehicle Parts & Supplies
5013	Wholesale-Motor Vehicle Supplies & New Parts
5020	Wholesale-Furniture & Home Furnishings
5030	Wholesale-Lumber & Other Construction Materials
5031	Wholesale-Lumber, Plywood, millwork & Wood Panels
5040	Wholesale-Professional & Commercial Equipment & Supplies
5045	Wholesale-Computers & Peripheral Equipment & Software
5047	Wholesale-Medical, Dental & Hospital Equipment & Supplies
5050	Wholesale-Metals & Minerals (No Petroleum)
5051	Wholesale-Metals Service Centres & Offices
5063	Wholesale-Electrical Apparatus & Equipment, Wiring Supplies
5064	Wholesale-Electrical Appliances, TV & Radio Sets
5065	Wholesale-Electronic Parts & Equipment, NEC
5070	Wholesale-Hardware & Plumbing & Heating Equipment & Supplies
5072	Wholesale-Hardware
5080	Wholesale-Machinery, Equipment & Supplies
5082	Wholesale-Construction & Mining (No Petro) Machinery & Equip
5084	Wholesale-Industrial Machinery & Equipment
5090	Wholesale-Misc Durable Goods
5094	Wholesale-Jewellery, Watches, Precious Stones & Metals
5099	Wholesale-Durable Goods, NEC
5110	Wholesale-Paper & Paper Products
5122	Wholesale-Drugs, Proprietaries & Druggists' Sundries
5130	Wholesale-Apparel, Piece Goods & Notions
5140	Wholesale-Groceries & Related Products
5141	Wholesale-Groceries, General Line (merchandise)
5150	Wholesale-Farm Product Raw Materials

Contd...

SIC Code	***Industry***
5160	Wholesale-Chemicals & Allied Products
5171	Wholesale-Petroleum Bulk Stations & Terminals
5172	Wholesale-Petroleum & Petroleum Products (No Bulk Stations)
5180	Wholesale-Beer, Wine & Distilled Alcoholic Beverages
5190	Wholesale-Miscellaneous Non-durable Goods
5200	Retail-Building Materials, Hardware, Garden Supply
5211	Retail-Lumber & Other Building Materials Dealers
5271	Retail-Mobile Home Dealers
5311	Retail-Department Stores
5331	Retail-Variety Stores
5399	Retail-Misc General Merchandise Stores
5400	Retail-Food Stores
5411	Retail-Grocery Stores
5412	Retail-Convenience Stores
5500	Retail-Auto Dealers & Gasoline Stations
5531	Retail-Auto & Home Supply Stores
5600	Retail-Apparel & Accessory Stores
5621	Retail-Women's Clothing Stores
5651	Retail-Family Clothing Stores
5661	Retail-Shoe Stores
5700	Retail-Home Furniture, Furnishings & Equipment Stores
5712	Retail-Furniture Stores
5731	Retail-Radio, TV & Consumer Electronics Stores
5734	Retail-Computer & Computer Software Stores
5735	Retail-Record & Prerecorded Tape Stores
5810	Retail-Eating & Drinking Places
5812	Retail-Eating Places
5900	Retail-Miscellaneous Retail
5912	Retail-Drug Stores and Proprietary Stores
5940	Retail-Miscellaneous Shopping Goods Stores
5944	Retail-Jewellery Stores
5945	Retail-Hobby, Toy & Game Shops
5960	Retail-Nonstore Retailers

Contd...

SIC Code	***Industry***
5961	Retail-Catalog & Mail-Order Houses
5990	Retail-Retail Stores, NEC
6021	National Commercial Banks
6022	State Commercial Banks
6029	Commercial Banks, NEC
6035	Savings Institution, Federally Chartered
6036	Savings Institutions, Not Federally Chartered
6099	Functions Related To Depository Banking, NEC
6111	Federal & Federally Sponsored Credit Agencies
6141	Personal Credit Institutions
6153	Short-Term Business Credit Institutions
6159	Miscellaneous Business Credit Institution
6162	Mortgage Bankers & Loan Correspondents
6163	Loan Brokers
6172	Finance Lessors
6189	Asset-Backed Securities
6199	Finance Services
6200	Security & Commodity Brokers, Dealers, Exchanges & Services
6211	Security Brokers, Dealers & Flotation Companies
6221	Commodity Contracts Brokers & Dealers
6282	Investment Advice
6311	Life Insurance
6321	Accident & Health Insurance
6324	Hospital & Medical Service Plans
6331	Fire, Marine & Casualty Insurance
6351	Surety Insurance
6361	Title Insurance
6399	Insurance Carriers, NEC
6411	Insurance Agents, Brokers & Service
6500	Real Estate
6510	Real Estate Operators (No Developers) & Lessors
6512	Operators of Nonresidential Buildings
6513	Operators of Apartment Buildings

Contd...

SIC Code	***Industry***
6519	Lessors of Real Property, NEC
6531	Real Estate Agents & Managers (For Others)
6532	Real Estate Dealers (For Their Own Account)
6552	Land Subdividers & Developers (No Cemeteries)
6770	Blank Checks
6792	Oil Royalty Traders
6794	Patent Owners & Lessors
6795	Mineral Royalty Traders
6798	Real Estate Investment Trusts
6799	Investors, NEC
7000	Hotels, Rooming Houses, Camps & Other Lodging Places
7011	Hotels & Motels
7200	Services-Personal Services
7310	Services-Advertising
7311	Services-Advertising Agencies
7320	Services-Consumer Credit Reporting, Collection Agencies
7330	Services-Mailing, Reproduction, Commercial Art & Photography
7331	Services-Direct Mail Advertising Services
7334	Services-Photocopying and Duplicating Services
7340	Services-To Dwellings & Other Buildings
7350	Services-Miscellaneous Equipment Rental & Leasing
7359	Services-Equipment Rental & Leasing, NEC
7361	Services-Employment Agencies
7363	Services-Help Supply Services
7370	Services-Computer Programming, Data Processing, Etc.
7371	Services-Computer Programming Services
7372	Services-Prepackaged Software
7373	Services-Computer Integrated Systems Design
7374	Services-Computer Processing & Data Preparation
7377	Services-Computer Rental & Leasing
7380	Services-Miscellaneous Business Services
7381	Services-Detective, Guard & Armored Car Services
7384	Services-Photofinishing Laboratories

Contd...

SIC Code	*Industry*
7385	Services-Telephone Interconnect Systems
7389	Services-Business Services, NEC
7500	Services-Automotive Repair, Services & Parking
7510	Services-Auto Rental & Leasing (No Drivers)
7600	Services-Miscellaneous Repair Services
7812	Services-Motion Picture & Video Tape Production
7819	Services-Allied To Motion Picture Production
7822	Services-Motion Picture & Video Tape Distribution
7829	Services-Allied To Motion Picture Distribution
7830	Services-Motion Picture Theaters
7841	Services-Video Tape Rental
7900	Services-Amusement & Recreation Services
7948	Services-Racing, Including Track Operation
7990	Services-Miscellaneous Amusement & Recreation
7994	Services-Video Game Arcades
7995	Services-Gambling Transactions
7996	Services-Amusement Parks
7997	Services-Membership Sports & Recreation Clubs
8000	Services-Health Services
8011	Services-Offices & Clinics of Doctors of Medicine
8050	Services-Nursing & Personal Care Facilities
8051	Services-Skilled Nursing Care Facilities
8060	Services-Hospitals
8062	Services-General Medical & Surgical Hospitals, NEC
8071	Services-Medical Laboratories
8082	Services-Home Health Care Services
8090	Services-Misc Health & Allied Services, NEC
8093	Services-Speciality Outpatient Facilities, NEC
8111	Services-Legal Services
8200	Services-Educational Services
8300	Services-Social Services
8351	Services-Child Day Care Services
8600	Services-Membership organizations

Contd...

SIC Code	***Industry***
8700	Services-Engineering, Accounting, Research, Management
8711	Services-Engineering Services
8731	Services-Commercial Physical & Biological Research
8734	Services-Testing Laboratories
8741	Services-Management Services
8742	Services-Management Consulting Services
8744	Services-Facilities Support Management Services
8748	Business Consulting Services, Not Elsewhere Classified
8880	American Depositary Receipts
8888	Foreign Governments
8900	Services-Services, NEC
9721	International Affairs
9995	Non-Operating Establishments

10

Natural Resources: Renewable and Non-renewable

Natural resources occur naturally within environments that exist relatively undisturbed by mankind, in a natural form. A natural resource is often characterized by amounts of biodiversity and geodiversity existent in various ecosystems.

Natural resources are derived from the environment. Some of them are essential for our survival while most are used for satisfying our wants. Natural resources may be further classified in different ways. Natural resources are materials and components (something that can be used) that can be found within the environment. Every man-made product is composed of natural resources (at its fundamental level). A natural resource may exist as a separate entity such as fresh water, and air, as well as a living organism such as a fish, or it may exist in an alternate form which must be processed to obtain the resource such as metal ores, oil, and most forms of energy.

There is much debate worldwide over natural resource allocations, this is partly due to increasing scarcity (depletion of resources) but also because the exportation of natural resources is the basis for many economies (particularly for developed nations such as Australia).

Some natural resources such as sunlight and air can be found everywhere, and are known as ubiquitous resources. However, most resources only occur in small sporadic areas, and are referred to as localized resources. There are very few resources that are considered inexhaustible (will not run out in foreseeable future) – these are solar radiation, geothermal energy, and air (though access to clean air may not be). The vast majority of resources are exhaustible, which means they have a finite quantity, and can be depleted if managed improperly.

Classification

There are various methods of categorizing natural resources, these include source of origin, stage of development, and by their renewability. These classifications are described below. On the basis of origin, resources may be divided into:

- Biotic – Biotic resources are obtained from the biosphere (living and organic material), such as forests and animals, and the materials that can be obtained from them. Fossil fuels such as coal and petroleum are also included in this category because they are formed from decayed organic matter.
- Abiotic – Abiotic resources are those that come from non-living, non-organic material. Examples of abiotic resources include land, fresh water, air and heavy metals including ores such as gold, iron, copper, silver, etc.

Considering their stage of development, natural resources may be referred to in the following ways:

- *Potential Resources* – Potential resources are those that exist in a region and may be used in the future. For example, petroleum may exist in many parts of India, having sedimentary rocks but until the time it is actually drilled out and put into use, it remains a potential resource.
- *Actual Resources* – Actual resources are those that have been surveyed, their quantity and quality determined and are being used in present times. The development of an actual resource, such as wood processing depends upon the technology available and the cost involved.
- *Reserve Resources* – The part of an actual resource which can be developed profitably in the future is called a reserve resource.
- *Stock Resources* – Stock resources are those that have been surveyed but cannot be used by organisms due to lack of technology. For example: hydrogen.

Renewability is a very popular topic and many natural resources can be categorized as either renewable or non-renewable:

- Renewable resources are ones that can be replenished naturally. Some of these resources, like sunlight, air, wind, etc., are continuously available and their quantity is not noticeably affected by human consumption. Though many renewable resources do not have such a rapid recovery rate, these resources are susceptible to depletion by over-use. Resources from a human use perspective are classified as renewable only so long as the rate of replenishment/recovery exceeds that of the rate of consumption.

- Non-renewable resources are resources that form extremely slowly and those that do not naturally form in the environment. Minerals are the most common resource included in this category. By the human perspective, resources are non-renewable when their rate of consumption exceeds the rate of replenishment/recovery; a good example of this are fossil fuels, which are in this category because their rate of formation is extremely slow (potentially millions of years), meaning they are considered non-renewable. Some resources actually naturally deplete in amount without human interference, the most notable of these being radio-active elements such as uranium, which naturally decay into heavy metals. Of these, the metallic minerals can be re-used by recycling them, but coal and petroleum cannot be recycled.

Extraction

Resource extraction involves any activity that withdraws resources from nature. This can range in scale from the traditional use of preindustrial societies, to global industry. Extractive industries are, along with agriculture, the basis of the primary sector of the economy. Extraction produces raw material which is then processed to add value. Examples of extractive industries are hunting and trapping, mining, oil and gas drilling, and forestry. Natural resources can add substantial's to a country's wealth, however a sudden inflow of money caused by a resource boom can create social problems including inflation harming other industries ("Dutch disease") and corruption, leading to inequality and underdevelopment, this is known as the "resource curse".

Depletion

In recent years, the depletion of natural resources has become a major focus of governments and organizations such as the United Nations (UN). This is evident in the UN's Agenda 21 Section Two, which outlines the necessary steps to be taken by countries to sustain their natural resources. The depletion of natural resources is considered to be a sustainable development issue. The term sustainable development has many interpretations, most notably the Brundtland Commission's 'to ensure that it meets the needs of the present without compromising the ability of future generations to meet their own needs', however in broad terms it is balancing the needs of the planet's people and species now and in the future. In regards to natural resources, depletion is of concern for sustainable development as it has the ability to degrade current environments and potential to impact the needs of future generations.

Depletion of Natural Resources is associated with social inequity. Considering most biodiversity are located in developing countries, depletion of this resource could result in losses of ecosystem services for these countries. Some view this depletion as a major source of social unrest and conflicts in developing nations.

At present, with it being the year of the forest, there is particular concern for rainforest regions which hold most of the Earth's biodiversity. According to Nelson deforestation and degradation affect 8.5% of the world's forests with 30% of the Earth's surface already cropped. If we consider that 80% of people rely on medicines obtained from plants and ¾ of the world's prescription medicines have ingredients taken from plants, loss of the world's rainforests could result in a loss of finding more potential life saving medicines.

The depletion of natural resources is caused by 'direct drivers of change' such as Mining, petroleum extraction, fishing and forestry as well as 'indirect drivers of change' such as demography, economy, society, politics and technology. The current practice of Agriculture is another factor causing depletion of natural resources. For example the depletion of nutrients in the soil due to excessive use of nitrogen and desertification The depletion of natural resources is a continuing concern for society. This is seen in the cited quote given by Theodore Roosevelt, a well-known conservationist and former United States president, was opposed to unregulated natural resource extraction.

Protection

In 1982 the UN developed the World Charter for Nature in which it recognised the need to protect nature from further depletion due to human activity. They state the measures needed to be taken at all societal levels, from international right down to individual, to protect nature. They outline the need for sustainable use of natural resources and suggest that the protection of resources should be incorporated into the law system at state and international level. To look at the importance of protecting natural resources further. The World Ethic of Sustainability, developed by the IUCN, WWF and the UNEP in 1990 which set out eight values for sustainability, include the need to protect natural resources from depletion. Since these documents, there have been many measures taken to protect natural resources, some of these ways include Conservation biology and Habitat Conservation.

Conservation biology is the scientific study of the nature and status of Earth's biodiversity with the aim of protecting species, their habitats, and ecosystems from excessive rates of extinction. It is an interdisciplinary subject drawing on sciences, economics, and the practice of natural resource management. The term *conservation biology* was introduced as the title of a conference held University of California at San Diego in La Jolla, California in 1978 organized by biologists Bruce Wilcox and Michael Soulé.

Habitat conservation is a land management practice that seeks to conserve, protect and restore, habitat areas for wild plants and animals, especially conservation reliant species, and prevent their extinction, fragmentation or reduction in range.

Environmental Protection

Environmental protection is a practice of protecting the natural environment on individual, organizational or governmental levels, for the benefit of the natural environment and humans. Due to the pressures of population and technology, the biophysical environment is being degraded, sometimes permanently. This has been recognized, and governments have begun placing restraints on activities that cause environmental degradation. Since the 1960's, activity of environmental movements has created awareness of the various environmental issues. There is no agreement on the extent of the environmental impact of human activity, and protection measures are occasionally criticized.

Academic institutions now offer courses, such as environmental studies, environmental management and environmental engineering, that teach the history and methods of environment protection. Protection of the environment is needed due to various human activities. Waste production, air pollution, and loss of biodiversity (resulting from the introduction of invasive species and species extinction) are some of the issues related to environmental protection.

Environmental protection is influenced by three interwoven factors: environmental legislation, ethics and education. Each of these factors plays its part in influencing national-level environmental decisions and personal-level environmental values and behaviours. For environmental protection to become a reality, it is important for societies to develop each of these areas that, together, will inform and drive environmental decisions.

Approaches to Environmental Protection

Voluntary Environmental Agreements: In industrialized countries, voluntary environmental agreements often provide a platform for companies to be recognized for moving beyond the minimum regulatory standards and, thus, support the development of best environmental practice.

In developing countries, such as throughout Latin America, these agreements are more commonly used to remedy significant levels of non-compliance with mandatory regulation. The challenges that exist with these agreements lie in establishing baseline data, targets, monitoring and reporting.

Due to the difficulties inherent in evaluating effectiveness, their use is often questioned and, indeed, the environment may well be adversely affected as a result. The key advantage of their use in developing countries is that their use helps to build environmental management capacity.

Ecosystems Approach

An ecosystems approach to resource management and environmental protection aims to consider the complex interrelationships of an entire ecosystem in decision making rather than simply responding to specific issues and challenges. Ideally the decision-making processes under such an approach would be a collaborative approach to planning and decision making that involves a broad range of stakeholders across all relevant governmental departments, as well as representatives of industry, environmental groups and community. This approach ideally supports a better exchange of information, development of conflict-resolution strategies and improved regional conservation.

International Environmental Agreements

Many of the earth's resources are especially vulnerable because they are influenced by human impacts across many countries. As a result of this, many attempts are made by countries to develop agreements that are signed by multiple governments to prevent damage or manage the impacts of human activity on natural resources.

This can include agreements that impact factors such as climate, oceans, rivers and air pollution. These international environmental agreements are sometimes legally binding documents that have legal implications when they are not followed and, at other times, are more agreements in principle or are for use as codes of conduct.

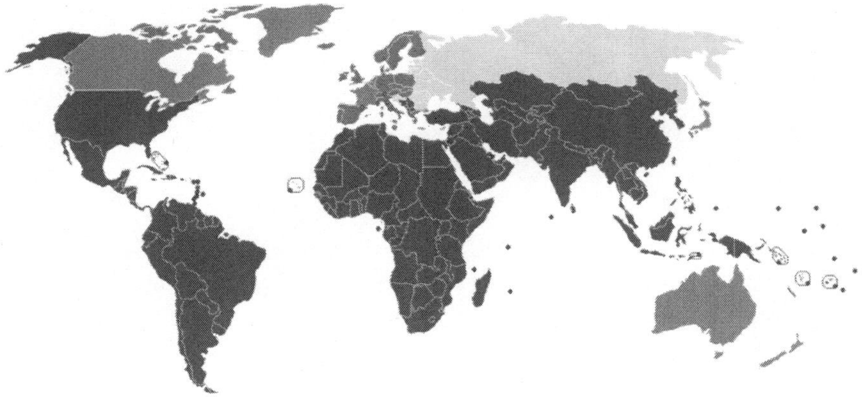

Figure: *Kyoto Protocol Commitment map 2010*

These agreements have a long history with some multinational agreements being in place from as early as 1910 in Europe, America and Africa. Some of the most well-known multinational agreements include: the Kyoto Protocol, Vienna Convention on the Protection of the Ozone Layer and Rio Declaration on Environment and Development

Government

Discussion concerning environmental protection often focuses on the role of government, legislation and law enforcement. However, in its broadest sense, environmental protection may be seen to be the responsibility of all people and not simply that of government.

Decisions that impact the environment will ideally involve a broad range of stakeholders, including industry, indigenous groups, environmental group and community representatives. Gradually, environmental decision-making processes are evolving to reflect this broad base of stakeholders and are becoming more collaborative in many countries.

Many constitutions acknowledge the fundamental right to environmental protection, and many international treaties acknowledge the right to live in a healthy environment. Also, many countries have organizations and agencies devoted to environmental protection. There are international environmental protection organizations, as the United Nations Environment Programme.

Although environmental protection is not simply the responsibility of government agencies, most people view these agencies as being of prime importance in establishing and maintaining basic standards that protect both the environment and the people interacting with it.

Management

Natural resource management is a discipline in the management of natural resources such as land, water, soil, plants and animals, with a particular focus on how management affects the quality of life for both present and future generations.

Management of natural resources involves identifying who has the right to use the resources and who does not for defining the boundaries of the resource. The resources are managed by the users according to the rules governing of when and how the resource is used depending on local condition.

A successful management of natural resources should engage the community because of the nature of the shared resources the individuals who are affected by the rules can participate in setting or changing them. The users have the rights to device their own management institutions and plans under the recognition by the government. The right to resources includes land, water, fisheries and pastoral rights. The users or parties accountable to the users have to actively monitor and ensure the utilisation of the resource compliance with the rules and to impose penalty on those peoples who violates the rules. These conflicts are resolved in a quick and low cost manner by the local institution according to the seriousness and context of the offence.. The global science-based platform to discuss natural resources management is the World Resources Forum, based in Switzerland.

Renewable Resource

A renewable resource is a natural resource which can replenish with the passage of time, either through biological reproduction or other naturally recurring processes. Renewable resources are a part of Earth's natural environment and the largest components of its ecosphere. A positive life cycle assessment is a key indicator of a resource's sustainability. In 1962, Paul Alfred Weiss defined Renewable Resources as: "*The total range of living organisms providing man with food, fibres, drugs, etc...*".

Renewable resources may be the source of power for renewable energy. However, if the rate at which the renewable resource is consumed exceeds its renewal rate, renewal and sustainability will not be ensured. The term renewable resource also describes systems like sustainable agriculture and water resources. Sustainable harvesting of renewable resources (i.e., maintaining a positive renewal rate) can reduce air pollution, soil contamination, habitat destruction and land degradation. Gasoline, coal, natural gas, diesel and other commodities derived from fossil fuels, as well as minerals like copper and others, are non-renewable resources without a sustainable yield.

Renewable Resources Endangered by the Industrial World

Overfishing :

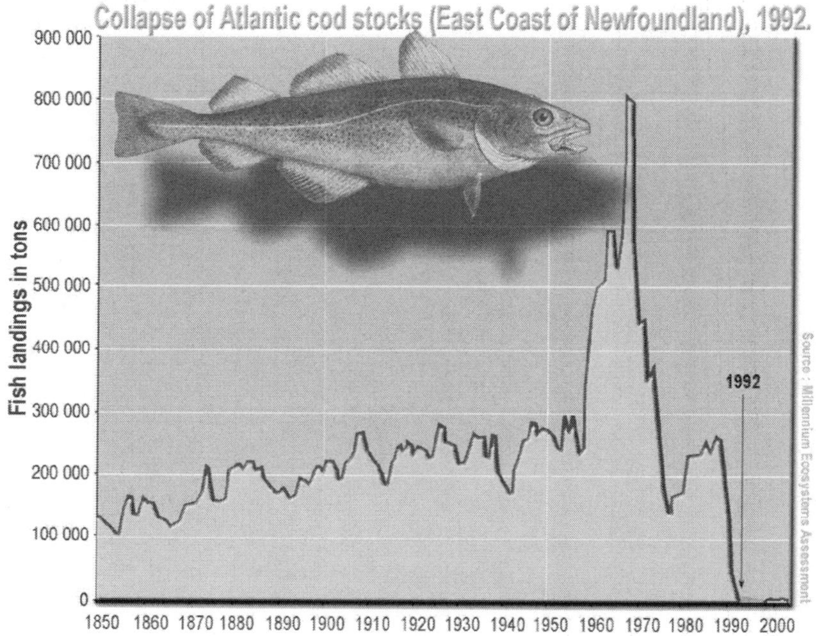

Figure: *Atlantic cod stocks severely overfished leading to abrupt collapse*

"Ocean overfishing is simply the taking of wildlife from the sea at rates too high for fished species to replace themselves." Tuna meat is driving overfishing as to endanger some species like the bluefin tuna. The European Community and other organisations are trying to regulate fishery as to protect species and to prevent their extinctions. The United Nations Convention on the Law of the Sea treaty deals with aspects of overfishing in articles 61, 62, and 65. Examples of overfishing exist in areas such as the North Sea of Europe, the Grand Banks of North America and the East China Sea of Asia.

The decline of penguin population is caused in part by overfishing, caused by human competition over the same renewable resources.

Sustainable Agriculture

The phrase sustainable agriculture was coined by Australian agricultural scientist Gordon McClymont. It has been defined as "an integrated system of plant and animal production practices having a site-specific application that will last over the long term. Expansion of agricultural land has an impact on biodiversity and contributes to deforestation. The Food and Agriculture Organisation of the United Nations estimates that in coming decades, cropland will continue to be lost to industrial and urban development, along with reclamation of wetlands, and conv ersion of forest to cultivation, resulting in the loss of biodiversity and increased soil erosion.

Although air and sunlight are available everywhere on Earth, crops also depend on soil nutrients and the availability of water. Monoculture is a method of growing only one crop at a time in a given field, which can damage land and cause it to become either unusable or suffer from reduced yields. Monoculture can also cause the build-up of pathogens and pests that target one specific species. The Great Irish Famine (1845–1849) is a well-known example of the dangers of monoculture.

Crop rotation and long-term crop rotations confer the replenishment of nitrogen through the use of green manure in sequence with cereals and other crops, and can improve soil structure and fertility by alternating deep-rooted and shallow-rooted plants. Other methods to combat lost soil nutrients are returning to natural cycles that annually flood cultivated lands (returning lost nutrients indefinitely) such as the Flooding of the Nile, the long-term use of biochar, and use of crop and livestock landraces that are adapted to less than ideal conditions such as pests, drought, or lack of nutrients.

Agricultural practices are the single greatest contributor to the global increase in soil erosion rates. It is estimated that "more than a thousand million tonnes of southern Africa's soil are eroded every year. Experts predict that crop yields will be halved within thirty to fifty years if erosion continues at present rates." The Dust Bowl phenomenon in the 1930s was caused by severe drought combined with farming methods that did not include crop rotation, fallow fields, cover crops, soil terracing and wind-breaking trees to prevent wind erosion.

The tillage of agricultural lands is one of the primary contributing factors to erosion, due to mechanized agricultural equipment that allows for deep plowing, which severely increases the amount of soil that is available for transport by water erosion. The phenomenon called *Peak Soil* describes how large-scale factory farming techniques are jeopardizing humanity's ability to grow food in the present and in the future. Without efforts to improve soil management practices, the availability of arable soil will become increasingly problematic.

Methods to combat erosion include no-till farming, using a keyline design, growing wind breaks to hold the soil, and widespread use of compost. Chemical fertilizer and pesticides can also have an effect of soil erosion, which can contribute to soil salinity and prevent other species from growing. Phosphate is a primary component in the chemical fertilizer applied most commonly in modern agricultural production. However, scientists estimate that rock phosphate reserves will be depleted in 50–100 years and that *Peak Phosphate* will occur in about 2030.

Industrial processing and logistics also have an effect on agriculture's sustainability. The way and locations crops are sold requires energy for transportation, as well as the energy cost for materials, labour, and transport. Food sold at a local location, such a farmers' market, have reduced energy overheads.

Deforestation

The destruction of rain forests is one of the critical causes of climate change. Deforestation causes carbon dioxide to linger in the atmosphere. As carbon dioxide accrues, it produces a layer in the atmosphere that traps radiation from the sun. The radiation converts to heat which causes global warming, which is better known as the greenhouse effect. Trees are renewable resources as they protect our environment by absorbing carbon dioxide and by creating oxygen.

Deforestation also affects the water cycle. It reduces the content of water in the soil and groundwater as well as atmospheric moisture. Deforestation reduces soil cohesion, so that erosion, flooding and landslides ensue.

Rain forests are also sheltering many species and organism providing local populations with food and other commodities. Are biofuel sustainable if they contribute to deforestation?

Endangered Species

Some renewable resources, species and organisms are facing a very high risk of extinction caused by growing human population and over-consumption. It has been estimated that over 40% of all living species on Earth are at risk of going extinct. Many nations have laws to protect hunted species and to restrict the practice of hunting. Other conservation methods includes restricting land development or creating preserves. The IUCN Red List of Threatened Species is the best-known worldwide conservation status listing and ranking system. Internationally, 199 countries have signed an accord agreeing to create Biodiversity Action Plans to protect endangered and other threatened species.

Water Resources

Water can be considered a renewable material when carefully controlled usage, treatment, and release are followed. If not, it would become a non-renewable resource at that location. For example, groundwater is usually removed from an aquifer at a rate much greater than its very slow natural recharge, and so groundwater is considered non-renewable. Removal of water from the pore spaces may cause permanent compaction (subsidence) that cannot be renewed. 97% of the water on the Earth is salt water, and 3% is fresh water; slightly over two thirds of this is frozen in glaciers and polar ice caps. The remaining unfrozen freshwater is found mainly as groundwater, with only a small fraction (0,008%) present above ground or in the air.

Water pollution is one of the main concerns regarding water resources. It is estimated that 22% of worldwide water is used in industry. Major industrial users include hydroelectric dams, thermoelectric power plants, which use water for cooling, ore and oil refineries, which use water in chemical processes, and manufacturing plants, which use water as a solvent.

Renewable Energy

Renewable energy is energy from natural resources such as sunlight, wind, rain, tides, waves and geothermal heat. Common applications of renewable energies are electricity generation and motor fuels. The reported problem with these renewable resources is that it is difficult and expensive to harness enough power from them to match the effectiveness of non-renewable resources.

Solar Energy

Solar energy is the most abundant and easily available renewable resource, and has been harnessed by humans since ancient times. In one year, the Sun delivers more than 10,000 times the energy that humans currently use, and almost twice the amount of energy that will ever be obtained from all of the planet's non-renewable resources.

Solar power is the conversion of sunlight into electricity, either directly using photovoltaics (PV), or indirectly using concentrated solar power (CSP). Concentrated solar power systems use lenses or mirrors and tracking systems to focus a large area of sunlight into a small beam. Photovoltaics convert light into electric current using the photoelectric effect.

There are many domestic applications of solar power including solar cookers, solar stills, solar water heating, solar heating and air conditioning.

Wind Power

Wind power is the conversion of wind energy into a useful form of energy. Most modern electrical wind power is generated by converting the rotation of turbine blades into electrical currents by means of an electrical generator.

Windmills provide mechanical power, and were originally developed for milling grain for food production. Other industrial uses of windmill machinery are windpumps, used for water pumping or drainage.

Wind power is also used to propel ships using sails.

Hydropower

Hydropower is energy derived from the movement of water in rivers and oceans, originally used for irrigation and the operation of various mechanical devices. Since the early 20th century, the term is used almost exclusively in conjunction with the modern development of hydro-electric power. Conventional hydroelectric power involves creating a dam, and using the resulting water force to turn a water turbine and generator. Other electricity generating methods are run-of-the-river hydroelectricity, which captures the kinetic energy in rivers or streams, without the use of dams, and pumped-storage hydroelectricity, which stores water pumped during periods of low demand to be released for generation when demand is high.

Geothermal Energy

Geothermal energy comes from the Earth's crust and originates from the original formation of the planet (20%) and from radioactive decay of minerals (80%). The available energy from the Earth's crust and mantle is approximately equal to that of incoming solar energy.

Geothermal heating is the direct use of geothermal energy for heating applications. Since paleolithic times, naturally occurring Hot springs have been used for bathing.

Geothermal electricity is electricity generated from geothermal energy using technologies like superheaters, flash steam power plants and binary cycle power plants. The first geothermal power station was built at Landrello, Italy. Other countries that have geothermal power stations are Japan, Iceland, the Philippines and the United States. In Iceland, geothermal energy is used for electricity and heat.

Biofuel

A biofuel is a type of fuel whose energy is derived from biological carbon fixation. Biofuels include fuels derived from biomass conversion, as well as solid biomass, liquid fuels and various biogases.

Bioethanol is an alcohol made by fermentation, mostly from carbohydrates produced in sugar or starch crops such as corn, sugarcane or switchgrass.

Biodiesel is made from vegetable oils and animal fats. Biodiesel is produced from oils or fats using transesterification and is the most common biofuel in Europe.

Biogas is methane produced by the process of anaerobic digestion of organic material by anaerobes., etc. is also a renewable source of energy.

Renewable Materials

Biomass

Biomass is biological material from living, or recently living organisms, most often referring to plants or plant-derived materials. As a renewable energy source, biomass can either be used directly, or indirectly—once or converted into another type of energy product such as biofuel. The use of biomass helps to sustain climate change, increase energy efficiency, and decrease greenhouse gas emission. Biomass is all biologically produced matter based in carbon, hydrogen and oxygen. The estimated biomass production in the world is 146 billion tons a year, consisting of mostly wild plant growth. Biomass energy is derived from six distinct energy sources: garbage, wood, plants, waste, landfill gases, and alcohol fuels. Historically, humans have harnessed biomass derived energy since the advent of burning wood to make fire, and wood remains the largest biomass energy source today.

The biomass used for electricity generation varies by region. Forest by-products, such as wood residues, are common in the United States. Agricultural waste is common in Mauritius (sugar cane residue) and Southeast Asia (rice husks). Animal husbandry residues, such as poultry litter, are common in the UK. The biomass power generating industry in the United States, which consists of approximately 11,000 MW of summer operating capacity actively supplying power to the grid, produces about 1.4 percent of the U.S. electricity supply.

Bioplastics

Bioplastics are a form of plastics derived from renewable biomass sources, such as vegetable fats and oils, corn starch, pea starch or microbiota. The most common form of bioplastic is thermoplastic starch. Other forms include Cellulose bioplastics, biopolyester, Polylactic acid, and bio-derived polyethylene.

The production and use of bioplastics is generally regarded as a more sustainable activity when compared with plastic production from petroleum (petroplastic), however manufacturing of bioplastic materials is often still reliant upon petroleum as an energy and materials source. Because of the fragmentation in the market and ambiguous definitions it is difficult to describe the total market size for bioplastics, but estimates put global production capacity at 327,000 tonnes. In contrast, global consumption of all flexible packaging is estimated at around 12.3 million tonnes.

Bioasphalt

Bioasphalt is an asphalt alternative made from non-petroleum based renewable resources. Manufacturing sources of bioasphalt include sugar, molasses and rice, corn and potato starches, and vegetable oil based waste. Asphalt made with vegetable oil based binders was patented by Colas SA in France in 2004.

Non-renewable Resource

A non-renewable resource (also known as a finite resource) is a resource that does not renew itself at a sufficient rate for sustainable economic extraction in meaningful human timeframes. An example is carbon-based, organically-derived fuel. The original organic material, with the aid of heat and pressure, becomes a fuel such as oil or gas.

Fossil fuels (such as coal, petroleum, and natural gas), and certain aquifers are all examples of non-renewable resources.

Metal ores are other examples of non-renewable resources. The metals themselves are present in vast amounts in the earth's crust which can never be exhausted, and which are continually being concentrated and replenished over time scales of millions of years, however their extraction by humans only occurs where they are concentrated by natural processes (such as heat, pressure, organic activity, weathering and other processes) to a level that is economically extractable, and where these processes occur, or are brought near, the earth's surface, generally over tens of thousands to millions of years. As such, localised deposits of metal ores near the surface which can be extracted economically by humans are non-renewable in human timeframes, but on a world scale metal ores as a whole are inexhaustible, because the amount ultimately available vastly exceeds human demand, on all timeframes. In other words, metal ores are non-renewable, but generally inexhaustible. In this respect, metal ores are considered vastly greater in supply to fossil fuels because metal ores are formed by crustal scale processes which make up a much larger portion of the earth's near-surface environment than those that form fossil fuels, and without the need for specialized conditions where carbon based life flourishes and fossil fuels can form.

In contrast, resources such as timber (when harvested sustainably) and wind (used to power energy conversion systems) are considered renewable resources, largely because their localized replenishment can occur within timeframes meaningful to humans.

Fossil Fuel

Natural resources such as coal, petroleum (crude oil) and natural gas take thousands of years to form naturally and cannot be replaced as fast as they are being consumed. Eventually it is considered that fossil-based resources will become too costly to harvest and humanity will need to shift its reliance to other sources of energy. These resources are yet to be named.

An alternative hypothesis is that carbon based fuel is virtually inexhaustible in human terms, if one includes all sources of carbon-based energy such as methane hydrates on the sea floor, which are vastly greater than all other carbon based fossil fuel resources combined. These sources of carbon are also considered non-renewable, although their rate of formation/replenishment on the sea floor is not known. However their extraction at economically viable costs and rates has yet to be determined.

At present, the main energy source used by humans is non-renewable fossil fuels. Since the dawn of internal combustion engine technologies in the 17th century, petroleum and other fossil fuels have remained in continual demand. As a result, conventional infrastructure and transport systems, which are fitted to combustion engines, remain prominent throughout the globe. The continual use of fossil fuels at the current rate is believed to increase global warming and cause more severe climate change.

Radioactive Fuel

The use of nuclear technology requires a radioactive fuel. Uranium ore is present in the ground at relatively low concentrations and mined in 19 countries. This mined uranium is used to fuel energy-generating nuclear reactors with fissionable uranium-238 which generates heat that is ultimately used to power turbines to generate electricity.

Nuclear power provides about 6% of the world's energy and 13–14% of the world's electricity. The expense of the nuclear industry remains predominantly reliant on subsidies and indirect insurance subsidies to continue. Nuclear energy production is associated with potentially dangerous radioactive contamination as it relies upon unstable elements. In particular, nuclear power facilities produce about 200,000 metric tons of low and intermediate level waste (LILW) and 10,000 metric tons of high level waste (HLW) (including spent fuel designated as waste) each year worldwide.

The use of nuclear fuel and the high-level radioactive waste the nuclear industry generates is highly hazardous to people and wildlife. Radiocontaminants in the environment can enter the food chain and become bioaccumulated. Internal or external exposure can cause mutagenic DNA breakage producing teratogenic generational birth defects, cancers and other damage. The United Nations (UNSCEAR) estimated in 2008 that average annual human radiation exposure includes 0.01 mSv (milli-Sievert) from the legacy of past atmospheric nuclear testing plus the Chernobyl disaster and the nuclear fuel cycle, along with 2.0 mSv from natural radioisotopes and 0.4 mSv from cosmic rays; all exposures vary by location. Some radioisotopes in nuclear waste emit harmful radiation for the prolonged period of 4.5 billion years or more, and storage has risks of containment. The storage of waste, health implications and dangers of radioactive fuel continue to be a topic of debate, resulting in a controversial and unresolved industry.

Renewable Resources

Natural resources, called renewable resources, are replaced by natural processes and forces persistent in the natural environment. There are intermittent and reoccurring renewables, and recyclable materials, which are utilized during a cycle across a certain amount of time, and can be harnessed for any number of cycles.

The production of goods and services by manufacturing products in economic systems creates many types of waste during production and after the consumer has made use of it. The material is then either incinerated, buried in a landfill or recycled for reuse. Recycling turns materials of value that would otherwise become waste into valuable resources again.

The natural environment, with soil, water, forests, plants and animals are all renewable resources, as long as they are adequately monitored, protected and conserved. Sustainable agriculture is the cultivation of plant materials in a manner that preserves plant and animal ecosystems over the long term. The overfishing of the oceans is one example of where an industry practice or method can threaten an ecosystem, endanger species and possibly even determine whether or not a fishery is sustainable for use by humans. An unregulated industry practice or method can lead to a complete resource depletion.

The renewable energy from the sun, wind, wave, biomass and geothermal energies are based on renewable resources. Renewable resources such as the movement of water (hydropower, tidal power and wave power), wind and radiant energy from geothermal heat (used for geothermal power) and solar energy (used for solar power) are practically infinite and cannot be depleted, unlike their non-renewable counterparts, which are likely to run out if not used sparingly. The potential wave energy on coastlines can provide 1/5 of world demand. Hydroelectric power can supply 1/3 of our total energy global needs. Geothermal energy can provide 1.5 more times the energy we need. There is enough wind to power the planet 30 times over, wind power could power all of humanity's needs alone. Solar currently supplies only 0.1% of our world energy needs, but there is enough out there to power humanity's needs 4,000 times over, the entire global projected energy demand by 2050.

Renewable energy and energy efficiency are no longer niche sectors that are promoted only by governments and environmentalists. The increasing levels of investment and that more of the capital is from conventional financial actors, both suggest that sustainable energy has become mainstream and the future of energy production, as non-renewable resources decline. This is reinforced by climate change concerns, nuclear dangers and accumulating radioactive waste, high oil prices, peak oil and increasing government support for renewable energy. These factors are commercializing renewable energy, enlarging the market and growing demand, the adoption of new products to replace obsolete technology and the conversion of existing infrastructure to a renewable standard.

Economic Models

In economics, a non-renewable resource is defined as goods, where greater consumption today implies less consumption tomorrow. David Ricardo in his early works analysed the pricing of exhaustible resources, where he argued that the price of a mineral resource should increase over time. He argued that the spot price is always determined by the mine with the highest cost of extraction, and mine owners with lower extraction costs benefit from a differential rent. The first model is defined by Hotelling's rule, which is a 1931 economic model of non-renewable resource management by Harold Hotelling. It shows that efficient exploitation of a nonrenewable and nonaugmentable resource would, under otherwise stable conditions, lead to a depletion of the resource. The rule states that this would lead to a net price or "Hotelling rent" for it that rose annually at a rate equal to the rate of interest, reflecting the increasing scarcity of the resources. The Hartwick's rule provides an important result about the sustainability of welfare in an economy that uses non-renewable source.

However, all metal prices have been declining over time, because of a number of false assumptions in the above. Firstly, metal resources are non-renewable, but on a world scale, inexhaustible. They are present throughout the earth's crust on a vast scale, far exceeding human demand on all time scales. Metal ores however, are only extracted in those areas where nature has concentrated the metal in the crust to a level whereby it is locally economic to extract. This also depends on the available technology for both finding the metal ores as well as extracting them, which is constantly changing. If the technology or demand changes, vast amounts of metal previously ignored can become economically extractable. This is why Ricardo's simplistic notion that the price of a mineral resource should increase over time has in fact turned out to be the opposite, all metal ores have decreased in price since the early 20th century. The main reason he was wrong is that he assumed that metals are exhaustible on a world scale, in human terms the amount of metal in the earth's crust is essentially limitless. It is only in localized areas that metal ores can become depleted, as these local areas compete with extraction costs of resources elsewhere, which has ramifications for the sustainability of local economies.

Conservation of Resources

Management of the human use of natural resources to provide the maximum benefit to current generations while maintaining capacity to meet the needs of future generations. Conservation includes both the protection and rational use of natural resources.

Earth's natural resources are either nonrenewable, such as minerals, oil, gas, and coal, or renewable, such as water, timber, fisheries, and agricultural crops. The combination of growing populations and increasing levels of resource consumption is degrading and depleting the natural resource base. The world's population stood at 850 million at the onset of the industrial age. The global population has grown to nearly seven times as large (6 billion), and the level of consumption of resources is far greater. This human pressure now exceeds the carrying capacity of many natural resources.

Nonrenewable resources, such as fossil fuels, are replaced over geologic time scales of tens of millions of years. Human societies will eventually use up all of the economically available stock of many nonrenewable resources, such as oil. Conservation entails actions to use these resources most efficiently and thereby extend their life as long as possible. By recycling aluminum, for example, the same piece of material is reused in a series of products, reducing the amount of aluminium ore that must be mined. Similarly, energy-efficient products help to conserve fossil fuels since the same energy services, such as lighting or transportation, can be attained with smaller amounts of fuel. It may be expected that the biggest challenge of resource conservation would involve nonrenewable resources, since renewable resources can replenish themselves after harvesting. In fact, the opposite is the case. Historically, when nonrenewable resources have been depleted, new technologies have been developed that effectively substitute for the depleted resources. Indeed, new technologies have often reduced pressure on these resources even before they are fully depleted. Fibre optics, for example, has substituted for copper in many electrical applications, and it is anticipated that renewable sources of energy, such as photovoltaic cells, wind power, and hydropower, will ultimately take the place of fossil fuels when stocks are depleted. Renewable resources, in contrast, can be seriously depleted if they are subjected to excessive harvest or otherwise degraded, and no substitutes are available for, say, clean water or food products such as fish or agricultural crops. Moreover, when the misuse of biological resources causes the complete extinction of a species or the loss of a particular habitat, there can be no substitute for that diversity of life.

"Conservation" is sometimes used synonymously with "protection." More appropriately, however, it refers to the protection and sustainable use of resources. Critical elements of the effective conservation of natural resources include sustainable resource management, establishment of protected areas, and ex situ (off-site) conservation.

11

Resource Based and Footloose Industries

The term and meaning of a Resource Based Economy was originated by Jacque Fresco. It is a holistic socio-economic system in which all goods and services are available without the use of money, credits, barter or any other system of debt or servitude. All resources become the common heritage of all of the inhabitants, not just a select few. The premise upon which this system is based is that the Earth is abundant with plentiful resource; our practice of rationing resources through monetary methods is irrelevant and counter productive to our survival. Modern society has access to highly advanced technology and can make available food, clothing, housing and medical care; update our educational system; and develop a limitless supply of renewable, non-contaminating energy. By supplying an efficiently designed economy, everyone can enjoy a very high standard of living with all of the amenities of a high technological society.

A resource-based economy would utilize existing resources from the land and sea, physical equipment, industrial plants, etc. to enhance the lives of the total population. In an economy based on resources rather than money, we could easily produce all of the necessities of life and provide a high standard of living for all. Consider the following examples: At the beginning of World War II the US had a mere 600 or so first-class fighting aircraft. We rapidly overcame this short supply by turning out more than 90,000 planes a year. The question at the start of World War II was: Do we have enough funds to produce the required implements of war? The answer was no, we did not have enough money, nor did we have enough gold; but we did have more than enough resources. It was the available resources that enabled the US to achieve the high production and efficiency required to win the war. Unfortunately this is only considered in times of war.

In a resource-based economy all of the world's resources are held as the common heritage of all of Earth's people, thus eventually outgrowing the need for the artificial boundaries that separate people. This is the unifying imperative. Natural resource economics deals with the supply, demand, and allocation of the Earth's natural resources. One main objective of natural resource economics is to better understand the role of natural resources in the economy in order to develop more sustainable methods of managing those resources to ensure their availability to future generations. Resource economists study interactions between economic and natural systems, with the goal of developing a sustainable and efficient economy.

We must emphasize that this approach to global governance has nothing whatever in common with the present aims of an elite to form a world government with themselves and large corporations at the helm, and the vast majority of the world's population subservient to them. Our vision of globalization empowers each and every person on the planet to be the best they can be, not to live in abject subjugation to a corporate governing body. Our proposals would not only add to the well being of people, but they would also provide the necessary information that would enable them to participate in any area of their competence. The measure of success would be based on the fulfilment of one's individual pursuits rather than the acquisition of wealth, property and power. At present, we have enough material resources to provide a very high standard of living for all of Earth's inhabitants. Only when population exceeds the carrying capacity of the land do many problems such as greed, crime and violence emerge. By overcoming scarcity, most of the crimes and even the prisons of today's society would no longer be necessary.

A resource-based economy would make it possible to use technology to overcome scarce resources by applying renewable sources of energy, computerizing and automating manufacturing and inventory, designing safe energy-efficient cities and advanced transportation systems, providing universal health care and more relevant education, and most of all by generating a new incentive system based on human and environmental concern. Many people believe that there is too much technology in the world today, and that technology is the major cause of our environmental pollution. This is not the case. It is the abuse and misuse of technology that should be our major concern. In a more humane civilization, instead of machines displacing people they would shorten the workday, increase the availability of goods and services, and lengthen vacation time. If we utilize new technology to raise the standard of living for all people, then the infusion of machine technology would no longer be a threat.

A resource-based world economy would also involve all-out efforts to develop new, clean, and renewable sources of energy: geothermal; controlled fusion; solar; photovoltaic; wind, wave, and tidal power; and even fuel from the oceans. We would eventually be able to have energy in unlimited quantity that could propel civilization for thousands of years. A resource-based economy must also be committed to the redesign of our cities, transportation systems, and industrial plants, allowing them to be energy efficient, clean, and conveniently serve the needs of all people. What else would a resource-based economy mean? Technology intelligently and efficiently applied, conserves energy, reduces waste, and provides more leisure time. With automated inventory on a global scale, we can maintain a balance between production and distribution. Only nutritious and healthy food would be available and planned obsolescence would be unnecessary and non-existent in a resource-based economy.

As we outgrow the need for professions based on the monetary system, for instance lawyers, bankers, insurance agents, marketing and advertising personnel, salespersons, and stockbrokers, a considerable amount of waste will be eliminated. Considerable amounts of energy would also be saved by eliminating the duplication of competitive products such as tools, eating utensils, pots, pans and vacuum cleaners. Choice is good. But instead of hundreds of different manufacturing plants and all the paperwork and personnel required to turn out similar products, only a few of the highest quality would be needed to serve the entire population. Our only shortage is the lack of creative thought and intelligence in ourselves and our elected leaders to solve these problems. The most valuable, untapped resource today is human ingenuity. With the elimination of debt, the fear of losing one's job will no longer be a threat. This assurance, combined with education on how to relate to one another in a much more meaningful way, could considerably reduce both mental and physical stress and leave us free to explore and develop our abilities. If the thought of eliminating money troubles you, consider this: If a group of people with gold, diamonds and money were stranded on an island that had no resources such as food, clean air and water, their wealth would be irrelevant to their survival. It is only when resources are scarce that money can be used to control their distribution. One could not, for example, sell the air we breathe or water abundantly flowing down from a mountain stream. Although air and water are valuable, in abundance they cannot be sold.

Money is only important in a society when certain resources for survival must be rationed and the people accept money as an exchange medium for the scarce resources. Money is a social convention, an agreement if you will. It is neither a natural resource nor does it represent one. It is not necessary for survival unless we have been conditioned to accept it as such. Coconino County has a wealth of natural resources — in agricultural and range lands, grasslands and forests — that could support sustainable economic development while helping to restore natural systems.

The Resource Based Industries Team is currently concentrating on developing collaborations that will help to identify and value the ecosystem services provided by the conservation efforts of major landscape-scale property owners as a way of enabling those stewards to remain on the land and continue making their contributions to local communities and environmental sustainability.

The Goal of this effort is to create economically viable, resource-based opportunities to support a thriving local / regional economy while maintaining stewardship of natural resources. This team:

- Encourages and promote the development and expansion of sustainable wood based industries in the area, including the production of electricity and steam that use all wood products (saw timber, round wood, biomass). This includes pinyon pine and juniper as well as ponderosa pine and Douglas-fir.
- Supports the establishment of long-term, large land management agency contracts to appropriately treat Northern Arizona forests and woodlands. Long-term contracts are a critical element in the creation and retention of a durable wood products based industry.
- Supports the establishment of viable, sustainable niche markets for speciality woods and products.
- Promotes the concept of healthy forests.
- Supports the creation of jobs with wages and benefits that provide adequately for families and contribute to community.

- Explores opportunities for acquiring conservation easements.
- Supports legislation that will enable exchanges between federal and state lands for the protection of open space.
- Develops and adopt a Coconino County *Transfer of Development Rights Ordinance.*
- Explores opportunities in Natural Heritage Area initiatives.
- Supports and seek to remove barriers to sustainable agriculture efforts.
- Supports a process by which the economic value of healthy watersheds is determined.
- Implements a market-based approach for large-scale watershed restoration.
- Encourages best-use practices and technologies for the use of reclaimed water and for water conservation.

Resource-based View

The resource-based view (RBV) as a basis for a competitive advantage of a firm lies primarily in the application of the bundle of valuable interchangeable and intangible tangible resources at the firm's disposal (Mwailu & Mercer, 1983 p142, Wernerfelt, 1984, p172; Rumelt, 1984, p557-558; Penrose, 1959). To transform a short-run competitive advantage into a sustained competitive advantage requires that these resources are heterogeneous in nature and not perfectly mobile (: p105-106; Peteraf, 1993, p180). Effectively, this translates into valuable resources that are neither perfectly imitable nor substitutable without great effort (Barney, 1991;: p117). If these conditions hold, the bundle of resources can sustain the firm's above average returns. The VRIO and VRIN model also constitutes a part of RBV. There is strong evidence that supports the RBV (Crook et al., 2008).

Key Points

The key points of the theory are:

1. Identify the firm's potential key resources.
2. Evaluate whether these resources fulfill the following criteria (referred to as *VRIN*):
   - o *Valuable* – A resource must enable a firm to employ a value-creating strategy, by either outperforming its competitors or reduce its own weaknesses (: p99;: p36). Relevant in this perspective is that the transaction costs associated with the

investment in the resource cannot be higher than the discounted future rents that flow out of the value-creating strategy (Mahoney and Prahalad, 1992, p370; Conner, 1992, p131).

- o *Rare* – To be of value, a resource must be rare by definition. In a perfectly competitive strategic factor market for a resource, the price of the resource will be a reflection of the expected discounted future above-average returns (Barney, 1986a, p1232-1233; Dierickx and Cool, 1989, p1504;: p100).
- o *In-imitable* – If a valuable resource is controlled by only one firm it could be a source of a competitive advantage (: p107). This advantage could be sustainable if competitors are not able to duplicate this strategic asset perfectly (Peteraf, 1993, p183; Barney, 1986b, p658). The term isolating mechanism was introduced by Rumelt (1984, p567) to explain why firms might not be able to imitate a resource to the degree that they are able to compete with the firm having the valuable resource (Peteraf, 1993, p182-183; Mahoney and Pandian, 1992, p371). An important underlying factor of inimitability is causal ambiguity, which occurs if the source from which a firm's competitive advantage stems is unknown (Peteraf, 1993, p182; Lippman and Rumelt, 1982, p420). If the resource in question is knowledge-based or socially complex, causal ambiguity is more likely to occur as these types of resources are more likely to be idiosyncratic to the firm in which it resides (Peteraf, 1993, p183; Mahoney and Pandian, 1992, p365;: p110). Conner and Prahalad go so far as to say knowledge-based resources are "*...the essence of the resource-based perspective*" (1996, p477).
- o *Non-substitutable* – Even if a resource is rare, potentially value-creating and imperfectly imitable, an equally important aspect is lack of substitutability (Dierickx and Cool, 1989, p1509;: p111). If competitors are able to counter the firm's value-creating strategy with a substitute, prices are driven down to the point that the price equals the discounted future rents (Barney, 1986a, p1233; sheikh, 1991, p137), resulting in zero economic profits.

3. Care for and protect resources that possess these evaluations, because doing so can improve organizational performance (Crook, Ketchen, Combs, and Todd, 2008).

The VRIN characteristics mentioned are individually necessary, but not sufficient conditions for a sustained competitive advantage (Dierickx and Cool, 1989, p1506; Priem and Butler, 2001a, p25). Within the framework of the resource-based view, the chain is as strong as its weakest link and therefore requires the resource to display each of the four characteristics to be a possible source of a sustainable competitive advantage (: 105-107).

Definitions

A subsequent distinction, made by Amit & Schoemaker (1993), is that the encompassing construct previously called "resources" can be divided into resources and capabilities. In this respect, resources are tradable and non-specific to the firm, while capabilities are firm-specific and are used to engage the resources within the firm, such as implicit processes to transfer knowledge within the firm (Makadok, 2001, p388-389; Hoopes, Madsen and Walker, 2003, p890). This distinction has been widely adopted throughout the resource-based view literature (Conner and Prahalad, 1996, p477; Makadok, 2001, p338; Barney, Wright and Ketchen, 2001, p630-31).

What Constitutes a "Capability"?

Makadok (2001) emphasizes the distinction between capabilities and resources by defining capabilities as "a special type of resource, specifically an organizationally embedded non-transferable firm-specific resource whose purpose is to improve the productivity of the other resources possessed by the firm" (p389). "[R]esources are stocks of available factors that are owned or controlled by the organization, and capabilities are an organization's capacity to deploy resources": p. 35. Essentially, it is the bundling of the resources that builds capabilities.

What Constitutes "Competitive Advantage"?

A competitive advantage can be attained if the current strategy is value-creating, and not currently being implemented by present or possible future competitors (: 102). Although a competitive advantage has the ability to become sustained, this is not necessarily the case. A competing firm can enter the market with a resource that has the ability to invalidate the prior firm's competitive advantage, which results in reduced (read: normal) rents (Barney, 1986b, p658). Sustainability in the context of a sustainable competitive advantage is independent with regard to the time frame. Rather, a competitive advantage is sustainable when the efforts by competitors to render the competitive advantage redundant have ceased (: p102; Rumelt, 1984, p562). When the imitative actions have come to an end without disrupting the firm's competitive advantage, the firm's strategy can be called sustainable. This is in contrast to views of others (e.g., Porter) that a competitive advantage is sustained when it provides above-average returns in the long run. (1985).

History of the Resource-based View

Some aspects of theories are thought of long before they are formally adopted and brought together into the strict framework of an academic theory. The same could be said with regard to the resource-based view.

While this influential body of research within the field of Strategic Management was named by Birger Wernerfelt in his article A Resource-Based View of the Firm (1984), the origins of the resource-based view can be traced back to earlier research. Retrospectively, elements can be found in works by Coase (1937), Selznick (1957), Penrose (1959), Stigler (1961), Chandler (1962, 1977), and Williamson (1975), where emphasis is put on the importance of resources and its implications for firm performance (Conner, 1991, p122; Rumelt, 1984, p557; Mahoney and Pandian, 1992, p263; Rugman and Verbeke, 2002). This paradigm shift from the narrow neoclassical focus to a broader rationale, and the coming closer of different academic fields (industrial organization economics and organizational economics being most prominent) was a particular important contribution.

Two publications closely following Wernerfelt's initial article came from Barney (1986a, 1986b). Even though Wernerfelt was not referenced directly, the statements made by Barney about strategic factor markets and the role of expectations can clearly be seen within the resource-based framework as later developed by Barney (1991). Other concepts that were later integrated into the resource-based framework have been articulated by Lippman and Rumelt (uncertain imitability, 1982), Rumelt (isolating mechanisms, 1984) and Dierickx and Cool (inimitability and its causes, 1989). Barney's framework proved a solid foundation upon which others might build, and its theoretical underpinnings were strengthened by Conner (1991), Mahoney and Pandian (1992), Conner and Prahalad (1996) and Makadok (2001), who positioned the resource-based view with regard to various other research fields. More practical approaches were provided for by Amit and Shoemaker (1993), while later criticism came from among others from Priem and Butler (2001a, 2001b) and Hoopes, Madsen and Walker (2003).

The resource based view has been a common interest for management researchers and numerous writings could be found for same. A resource-based view of a firm explains its ability to deliver sustainable competitive advantage when resources are managed such that their outcomes can not be imitated by competitors, which ultimately creates a competitive barrier (Mahoney and Pandian 1992 cited by Hooley and Greenley 2005, p. 96, Smith and Rupp 2002, p. 48). RBV explains that a firm's sustainable competitive advantage is reached by virtue of unique resources being rare, valuable, inimitable, non-tradable, and non-substitutable, as well as firm-specific (Barney 1999 cited by Finney et al.2004, p. 1722, Makadok 2001, p. 94).

These authors write about the fact that a firm may reach a sustainable competitive advantage through unique resources which it holds, and these resources cannot be easily bought, transferred, or copied, and simultaneously, they add value to a firm while being rare. It also highlights the fact that not all resources of a firm may contribute to a firm's sustainable competitive advantage.

Varying performance between firms is a result of heterogeneity of assets (Lopez 2005, p. 662, Helfat and Peteraf 2003, p. 1004) and RBV is focused on the factors that cause these differences to prevail (Grant 1991, Mahoney and Pandian 1992, cited by Lopez 2005, p. 662).

Fundamental similarity in these writings is that unique value-creating resources will generate a sustainable competitive advantage to the extent that no competitor has the ability to use the same type of resources, either through acquisition or imitation. Major concern in RBV is focused on the ability of the firm to maintain a combination of resources that cannot be possessed or built up in a similar manner by competitors. Further such writings provide us with the base to understand that the sustainability strength of competitive advantage depends on the ability of competitors to use identical or similar resources that make the same implications on a firm's performance. This ability of a firm to avoid imitation of their resources should be analyzed in depth to understand the sustainability strength of a competitive advantage.

Barriers to Imitation of Resources

Resources are the inputs or the factors available to a company which helps to perform its operations or carry out its activities (, Black and Boal 1994, Grant 1995 cited by Ordaz et al.2003, p. 96). Also, these authors state that resources, if considered as isolated factors, do not result in productivity; hence, coordination of resources is important. The ways a firm can create a barrier to imitation are known as "isolating mechanisms", and are reflected in the aspects of corporate culture, managerial capabilities, information asymmetries and property rights (Hooley and Greenlay 2005, p. 96, Winter 2003,p. 992). Further, they mention that except for legislative restrictions created through property rights, the other three aspects are direct or indirect results of managerial practices.

King (2007, p. 156) mentions inter-firm causal ambiguity may results in sustainable competitive advantage for some firms. Causal ambiguity is the continuum that describes the degree to which decision makers understand the relationship between organizational inputs and outputs (Ghinggold and Johnson 1998,p. 134,Lippman and Rumelt 1982 cited by King 2007, p. 156, Matthyssens and Vandenbempt 1998, p. 46). Their argument is that inability of competitors to understand what causes the superior performance of another (inter-firm causal ambiguity), helps to reach a sustainable competitive advantage for the one who is presently performing at a superior level. Holley and Greenley (2005, p. 96) state that social context of certain resource conditions act as an element to create isolating mechanisms and quote Wernerfelt (1986) that tacitness (accumulated skill-based resources acquired through learning by doing) complexity (large number of inter-related resources being used) and specificity (dedication of certain resources to specific activities) and ultimately, these three characteristics will result in a competitive barrier.

Referring back to the definitions stated previously regarding the competitive advantage that mentions superior performance is correlated to resources of the firm (Christensen and Fahey 1984, Kay 1994, Porter 1980 cited by Chacarbaghi and Lynch 1999, p. 45) and consolidating writings of King (2007, p. 156) stated above, we may derive the fact that inter-firm causal ambiguity regarding resources will generate a competitive advantage at a sustainable level. Further, it explains that the depth of understanding of competitors—regarding which resources underlie the superior performance—will determine the sustainability strength of a competitive advantage. Should a firm be unable to overcome the inter-firm causal ambiguity, this does not necessarily result in imitating resources. As to Johnson (2006, p. 02) and Mahoney (2001, p. 658), even after recognizing competitors' valuable resources, a firm may not imitate due to the social context of these resources or availability of more pursuing alternatives. Certain resources, like company reputation, are path-dependent and are accumulated over time, and a competitor may not be able to perfectly imitate such resources (Zander and Zander 2005, p. 1521, Santala and Parvinen 2007, p. 172).

They argue on the basis that certain resources, even if imitated, may not bring the same impact, since the maximum impact of the same is achieved over longer periods of time. Hence, such imitation will not be successful. In consideration of the reputation of fact as a resource and whether a late entrant may exploit any opportunity for a competitive advantage, Kim and Park (2006, p. 45) mention three reasons why new entrants may be outperformed by earlier entrants. First, early entrants have a technological know-how which helps them to perform at a superior level. Secondly, early entrants have developed capabilities with time that enhance their strength to out-perform late entrants. Thirdly, switching costs incurred to customers, if they decide to migrate, will help early entrants to dominate the market, evading the late entrants' opportunity to capture market share. Customer awareness and loyalty is another rational benefit early entrants enjoy.

However, first mover advantage is active in evolutionary technological transitions, which are technological innovations based on previous developments. The same authors further argue that revolutionary technological changes (changes that significantly disturb the existing technology) will eliminate the advantage of early entrants. Such writings elaborate that though early entrants enjoy certain resources by virtue of the forgone time periods in the markets, rapidly changing technological environments may make those resources obsolete and curtail the firm's dominance. Late entrants may comply with the technological innovativeness and increased pressure of competition, seeking a competitive advantage by making the existing competencies and resources of early entrants invalid or outdated. In other words, innovative technological implications will significantly change the landscape of the industry and the market, making early movers' advantage minimal. However, in a market where technology does not play a dynamic role, early mover advantage may prevail.

Analyzing the above-developed framework for the Resource-Based View, it reflects a unique feature, namely, that sustainable competitive advantage is achieved in an environment where competition does not exist. According to the characteristics of the Resource-based view, rival firms may not perform at a level that could be identified as considerable competition for the incumbents of the market, since they do not possess the required resources to perform at a level that creates a threat and competition. Through barriers to imitation, incumbents ensure that rival firms do not reach a level at which they may perform in a similar manner to the former. In other words, the sustainability of the winning edge is determined by the strength of not letting other firms compete at the same level. The moment competition becomes active, competitive advantage becomes ineffective, since two or more firms begin to perform at a superior level, evading the possibility of single-firm dominance; hence, no firm will enjoy a competitive advantage. Ma agrees stating that, by definition, the sustainable competitive advantage discussed in the Resource based view is anti-competitive. Further such sustainable competitive advantage could exist in the world of no competitive imitation.

Based on the empirical writings stated above, RBV provides the understanding that certain unique existing resources will result in superior performance and ultimately build a competitive advantage. Sustainability of such an advantage will be determined by the ability of competitors to imitate such resources. However, the existing resources of a firm may not be adequate to facilitate the future market requirement, due to volatility of the contemporary markets. There is a vital need to modify and develop resources in order to encounter the future market competition. An organization should exploit existing business opportunities using the present resources while generating and developing a new set of resources to sustain its competitiveness in the future market environments; hence, an organization should be engaged in resource management and resource development (Chaharbaghi and Lynch 1999, p. 45, Song et al., 2002, p. 86). Their writings explain that in order to sustain the competitive advantage, it is crucial to develop resources that will strengthen the firm's ability to continue the superior performance. Any industry or market reflects high uncertainty and, in order to survive and stay ahead of competition, new resources become highly necessary. Morgan (2000 cited by Finney et al.2004, p. 1722) agrees, stating that the need to update resources is a major management task since all business environments reflect highly unpredictable market and environmental conditions. The existing winning edge needed to be developed since various market dynamics may make existing value-creating resources obsolete.

Criticism

Priem and Butler (2001) raised four key points of criticism:

- The RBV is tautological, or self-verifying. Barney has defined a competitive advantage as a value-creating strategy that is based on resources that are, among other characteristics, valuable

(1991, p106). This reasoning is circular and therefore operationally invalid (Priem and Butler, 2001a, p31).

- Different resource configurations can generate the same value for firms and thus would not be competitive advantage
- The role of product markets is underdeveloped in the argument
- The theory has limited prescriptive implications

However, Barney (2001) provided counter-arguments to these points of criticism.

Further criticisms are:

- It is perhaps difficult (if not impossible) to find a resource which satisfies all of the Barney's VRIN criteria.
- There is the assumption that a firm can be profitable in a highly competitive market as long as it can exploit advantageous resources, but this may not necessarily be the case. It ignores external factors concerning the industry as a whole; a firm should also consider Porter's Industry Structure Analysis (Porter's Five Forces).
- Long-term implications that flow from its premises: A prominent source of sustainable competitive advantages is causal ambiguity (Lippman & Rumelt, 1982, p420). While this is undeniably true, this leaves an awkward possibility: the firm is not able to manage a resource it does not know exists, even if a changing environment requires this (Lippman & Rumelt, 1982, p420). Through such an external change, the initial sustainable competitive advantage could be nullified or even transformed into a weakness (Priem and Butler, 2001a, p33; Peteraf, 1993, p187; Rumelt, 1984, p566).
- Premise of efficient markets: Much research hinges on the premise that markets in general or factor markets are efficient, and that firms are capable of precisely pricing in the exact future value of any value-creating strategy that could flow from the resource (Barney, 1986a, p1232). Dierickx and Cool argue that purchasable assets cannot be sources of sustained competitive advantage, just because they can be purchased. Either the price of the resource will increase to the point that it equals the future above-average return, or other competitors will purchase the resource as well and use it in a value-increasing strategy that diminishes rents to zero (Peteraf, 1993, p185; Conner, 1991, p137).

- The concept of rarity is obsolete: Although prominently present in Wernerfelt's original articulation of the resource-based view (1984) and Barney's subsequent framework (1991), the concept that resources need to be rare to be able to function as a possible source of a sustained competitive advantage is unnecessary (Hoopes, Madsen and Walker, 2003, p890). Because of the implications of the other concepts (e.g. valuable, inimitable and nonsubstitutability) any resource that follows from the previous characteristics is inherently rare.
- Sustainable: The lack of an exact definition of sustainability makes its premise difficult to test empirically. Barney's statement (: p102-103) that the competitive advantage is sustained if current and future rivals have ceased their imitative efforts is versatile from the point of view of developing a theoretical framework, but is a disadvantage from a more practical point of view, as there is no explicit end-goal.

The relational view is an extension of the resource-based view for considering networks and dyads of firms as the unit of analysis to explain relational rents, i.e., superior individual firm performance generated within that network/dyad.

Areas of Discussion

Natural resource economics is a transdisciplinary field of academic research within economics that aims to address the connections and interdependence between human economies and natural ecosystems. Its focus is how to operate an economy within the ecological constraints of earth's natural resources. Resource economics brings together and connects different disciplines within the natural and social sciences connected to broad areas of earth science, human economics, and natural ecosystems. Economic models must be adapted to accommodate the special features of natural resource inputs. The traditional curriculum of natural resource economics emphasized fisheries models, forestry models, and minerals extraction models (i.e. fish, trees, and ore). In recent years, however, other resources, notably air, water, the global climate, and "environmental resources" in general have become increasingly important to policy-making.

Academic and policy interest has now moved beyond simply the optimal commercial exploitation of the standard trio of resources to encompass management for other objectives. For example, natural resources more broadly defined have recreational, as well as commercial values. They may also contribute to overall social welfare levels, by their mere existence. The economics and policy area focuses on the human aspects of environmental problems. Traditional areas of environmental and natural resource economics include welfare theory, pollution control, resource extraction, and non-market valuation, and also resource exhaustibility, sustainability, environmental management, and environmental policy. Research topics could include the environmental impacts of agriculture, transportation and urbanization, land use in poor and industrialized countries, international trade and the environment, climate change, and methodological advances in non-market valuation, to name just a few.

Hotelling's rule is a 1931 economic model of non-renewable resource management by Harold Hotelling. It shows that efficient exploitation of a nonrenewable and nonaugmentable resource would, under otherwise stable economic conditions, lead to a depletion of the resource. The rule states that this would lead to a net price or "Hotelling rent" for it that rose annually at a rate equal to the rate of interest, reflecting the increasing scarcity of the resource. Nonaugmentable resources of inorganic materials (i.e. minerals) are uncommon; most resources can be augmented by recycling and by the existence and use of substitutes for the end-use products. Vogely has stated that the development of a mineral resource occurs in five stages: (1) The current operating margin (rate of production) governed by the proportion of the reserve (resource) already depleted. (2) The intensive development margin governed by the trade-off between the rising necessary investment and quicker realization of revenue. (3) The extensive development margin in which extraction is begun of known but previously uneconomic deposits. (4) The exploration margin in which the search for new deposits (resources) is conducted and the cost per unit extracted is highly uncertain with the cost of failure having to be balanced against finding usable resources (deposits) that have marginal costs of extraction no higher than in the first three stages above. (5) The technology margin which interacts with the first four stages. The Gray-Hotelling (exhaustion) theory is a special case, since it covers only Stages 1–3 and not the far more important Stages 4 and 5.

Simon has stated that the supply of natural resources is infinite (i.e. perpetual) These conflicting views will be substantially reconciled by considering resource-related topics in depth in the next section, or at least minimized. Furthermore, Hartwick's rule provides insight to the sustainability of welfare in an economy that uses non-renewable resources.

Perpetual Resources vs. Exhaustibility

Background and Introduction: The perpetual resource concept is a complex one because the concept of resource is complex and changes with the advent of new technology (usually more efficient recovery), new needs, and to a lesser degree with new economics (e.g. changes in prices of the material, changes in energy costs, etc.). On the one hand, a material (and its resources) can enter a time of shortage and become a strategic and critical material (an immediate exhaustibility crisis), but on the other hand a material can go out of use, its resource can proceed to being perpetual if it was not before, and then the resource can become a paleoresource when the material goes almost completely out of use (e.g. resources of arrowhead-grade flint). Some of the complexities influencing resources of a material include the extent of recyclability, the availability of suitable substitutes for the material in its end-use products, plus some other less important factors. The Federal Government suddenly became compellingly interested in resource issues on December 7, 1941, shortly after which Japan cut the U.S. off from tin and rubber and made some other materials very difficult to obtain, such as tungsten. This was the worst case for resource availability, becoming a strategic and critical material. After the war a government stockpile of strategic and critical materials was set up, having around 100 different materials which were purchased for cash or obtained by trading off U.S. agricultural commodities for them. In the longer term, scarcity of tin later led to completely substituting aluminium foil for tin foil and polymer lined lined steel cans and aseptic packaging substituting for tin electroplated steel cans. Resources change over time with technology and economics; more efficient recovery leads to a drop in the ore grade needed. The average grade of the copper ore processed has dropped from 4.0% copper in 1900 to 1.63% in 1920, 1.20% in 1940, 0.73% in 1960, 0.47% in 1980, and 0.44% in 2000. Cobalt had been in an iffy supply status ever since the Belgian Congo (world's only significant source of cobalt) was given a hasty independence in 1960 and the cobalt-producing province seceded as Katanga, followed by several wars and insurgencies, local government removals, railroads destroyed, and nationalizations. This was topped off by an invasion of the province by Katangan rebels in 1978 that disrupted supply and transportation and caused the cobalt price to briefly triple. While the cobalt supply was disrupted and the price shot up, nickel and other substitutes were pressed into service.

Following this, the idea of a "Resource War" by the Soviets became popular. Rather than the chaos that resulted from the Zairean cobalt situation, this would be planned, a strategy designed to destroy economic activity outside the Soviet bloc by the acquisition of vital resources by noneconomic means (military?) outside the Soviet bloc (Third World?), then withholding these minerals from the West.

An important way of getting around a cobalt situation or a "Resource War" situation is to use substitutes for a material in its end-uses. Some criteria for a satisfactory substitute are (1) ready availability domestically in adequate quantities or availability from contiguous nations, or possibly from overseas allies, (2) possessing physical and chemical properties, performance, and longevity comparable to the material of first choice, (3) well-established and known behaviour and properties particularly as a component in exotic alloys, and (4) an ability for processing and fabrication with minimal changes in existing technology, capital plant, and processing and fabricating facilities. Some suggested substitutions were alunite for bauxite to make alumina, molybdenum and/or nickel for cobalt, and aluminium alloy automobile radiators for copper alloy automobile radiators. Materials can be eliminated without material substitutes, for example by using discharges of high tension electricity to shape hard objects that were formerly shaped by mineral abrasives, giving superior performance at lower cost, or by using computers/satellites to replace copper wire (land lines). An important way of replacing a resource is by synthesis, for example, industrial diamonds and many kinds of graphite, although a certain kind of graphite could be almost replaced by a recycled product. Most graphite is synthetic, for example, graphite electrodes, graphite fibre, graphite shapes (machined or unmachined), and graphite powder.

Another way of replacing or extending a resource is by recycling the material desired from scrap or waste. This depends on whether or not the material is dissipated or is available as a no longer usable durable product. Reclamation of the durable product depends on its resistance to chemical and physical breakdown, quantities available, price of availability, and the ease of extraction from the original product. For example, bismuth in stomach medicine is hopelessly scattered (dissipated) and therefore impossible to recover, while bismuth alloys can be easily recovered and recycled. A good example where recycling makes a big difference is the resource availability situation for graphite, where flake graphite can be recovered from a renewable resource called kish, a steelmaking waste created when carbon separates out as graphite within the kish from the molten metal along with slag. After it is cold, the kish can be processed.

Several other kinds of resources need to be introduced. If strategic and critical materials are the worst case for resources, unless mitigated by substitution and/or recycling, one of the best is an abundant resource. An abundant resource is one whose material has so far found little use, such as using high-aluminous clays or anorthosite to produce alumina, and magnesium before it was recovered from seawater. An abundant resource is quite similar to a perpetual resource. The reserve base is the part of an identified resource that has a reasonable potential for becoming economically available at a time beyond when currently proven technology and current economics are in operation. Identified resources are those whose location, grade, quality, and quantity are known or estimated from specific geologic evidence. Reserves are that part of the reserve base that can be economically extracted at the time of determination; reserves should not be used as a surrogate for resources because they are often distorted by taxation or the owning firm's public relations needs.

Comprehensive Natural Resource Models

Harrison Brown and associates stated that humanity will process lower and lower grade "ore". Iron will come from low-grade iron-bearing material such as raw rock from anywhere in an iron formation, not much different from the input used to make taconite pellets in North America and elsewhere today. As coking coal reserves decline, pig iron and steel production will use non-coke-using processes (i.e. electric steel). The aluminium industry could shift from using bauxite to using anorthosite and clay. Magnesium metal and magnesia consumption (i.e. in refractories), currently obtained from seawater, will increase. Sulphur will be obtained from pyrites, then gypsum or anhydrite. Metals such as copper, zinc, nickel, and lead will be obtained from manganese nodules or the Phosphoria formation (sic!). These changes could occur irregularly in different parts of the world. While Europe and North America might use anorthosite or clay as raw material for aluminium, other parts of the world might use bauxite, and while North America might use taconite, Brazil might use iron ore. New materials will appear (note: they have), the result of technological advances, some acting as substitutes and some with new properties. Recycling will become more common and more efficient (note: it has!). Ultimately, minerals and metals will be obtained by processing "average" rock. Rock, 100 tonnes of "average" igneous rock, will yield eight tonnes of aluminium, five tonnes of iron, and 0.6 tonnes of titanium.

The USGS model based on crustal abundance data and the reserve-abundance relationship of McKelvey, is applied to several metals in the Earth's crust (worldwide) and in the U.S. crust. The potential currently recoverable (present technology, economy) resources that come closest to the McKelvey relationship are those that have been sought for the longest time, such as copper, zinc, lead, silver, gold and molybdenum. Metals that do not follow the McKelvey relationship are ones that are byproducts (of major metals) or haven't been vital to the economy until recently (titanium, aluminium to a lesser degree). Bismuth is an example of a byproduct metal that doesn't follow the relationship very well; the 3% lead reserves in the western U.S. would have only 100 ppm bismuth, clearly too low-grade for a bismuth reserve. The world recoverable resource potential is 2,120 million tonnes for copper, 2,590 million tonnes for nickel, 3,400 million tonnes for zinc, 3,519 BILLION tonnes for aluminium, and 2,035 BILLION tonnes for iron.

Diverse authors have further contributions. Some think the number of substitutes is almost infinite, particularly with the flow of new materials from the chemical industry; identical end products can be made from different materials and starting points. Plastics can be good electrical conductors. Since all materials are 100 times weaker than they theoretically should be, it ought to be possible to eliminate areas of dislocations and greatly strengthen them, enabling lesser quantities to be used. To summarize, "mining" companies will have more and more diverse products, the world economy is moving away from materials towards services, and the population seems to be levelling, all of which implies a lessening of demand growth for materials; much of the materials will be recovered from somewhat uncommon rocks, there will be much more coproducts and byproducts from a given operation, and more trade in minerals and materials.

Trend Towards Perpetual Resources

As radical new technology impacts the materials and minerals world more and more powerfully, the materials used are more and more likely to have perpetual resources. There are already more and more materials that have perpetual resources and less and less materials that have nonrenewable resources or are strategic and critical materials. Some materials that have perpetual resources such as salt, stone, magnesium, and common clay were mentioned previously. Thanks to new technology, synthetic diamonds were added to the list of perpetual resources, since they can be easily made from a lump of carbon. Another form of carbon, synthetic graphite, is made in large quantities (graphite electrodes, graphite fibre) from carbon precursors such as petroleum coke or a textile fibre. A firm named Liquidmetal Technologies, Inc. is utilizing the removal of dislocations in a material with a technique that overcomes performance limitations caused by inherent weaknesses in the crystal atomic structure. It makes amorphous metal alloys, which retain a random atomic structure when the hot metal solidifies, rather than the crystalline atomic structure (with dislocations) that normally forms when hot metal solidifies. These amorphous alloys have much better performance properties than usual; for example, their zirconium-titanium Liquidmetal alloys are 250% stronger than a standard titanium alloy. The Liquidmetal alloys can supplant many high performance alloys.

Exploration of the ocean bottom in the last fifty years revealed manganese nodules and phosphate nodules in many locations. More recently, polymetallic sulfide deposits have been discovered and polymetallic sulfide "black muds" are being presently deposited from "black smokers" The cobalt scarcity situation of 1978 has a new option now: recover it from manganese nodules. A Korean firm plans to start developing a manganese nodule recovery operation in 2010; the manganese nodules recovered would average 27% to 30% manganese, 1.25% to 1.5% nickel, 1% to 1.4% copper, and 0.2% to 0.25% cobalt (commercial grade) Nautilus Minerals Ltd. is planning to recover commercial grade material averaging 29.9% zinc, 2.3% lead, and 0.5% copper from massive ocean-bottom polymetallic sulfide deposits using an underwater vacuum cleaner-like device that combines some current technologies in a new way. Partnering with Nautilus are Tech Cominco Ltd. and Anglo-American Ltd., world-leading international firms.

There are also other robot mining techniques that could be applied under the ocean. Rio Tinto is using satellite links to allow workers 1500 kilometers away to operate drilling rigs, load cargo, dig out ore and dump it on conveyor belts, and place explosives to subsequently blast rock and earth. The firm can keep workers out of danger this way, and also use fewer workers. Such technology reduces costs and offsets declines in metal content of ore reserves. Thus a variety of minerals and metals are obtainable from unconventional sources with resources available in huge quantities. Finally, what is a perpetual resource? The ASTM definition for a perpetual resource is "one that is virtually inexhaustible on a human time-scale". Examples given include solar energy, tidal energy, and wind energy, to which should be added salt, stone, magnesium, diamonds, and other materials mentioned above. A study on the biogeophysical aspects of sustainability came up with a rule of prudent practice that a resource stock should last 700 years to achieve sustainability or become a perpetual resource, or for a worse case, 350 years. If a resource lasting 700 or more years is perpetual, one that lasts 350 to 700 years can be called an abundant resource, and is so defined here. How long the material can be recovered from its resource depends on human need and changes in technology from extraction through the life cycle of the product to final disposal, plus recyclability of the material and availability of satisfactory substitutes. Specifically, this shows that exhaustibility does not occur until these factors weaken and play out: the availability of substitutes, the extent of recycling and its feasibility, more efficient manufacturing of the final consumer product, more durable and longer-lasting consumer products, and even a number of other factors.

The most recent resource information and guidance on the kinds of resources that must be considered is covered on the Resource Guide-Update.

Transitioning: Perpetual Resources to Paleoresources

Perpetual resources can transition to being a paleoresource. A paleoresource is one that has little or no demand for the material extracted from it; an obsolescent material, humans no longer need it. The classic paleoresource is an arrowhead-grade flint resource; no one makes flint arrowheads or spearheads anymore—making a sharpened piece of scrap steel and using it is much simpler. Obsolescent products include tin cans, tin foil, the schoolhouse slate blackboard, and radium in medical technology. Radium has been replaced by much cheaper Cobalt 60 and other radioisotopes in radiation treatment. Noncorroding lead as a cable covering has been replaced by plastics.

Pennsylvania anthracite is another material where the trend towards obsolescence and becoming a paleoresource can be shown statistically. Production of anthracite was 70.4 million tonnes in 1905, 49.8 million tonnes in 1945, 13.5 million tonnes in 1965, 4.3 million tonnes in 1985, and 1.5 million tonnes in 2005. The amount used per person was 84 kg per person in 1905, 7.1 kg in 1965, and 0.8 kg in 2005. Compare this to the USGS anthracite reserves of 18.6 billion tonnes and total resources of 79 billion tonnes; the anthracite demand has dropped so much that these resources are more than perpetual.

Since anthracite resources are so far into the perpetual resource range and demand for anthracite has dropped so far, is it possible to see how anthracite might become a paleoresource? Probably by customers continuing to disappear (i.e. convert to other kinds of energy for space heating), the supply network atrophy as anthracite coal dealers can't retain enough business to cover costs and close, and mines with too small a volume to cover costs also close. This is a mutually reinforcing process: customers convert to other forms of cleaner energy that produce less pollution and carbon dioxide, then the coal dealer has to close because of lack of enough sales volume to cover costs. The coal dealer's other customers are then forced to convert unless they can find another nearby coal dealer. Finally the anthracite mine closes because it doesn't have enough sales volume to cover its costs.

Footloose Industry

Footloose industry is a general term for an industry that can be placed and located at any location without effect from factors such as resources or transport.

These industries often have spatially fixed costs, which means that the costs of the products do not change despite where the product is assembled. Diamonds and computer chips are some examples of footloose industries.

These industries can be located at a wide variety of places, as these are not weight-losing nor raw-material-specific. Moreover, they produce in relatively small quantities, employing smaller workforces and are considered to be more efficient from an ecological point of view. These are generally not polluting industries.

The Idea of Footloose industries has changed along with the transformation from an industrial to a postindustrial economy. The core concept remains the same, however: A footloose industry does not have a strong locational preference because the resources, production skills, and consumers on which it depends can be found in numerous places. Such a company may therefore be more prone to relocation, hence the term footloose. Footloose industries became prevalent in geographic parlance during the quantitative approach in geography from the 1950s onward. Economic geographers interested in industrial location borrowed ideas and methodology from neo-classical economics. The basic premises of footloose industries are derived from the work of German economist Alfred Weber, who was probably the first to theorize on the location of industries in the beginning of the 20th century. First, we must assume that the most important factor in industrial location is the cost of transportation (however, this is less and less true over time). Some industries may have a strong resource orientation, that is, if the raw material used in a production process is heavy and bulky in character, it makes sense to be located close to those natural resources. Heavy manufacturing districts around the world (e.g., the steel industry in northeastern United States) are usually located near major coal deposits. Such a resource-oriented location is often combined with good access to important transportation routes. Other types of manufacturing can be market-oriented. (Traditionally, the footloose concept has been applied in manufacturing, once the dominant sector in the economy.) Let's take the example of a dairy. If we assume that cows can graze just about anywhere and that milk is a perishable commodity, dairy production should be located close to the consumers the industry serves. For both resource and market orientation, the locational choices of industries are limited, or dressed in more theoretical language, and the so-called spatial margins to profitability are narrow. The opposite is true for a footloose industry. If raw material is easily accessible in numerous locations, markets are dispersed, and the physical properties of the commodity are such that transportation cost makes up a small portion of total cost, the locational choice is much greater.

Information Flow

The locational logic described so far has become less powerful over time for a couple of reasons. Relative transportation costs have declined, which in effect expands the spatial margins to profitability for an increasing number of industries. Moreover, the contemporary postindustrial economy is more and more characterized by flow of information and people rather than bulky goods, which has made traditional transportation cost-based location analysis less relevant. The Internet and other forms of advanced communication technology are said to make location completely detached from both resource and market considerations.

The growth of footloose industries has some strong implications. Cities and regions that once occupied a relatively secure position in the national and global economy because they harbored few industries that could be characterized as footloose are now thrust into an economic environment that is much more insecure. Capital is more mobile where both existing industries relocate and new investment flows to previously bypassed areas. To cope with this reality, local governments increasingly offer incentives to lure footloose industries. Such incentives include tax subsidies, land to build on, and infrastructure accommodations. Not to be outcompeted by their neighbours, other cities answer with similar measures, which have brought an era of unparalleled interurban competition. As cities are more dependent on the capacity to capture mobile capital, urban policy has inevitably been more businessfriendly, and business interests have strengthened their position in urban governance.

Cities are even spending significant money to present themselves as good locations for footloose industries by marketing and advertising. But as cities often offer similar economic incentive packages, location decisions may be determined by other factors. Footloose industries are more likely to locate in places with a perceived high quality of life (i.e., cultural, recreational, climate, educational amenities), where a productive workforce can be attracted. On the other hand, the idea that relocating companies always look for the lowest-cost location has been challenged. For several reasons, industries may not be as footloose as sometimes portrayed. They usually have significant investments in physical infrastructure, they are dependent on local skills and capacities that have been built up over time, and they may share resources and support services with other companies. The hightech industry is sometimes considered a typical footloose industry because it is neither resource- or market-oriented. However, it tends to cluster for some of the above reasons and thus is not a good example of a contemporary footloose industry.

Globalization

A city's strategy is usually not to attract the most footloose of industries, because they often also produce the lowest-paying jobs. However, the situation is different from a global perspective. With the globalization of the economy, the spatial margins to profitability have widened to encompass large areas of the world. Particularly in industries that are labour intensive, where the products have high value per weight unit, and free trade is the norm, the propensity to frequently seek out new production sites is strong. The clothing industry, for example, is such a footloose industry that has developed a truly global pattern. If companies have the option to outsource much of their production, labour relations are also altered, circumscribing the bargaining position of labour in the United States and other developed nations.

Case Study: Footloose Industry in the UK

Footloose industries are not tied to a particular location. They include high-tech industries and are located near motorway junctions or on the edges of towns and cities in business parks. The products are often electronics and computer components.

Inputs and Outputs

- The M4 corridor stretches from Heathrow airport in the east to Bath and Bristol in the west. The corridor is home to companies such as Hewlett Packard and Sony who are involved in research and development (quaternary industry) and have links with universities who provide well-qualified graduates.
- Few raw materials are used and therefore transport costs are low, making the industries 'footloose'.

Advantages

- Land on the edge of cities is often cheaper than in the centre. The out of town surroundings and easy access to workers in the suburbs provides an ideal location for building science and business parks.
- Motorway links and railways also provide access for commuters and for transporting components and products.

Disadvantages

- Workers wanting to live near their place of work increases the demand for housing and puts pressure on green belt land.
- As demand grows, house prices increase. This means that less skilled and lower paid workers are priced out of the market in desirable areas.

Factors Affecting Location of Industries In India

Before an industry is located at any place, certain basic requirements have to be considered. Not all of them are required all the time for each and every industry; however, nor can the location of an industry be guided by a single factor. All these factors must be researched and analysed before an industry is established if the expectations of economic production are to be met. Raw materials are basic requirements for manufacturing industries. Weight-losing industries e.g., cement, sugar (to quintals of sugarcane is needed to produce 1 quintal of sugar) are located near the source of raw material. On the other hand, foot-loose industries are independent of raw material sources, e.g., garment and electronics industries, and can be established practically anywhere.

Power resources are important for energy-intensive industries such as aluminium and polythene bags industries which are located near the energy sources. Labour supply is another important factor particularly for the labour-intensive industry, e.g., construction industry. To an extent, labour can be brought to a site from other regions. Means of transportation and communication playa special role in bringing raw material to the factory and finished products to the market, e.g., cheap water transport has facilitated the development and concentration of jute mills in the Hooghly region.

Market facility also influences industries, many of which are located near large urban centres because the potential buyers are easy available. Other factors like financial facilities, climate, industrial incentives and government facilities also matter. In India one could get more subsidised raw material, very low rate of interest on capital and 9!her incentives for establishing an industry in the 'Backward Regions' or in 'No Industry District'.

Bibliography

Abler, R., J. Adams, and P. Gould: *Spatial Organization–The Geographer's View of the World*, Prentice-Hall, Englewood Cliffs, NJ, 1971.

Allen, John C. and Dillman, Don: *Against All Odds: Rural Community in the Information Age*, Boulder: Westview Press, 1994.

Arnott, Richard; McMillen, Daniel P.: *A Companion to Urban Economics*. Blackwell Publishing, Oxford, 2006.

Belden C.: *Landscapes of the Sacred: Geography and Narrative in American Spirituality*, New York: Paulist Press, 1988.

Benenson, I. and P. M. Torrens: *Geosimulation: Automata-Based Modeling of Urban Phenomena*, Wiley, New York, 2004.

Capello, Roberta; Nijkamp, Peter: *Urban Dynamics and Growth: Advances in Urban Economics*, Elsvier Inc., 2004.

Chaklader, Snehamoy: *Sociolinguistics: A Guide to Language Problems in India*, New Delhi, Mittal, 1990.

Damon, William: *Social and Personality Development, Infancy through Adolescence*, New York: Norton, 1983.

Davey, Kenneth J.: *Elements of Urban Management*, Urban Management Program Discussion, The World Bank, Washington DC, 1993.

Dicken, P.: *Global Shift: Reshaping the Global Economic Map in the 21st Century*, Guilford, New York, 2003.

Dicken, Peter: *Global Shift: Mapping the Changing Contours of the World Economy*, Guilford, New York, 2011.

Elangovan K.: *GIS, Fundamentals, Applications and Population Geography*, New India Publishing Agency, New Delhi 2006.

Florida, R.: *The Rise of the Creative Class: And How it's Transforming Work, Leisure, Community and Everyday Life*, Perseus Book Group, New York, 2002.

Fotheringham, A. S., C. Brunsdon and M. Charlton: *Quantitative Geography: Perspectives on Spatial Data Analysis*, Sage, London, 2000.

Gurukal, Rajan: *The Formation of Caste Society in Kerala*, Rawat Publications, New Delhi, 1994.

Haggett, Peter: *Geography: A Modern Synthesis*. New York: Harper and Row, 1975.

Jackson, Peter: *Maps of Meaning: An Introduction to Cultural Geography*. London and Boston: Unwin Hyman, 1989.

Kidokoro, Tetsuo: *Development Control Systems for Housing Development in Southeast Asian Cities*, Regional Development Dialogue, UNCRD, Nagoya, Japan, 1992.

Levine, N.: *CrimeStat: A Spatial Statistics Program for the Analysis of Crime Incident Locations*, Ned Levine & Associates, Houston, TX and the National Institute of Justice, Washington, DC, 2010.

MacEachren, A. M. and D. R. F. Taylor: *Visualization in Modern Cartography*, Pergamon, NJ, 1994.

Massey, D.: *Spatial Divisions of Labour, Social Structures and the Structure of Production*, MacMillan, London, 1984.

Miller, H. J. and J. Han: *Geographic Data Mining and Knowledge Discovery*, Taylor and Francis, 2001.

Neil, H.: *The Land of Contrasts: 1880-1901,* The American Culture 5. New York: G. Braziller, 1970.

Openshaw S and Abrahart RJ: *GeoComputation*, CRC Press, London, 2000.

Peck, J.: *Work-place: The Social Regulation of Labor Markets*. Guilford, New York, 1996.

Quaino, Massimo: *Geography and Marxism*. Translated by Alan Braley. Totowa, N.J.: Barnes and Noble, 1982.

Ray Allen: *The Far Western Frontier, 1830-1860*. The New American Nation Series. New York: Harper, 1956.

Robert Fisher and Peter Romanofsky: *Community Organizing for Urban Social Change, A Historical Perspective,* Greenwood Press, Delhi, 1981.

Stephen, D.: *Fields of Vision: Landscape Imagery and National Identity in England and the United States*. Cambridge: Polity, 1993.

Tulder, R.: *Cars, Carriers of Regionalism*, Palgrave Macmillan, New York, 2004.

Warf, Barney: *The World Economy: Geography, Business and Development*, Pearson Education, Upper Saddle River, NJ, 2011.

Worboys, Michael, and Matt Duckham.: *GIS, a Computing Perspective,* Boca Raton, CRC Press, 2004.

Yap Kioe Sheng: *Land-Sharing as a Low-Income Housing Policy, An Analysis of its Potential,* Habitat International, Pergamon Press, United Kingdom, 1989.

Index

❑❑❑